A passage to anthropology

D0143660

The postmodernist critique of Objectivism, Realism and Essentialism has somewhat shattered the foundations of anthropology, seriously questioning the legitimacy of studying others. By confronting the critique and turning it into a vital part of the anthropological debate, *A Passage to Anthropology* provides a rigorous discussion of central theoretical problems in anthropology that will find a readership in the social sciences and the humanities. It makes the case for a renewed and invigorated scholarly anthropology with extensive reference to recent anthropological debates in Europe and the US, as well as to new developments in linguistic theory and, especially, newer American philosophy.

Through discussions of the relationship between language and the world, of 'the empirical', of the nature of the anthropological imagination, of the point of raising cultural and theoretical awareness, it is shown that far from invalidating the scholarly, even scientific, ambition of anthropology, the recent insights into subjectivity, reflexivity and the writing of culture give the discipline a new life and a new pertinence in the world. Although still anchored in detailed ethnographies, the lasting significance of anthropology is located in its theoretical contribution.

Kirsten Hastrup is Professor of Anthropology at the Institute of Anthropology, University of Copenhagen, Denmark.

A passage to anthropology

Between experience and theory

Kirsten Hastrup

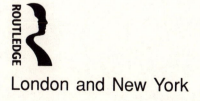

London and New York

First published 1995
by Routledge
11 New Fetter Lane, London EC4P 4EE

Simultaneously published in the USA and Canada
by Routledge
29 West 35th Street, New York, NY 10001

Reprinted in 1999

© 1995 Kirsten Hastrup
Phototypeset in Times by Intype, London
Printed and bound in Great Britain by
TJ International Ltd, Padstow, Cornwall

British Library Cataloguing in Publication Data
A catalogue record for this book is available from the British Library

Library of Congress Cataloging in Publication Data
A catalogue record for this book has been requested

ISBN 0–415–12922–2 (hbk)
ISBN 0–415–12923–0 (pbk)

This book is dedicated to my children,
Rasmus, Simon, Anders and Frida,
who have been with me all the way

Contents

Preface and acknowledgements

This book is the outcome of a long process of practising and thinking about anthropology in different intellectual settings. It is also a burst, however, or an eruption from professional routines, risking them in the attempt to ground them. In many ways my argument has the form of an implicit conversation with colleagues, primarily in anthropology but also in other human and social sciences. The conversation itself is part of my ambition, since my principal aim is to point to the permanent need to achieve a shared language so that we may actually feel part of a conversational community. Within such a community, ideas and values may be tried and measured, and provide common ground for agency. Conversation takes place between interested partners; it is appropriate, therefore, to specify my own interest as 'anthropology'.

It has become fashionable, at least in prefaces, to denounce one's discipline and make a plea for a general intellectual understanding. The hostility to academic specialization may be a peculiar reflection of the historical process of globalization, but even then it seems unproductive. I fail to see how academic specificity need be an obstacle to general intellectual understanding and broad scholarly conversation. Academic disciplines and scholarly traditions never were closed spaces; they are fields of knowledge with distinct centres of gravity. These centres may shift in the course of enquiry, of course, but it is important that disciplines be defined by their core values rather than by their boundaries. Specialized scholars are not gatekeepers but explorers of distinct fields. Their profound professional knowledge of one tradition constitutes for each their zero-point of perception; the perspective upon the world is premissed by this point, yet not limited by it, nor is it exclusive of other perspectives. Sharing insight does not imply reduction to a common denominator; on the contrary, the crossing of distinct perspectives may create double exposure of the subject.

My point is that it is only by being specific about one's point of perception and, by implication, one's intellectual perspective that one may enter into a meaningful scholarly conversation. Of course, one may talk, read, drop names, be inspired and inspire others quite irrespective of academic background. Yet in so far as we see our project as an essentially theoretical one, a shared intellectual interest in the world does not provide sufficient distinction to the fulfilment of the project. The conversational community that allows for meaningful action cannot be established by talking 'naturally' to each other about common interests. The arbitrariness of signs will not take us far enough.

This is why I do not hesitate to declare that there is such a thing as a distinct anthropological project, the object of which is to provide ground for comparison and generalization of social experience on the basis of concrete ethnography. The distinctiveness of ethnography lies precisely in its experiential character, which allows for a recognition of both difference and unity. While inhabiting different worlds and projecting different desires into our world, we share the capacity to experience relativity. This is the backbone of anthropology, straddling the gap between the particular and the general.

The often-noted crisis in anthropology, as we have traditionally known it, and the problems of practising it in a decolonized world, is here recast as part of our project. There is a distinct theoretical project to pursue, even if the discipline has either been declared obsolete or appropriated by various other fields with an interest in cultures. The theoretical project is based in concrete experience. This is why anthropology potentially is an important supplement to historical or literary modes of apprehending the world through texts. If, as one of my critics has said, the present work feels imperialist, this is a side-effect of my personal belief in the value of anthropology rather than a wish to denigrate other disciplines. In the course of my own professional life I have made extensive and invaluable excursions into the fields of linguistics, history and philosophy without which my anthropological insight would have been poorer. A true conversation does not presuppose similarity or identity between the conversational partners, however. It takes place between equals, speaking as distinct subjects. It is the distinction of anthropology with which I am concerned in this book, more than anything else. Once established it may be transformed; scholarly identities are no more static than cultural ones. And like culture, anthropology is not primarily what we see, but what we see with. This, of course, is why all academic disciplines are in some sense totalitarian. They are views of the world, and to get beyond the alleged crisis in academics, we need to investigate the multiple points of perception that frame this notion of crisis in the first place.

The book is a personal statement, which may be read as being addressed to fellow anthropologists. It may also be read as a statement *from* anthropology to colleagues in other fields. The idea is to open a multivocal conversation, and to do so from a particular and well-defined position, that of an invigorated anthropology.

The main bulk of this work is newly written, even if parts of some chapters have been integrated elements in previously published articles. Thus, parts of chapter 1 were previously published in my article 'The Ethnographic Present: A Reinvention', *Cultural Anthropology*, vol. 5, 1990 (copyright American Anthropological Association 1990); and chapter 6 is a reframed and slightly edited version of my article 'Out of Anthropology. The Anthropologist as an Object of Dramatic Representation', *Cultural Anthropology*, vol. 7, 1992 (copyright American Anthropological Association 1992). Reprinted with permission from *Cultural Anthropology*. Parts of chapter 8 were included in my article 'The Native Voice and the Anthropological Vision', *Social Anthropology/Anthropologie sociale*, vol. 1, 1993 (copyright European Association of Social Anthropologists).

I would also like to acknowledge King's College, Cambridge, and The Society of Authors as the literary representatives of the E. M. Forster estate for permission to quote from *A Passage to India*; Faber and Faber Ltd for permission to quote an extract from 'Burnt Norton', T. S. Eliot's *Collected Poems 1909–1962*; and Random House for permission to quote Karen Blixen's *Out of Africa*.

In the course of writing this book I have incurred many new debts in addition to old ones. Among the oldest and most profound, I shall mention the late Edwin Ardener of Oxford University, whose teaching had a formative influence upon my conception of the field, even if today he might not have recognized this. Shirley Ardener and other colleagues and friends in Britain have been intellectual companions since my first years in Oxford, and have contributed immensely by making me part of a long-standing community of anthropological conversation.

Among the newer ones, I wish first to acknowledge the unexpected and honorific support received from *Tagea Brandts Rejselegat* (1992), a generous travel grant which allowed me to spend almost three months at the University of California, Santa Cruz, during the winter 1992–1993, where this book was conceived. I want to thank Professor Richard Randolph, Department of Anthropology, and Cowell College for their hospitality and friendliness on that occasion and before. A short visit to Rice University, Texas, provided a welcome opportunity to test some of the ideas propounded in the book.

My profound gratitude also extends to friends and colleagues who invested precious time in reading the first draft of this book, helping me to see what I had actually written and to clarify certain points. They are Anthony Cohen, Tord Olsson, Marilyn Strathern and Preben Meulengracht Sørensen. At an earlier stage David Parkin also read some chapters. Each from their own perspective have provided me with insight and encouragement, for which I remain grateful.

There are others whom I wish to acknowledge, namely my students at the Institute of Anthropology, University of Copenhagen. With their intelligence and enthusiasm they have been my main sounding board over the past years, as well as my main critics. I thank them for their sharing my conviction that what we do has to be important.

My children Rasmus, Simon, Anders and Frida also have to be remembered at this occasion. They have shared extensive periods of study abroad, of fieldwork, and scores of shorter journeys with me. They have helped me keep a sense of proportion wherever we went. As they have come of age they have also to an increasing degree become intellectual partners, offering their own perspective on the world while challenging mine. At this particular point in time, when they begin leaving home to make their own

passage, it is only right to dedicate this book to them in acknow-
ledgement of their genuine contribution.

Finally, I thank Mogens Trolle Larsen for his loving appreciation
of my work, including his sceptical reading of this book and his
readiness to share his own learning with me.

Kirsten Hastrup
Copenhagen, Autumn 1994

Prologue
The itinerary

India a nation! What an apotheosis! Last comer to the drab
nineteenth-century sisterhood! Waddling in at this hour of the
world to take her seat! She, whose only peer was the Holy
Roman Empire, she shall rank with Guatemala and Belgium
perhaps! Fielding mocked again. And Aziz in an awful rage
danced this way and that, not knowing what to do, and cried:
'Down with the English anyhow. That's certain. Clear out, you
fellows, double quick, I say. We may hate one another, but we
hate you most. If I don't make you go, Ahmed will, Karim
will, if it's fifty five-hundred years we shall get rid of you, yes,
we shall drive every blasted Englishman into the sea, and then'
– he rode against him furiously – 'and then,' he concluded, half
kissing him, 'you and I shall be friends.'

(E. M. Forster, *A Passage to India*, 1924)[1]

At the time that E. M. Forster wrote his sun-baked novel on the
encounter between the British community of colonialists and
the mixed Indian group of colonized, anthropology as a distinct
kind of scholarship was still in the making. It was made precisely
from such encounters as that Forster described, however, and
which had been part and parcel of the European incorporation
of strange lands elsewhere since the doubling of the known world
in the Age of Discovery – lands that were not yet nations, and
which for the most part could not aspire to be either, because
they were not ready, or were simply on the wrong track. The
'white man's burden' was to remedy this, and to bring the lesser
nations into world history. They succeeded on all counts, including
the anthropological one, which until recently declared the colonized peoples to be without a history of their own (e.g. Wolf 1982).

The imperial eyes that first saw the others and recreated them in travel writing had but little idea of the nature of the contact zone as a zone of mutual implication. The European 'planetary consciousness' (Pratt 1992: 29), aimed at systematizing nature, was as hierarchical as the Linnean taxonomic system; *alter* was recognized through incorporation. The only logical alternative was open conflict (cf. Dumont 1986: 266).

Anthropology grew out of the contact zone; it is one of the principal heirs to transculturation. As such it has always been ill at ease with the hierarchical assumptions of the West, while also exploiting them, and even carrying them further. The 'imperialist nostalgia', identified by Renato Rosaldo (1989: 68ff.) as the mourning of the disappearance of what we, the imperialists, have ourselves transformed, and which still characterizes large areas of anthropology, stems from this. This particular nostalgia is conspicuous right from the beginnings of modern anthropology, around the time that Forster produced his key work on the complexity of the colonial encounter with the multicultural Indian subcontinent. While Forster's heroine Mrs Moore would die from her sudden insight in the Marabar Caves, because it could not be accommodated, the contemporary anthropological hero Malinowski was saved through his declaration of the 'native's point of view' as a legitimate, and even necessary, point of departure (Malinowski 1922: 25). The natives became persons with their own view of things. Generally, as a person anyone 'is "one of us" in a deeper way than that in which, because of his race, his caste or his fortune, he may be "not one of us" ' (Casey 1990: 5). Slaves, aborigines, Indians and shamans added to the complexity of our world, but as persons they had become irrevocably part of it.

The making of anthropology took on a new turn from then. The professional discoverers of human worlds switched from the external to the internal gaze, disquieting though it was. This shift made friendship between us and them theoretically possible. Friendship presupposes a degree of sameness and equality, which was still a far cry at Forster's time, and which nineteenth-century racism had effectively precluded. There remains, however, a paradox of friendship in the field that is not easily overcome, because it is profoundly embedded in the asymmetry between the knowledge projects of the friends (cf. Hendry 1992).

With its rightful emphasis on cultural distinction, anthropology more or less unwillingly came to cement, even exaggerate, difference (cf. Boon 1982). Given the imperialist and evolutionary legacy in the mental map of Europeans, such difference was not easily freed from connotations of race and inequality. The others were less worthy, less developed, less civilized specimen of ourselves. They represented us in the past tense (Fabian 1983).

Within anthropology, Orientalism (Said 1978) and related regionalisms (Fardon 1990) have organized the cultural differences into larger areas, amounting to bounded territories of knowledge, each with its own agenda. The rhetorical practices of Indianists, Americanists and Africanists have been grounded in region; concepts grew out of localized worlds. The result has been a curious topographical space, a map onto which constructed differences were written, and from whence they soon began to make differences of their own. Rhetorical and literary stereotypes were reproduced; peoples were recreated in the image of their neighbours. 'Evidence' was as much a question of regional genre as of social experience.

Neither imperialism nor regionalism have yet become wholly past, even if India long since became a nation, and later was split into yet more nations. As a figure of thought, imperialism will remain with us because all living societies are still deeply marked by the imperial regime (Said 1993), and regionalisms will prevail in some form because we still need to write about social life in a fashion that cannot but group local peculiarities into larger orders. The minutiae of daily life cannot be written out verbatim; first, because they are not words, and second, because they would already be gone before the text was produced. Analytical spaces that outlive particular events have to be created. Yet the cultural resilience of the colonized and the global cultural flows that are part of world history at the end of the second millennium still make us realize that histories are intertwined and territories overlapping; the Empire that englobed the peoples without history has been defrocked, yet it still connects peoples and places, if under a new name. Empirically, the world is a space marked by a continuity that is broken down only in theory – which must then account for the nature of rupture.

The world has lost its enchantment for many people since the time that Conrad's Kurtz and Forster's Fielding travelled distant continents, and could inspire the young science of social anthropology, impersonated by Malinowski. His story is an ambiguous one; the personal conflict between seeing the Trobriand others as inferior 'niggers' and becoming emotionally involved with them as fellow human beings reflects the Indian Aziz's craving for friendship amid hate of the British Fielding. At another level it reflects the double vision of anthropology: to observe the native culture and to participate in it at the same time. By 'native culture' I refer to any culture studied by anthropologists, including industrialized and western societies; all of us are natives to some culture as we shall discuss later (chapter 8). Observation is never neutral; the gaze is directed from a particular point of view. In Malinowski's time this view was still pervaded by notions of racism, while today the imperialist nostalgia seems to dominate the clinical gaze. There is no way of seeing from 'nowhere in particular'. Anthropology is seeing from a point that epitomizes the contact zone. 'There is no vantage point *outside* the actuality of relationships between cultures' (Said 1989: 216). Whence the performative contradiction of the discipline: the claim to objective, historical scholarship, including the criticism of imperialism, is at odds with the implications of the anthropological practice of studying the others by way of engagement.[2]

While most of us are ready to acknowledge the performative contradiction as such, we have failed to take theoretical advantage of it. We have lamented the loss of the others, while simultaneously contributing to their disenchantment ourselves. The sentimental pessimism, ruling large tracts of the anthropological territory, and collapsing the lives of the others within a global vision of western domination, has made the conquest complete (Greenblatt 1991: 152). The imperial naïveté has been traded in for melancholy (Sahlins 1993: 6). While, certainly, there is a call for humility in the face of the colonial transformation of local histories, there is no need to deny that local histories always transformed colonialism as well. While the contact zone may form a space of coercive relationships between peoples that were previously apart, the fact of coercion and inequality itself should not blur our vision from the noticeable feature that 'contact' implies an interactive copresence of historical subjects, responding to and improvising the encounter (Pratt 1992: 6–7).

It seems to me that there are two ways out of the impasse contained in the notion of imperialist nostalgia or sentimental pessimism: one of silence, and one of bringing the performative paradox to full methodological effect and ethical import. Silence invokes secrecy and shame, neither of which inspire solidarity.

The second route beyond the sentimental pessimism of anthropology therefore is more appealing; by no means an easy path, it still contains a promise of a new world. For the promise to materialize we have to reconsider the philosophical underpinnings of the discipline, in order that we might enter the performative paradox without fear. Melancholy must now be traded in for civil courage – to articulate and pursue a common good.

It is my contention that the performative paradox of anthropology implies a reconciliation of objectivity and solidarity. As noted by Richard Rorty, solidarity is not discovered by reflection but created through imaginative investment of one's own sensitivity to alien lifeways (Rorty 1989: xvi). The anthropological sensitivity to unfamiliar modes of life and reasoning makes it more difficult to marginalize these in general. The 'process of coming to see other human beings as "one of us" rather than "them" is a matter of detailed description of what unfamiliar people are like and of redescription of what we ourselves are like' (Rorty 1989: xvi). This clearly is a task for ethnography, and a task whose foundation is of a profoundly moral nature, even if the project is theoretical.

By a theoretical project I refer to a project that sets itself apart from the practical project of living; the theories of daily life part company from this life itself. Characteristically, anthropology in the past decade has largely renounced theory; it has been either all 'experience-near' ethnography or epistemological qualms. Solidarity has been waved about in the rhetoric of the former, while realism has been refuted by the latter. Sentimental pessimism has prevented their reconciliation at the cost of the theoretical project. This book is an attempt at clearing the ground for a renewed effort at theorizing in the contact zone, without destroying the autonomous cultural projects that are embedded in the practical lives of people inhabiting the zone. The centralist and nostalgic view of the 'tristes tropes' gives way to a vision of creativity and local cultural sabotage of the preconceived scheme (cf. Sahlins 1993: 13). This again paves the way for a new ethics of authenticity and of theory.

The ethics of authenticity takes a particular turn in anthropology, methodologically based as it is in a holism that refutes fragmentation and individualism. At the risk of sounding presumptuous, I would say that anthropology – potentially at least – provides a powerful potion in the curing of the three dominant malaises of present-day society, as identified by Charles Taylor (1991). The first is individualism and the loss of a moral community; the second, a dominance of instrumental reason, or efficiency, over other forms of rationality; and finally, the political culture arising from the combined effect of individualism and instrumental reason, a mild form of despotism which makes individual freedom of choice an illusion without destroying individualism. Whether one agrees with the identification of these modern malaises or not, I think they do point to an area of shared concern about alienation from one's own world of experience – including the experience of moral ambiguity.[3] This is where a repatriated anthropology may provide an antidote, I believe. The purpose is not simply to cure western malaises, contagiously transported to the rest of the world in the wake of imperialism, but to contribute to a healthier vocabulary that may serve as a shared language for identifying new standards for the common good.

Anthropology in general has abandoned the 'exotic' view of culture, largely equating the object of anthropology with distant, primitive or tribal others. We are ready to transcend the agenda set by our own imperialist nostalgia. Beyond this nostalgia, all too often part of the anthropological discourse in the past and still very conspicuous in ethnographic films for instance (Hastrup 1992b), 'culture' is no longer seen as a primordial entity, but as a particular analytical perspective. This shift has a correlate in a questioning of regionalism at the largest scale, namely, the division of the world into the West and the Rest.

In the process of this questioning, the categories of 'selves' and 'others' have been dismantled as substantially defined entities and redefined as categories of thought. The redefinition is one reason why anthropology has become transformed from the exclusive and exotic study of other cultures to a potentially critical analysis of one's own society. Phrased differently, the shift of anthropological interest is not only, and perhaps not even mainly, a result of vanishing worlds of primitives, but more significantly a result of new epistemological considerations that make all societies equally eligible as objects of analysis. Anthropology has left the 'savage slot' (Trouillot 1991) and come 'home' (Jackson 1987). The practice of anthropology is no longer bounded by alleged 'demands of the object', but by its attention to the demands of the purpose which a particular enquiry is supposed to serve (cf. Rorty 1991a: 110). The radical interpreter, and I would liken the anthropologist to one, provides an understanding that is not already given by the object, but which emerges in the process of theorizing (cf. Davidson 1984: 128).

The call for a 'repatriation' of anthropology made by some American anthropologists, notably Renato Rosaldo (1989) and George Marcus and Michael Fischer (1986: 111ff.), is part of a larger concern about making an explicit social or cultural critique of domestic matters part and parcel of the anthropological practice. In traditional (read 'exotic') anthropology, this critique was most often implicit; it was clad in reverence for difference, and in romanticizing a generalized other – Oriental, African or Gypsy. By their detailed descriptions of other cultures, anthropologists have contributed to a hidden agenda of critique of their own culture (Marcus and Fischer 1986: 111). In the words of James Boon, anthropology has aimed and, indeed, succeeded in the endeavour to 'make explicitly exotic populations appear implicitly familiar and explicitly familiar populations appear implicitly exotic' (Boon 1982: 9). Cultures juxtapose themselves to one another through an exaggeration of difference: anthropology cements this exaggeration (Boon 1982: 26; Hastrup 1985c). This implies that any description of a particular culture is implicitly comparative, and simultaneously a statement of what it is *not*. The call for 'repatriation' means bringing the strategy of defamiliarization to explicit domestic effect. This strategy must also be applied to the givens in the production of anthropological knowledge itself, that is, its practice.

Anthropological practice rests upon the performative paradox identified above. However much the others are dealt with as equal historical subjects, anthropology still has to objectify them in writing; the implicit process of 'othering' is at the heart of the current epistemological uncertainty in anthropology. It has been heavily criticized as profoundly alienating the others. My contention, however, is that we are now in a position to turn the concept of othering towards ourselves. It is for anthropology to assume the position of the 'radical other' in the world. It is a particular epistemological position in which we renounce continuity between our own words, conceptions, theories and conventions of representation and those of the people studied, whoever they are, and to whatever world they are native – including our own. From the position of the radical other, anthropology may help the world realize the extent to which local cultures are mutually implicated while also allowing for a recognition of difference and points of resistance. The position from which anthropology may now speak is one of deliberate eccentricity. The point is that the degree of centrality to our own belief system held by various propositions about the world is not a correlate to different degrees of reality (Rorty 1991a: 52). By its double vision, and through its speaking from the perceived periphery rather than the self-declared centre of reason, anthropology challenges received wisdom. Thus, it enables us to make the world new rather than to get it right (cf. Rorty 1991a: 44).

This evidently has to be demonstrated in practice. Ethnography and detailed empirical studies from all over the globe must be produced to that effect. Along with that, the epistemological assumptions of anthropology must be questioned and clarified. As noted by Pierre Bourdieu, progress of knowledge in the social sciences implies progress in our knowledge of the conditions of knowledge (Bourdieu 1990: 1). This book is addressed to an elucidation of some of the basic conditions for anthropological knowledge by the end of the twentieth century, at a time of scholarly uncertainty in the wake of a self-declared postmodernism that made of the world a paradox of unification and fragmentation – inaccessible for science, if ready for narration.

Given this paradox, the passage to anthropology is not easily made by way of a traditional map. Regionalism, grand theory and dogma that once provided fixed coordinates for orientation in the scholarly space are being replaced by moving frames of reference. This calls for an itinerary rather than a map.[4] The latter may show you where you are, while the former tells you where you are going. The itinerary indicates direction and places of reverence, and works on the experience of movement in space. This explains the organization of my book. The direction is towards anthropology as a vital theoretical project; the tour passes what I consider to be points of contemplative relevance as indicated by the chapter headings. It is neither a straight line of argument nor a fixed structure of certainties. It is a tour which – like a pilgrimage – counts by the effort as much as by the goal. At the end of the tour lies nothing but a rather simple point about the intrinsic value of the theoretical project of anthropology – apart from the knowledge that the passage has been made. A renewed confidence in the anthropological project may hopefully ensue upon return.

Chapter 1

The ethnographic present
On starting in time

In the context of modern world history the present tends to evade our gaze and to defy our language. 'The present' refers not only to the contemporary but also to the peculiar: what is not yet clear because of its uniqueness and interpretative ambiguity. Our present seems to be substantially different from the present that our predecessors confronted, just a short time ago (Fox 1991b: 1). Decentred, fragmented and compressed are some of the words in current use, signalling the nature of the difference. With the sense of substantial change goes an enlarged mental problem of assessing the present; as Marilyn Strathern has recently argued, it is always the present rather than the future that is the momentous unknown (Strathern 1992: 178). It is only the future that can tell us how to evaluate the present. And with the decentredness of the world, it seems more doubtful than ever that we shall be able to make a uniform future evaluation. The present is endlessly open for interpretation.

Nevertheless, the present is where we start from. Touring means setting out from a particular point in time and space. Trajectories may be made in all directions, but the anthropological traveller literally moves in the present and becomes part and parcel of the global unrest. The old treading stones have to be turned as a matter of course. Occasionally, this will give one a sense of losing one's footing, but the sense of direction is not necessarily threatened.

As implied by the prologue, recent epistemological turmoils in anthropology have been related to no less dramatic changes in the world order. Attempts have been made at recapturing the discipline before it disappears altogether (e.g. Fox 1991a). There has been a certain sense of panic resulting from the disappearance of the traditional object, and what seems to be the last burial of positivist virtue. In the context of modern world history, englobement seems complete: the 'others' have become sadly like 'us'. What is forgotten by the mourners is the fact that modernity was everywhere indigenized (Sahlins 1993). The present cultural projects of the peoples that earlier were deemed without history are not chance inventions of tradition but full-scale declarations of autonomy and authenticity. Anthropology must seek to contextualize this declaration from a theoretical standpoint, not just a sentimental one.

In a sense, there is no anthropology to recapture because it was never at the point of vanishing; not more than the world itself, that is. There has been a certain degree of epistemological *Angst*, and the death of the discipline has been announced often enough, but the fundamental continuity between anthropology and the world remains as real as ever. The changes experienced are, indeed, connected. The world changes and so must anthropology. Whether we like it or not, anthropology is one of the declarations made by the self-announcing species of *anthropos*.

The *Angst* expressed over the past decade or more bears witness to a temporary theoretical shortcoming of anthropology rather than to its imminent death. The 'obituary mode' is related to the somewhat painful fact that anthropological knowledge all too often has been used to supply us with parables for talking about ourselves, rather than to explore historical alternatives for the vast numbers of 'others' who live under critical conditions, be it due to poverty, famine, civil war, flight, torture, racism or totalitarianism. Thus, the mode is implicated by the theoretical legacy of anthropology, constructed on an idea of other societies as coherent wholes and thereby relegating chaos and disorder to the non-social, or at best to a temporary setback (cf. Davis 1992b). As I have argued elsewhere, this is no longer tenable (Hastrup 1993b). Theory has to catch up with the often distressful fact that the world is chaotic, rather than mechanical. The *Angst* must be faced, not evaded by means of disciplinary suicide.

The parables on ourselves were nourished by the eternal mimetic process taking place between ourselves and others, a process which for long – quite wrongly – was seen as a western privilege (Taussig 1993). To mime is to play the other; the western world and, with it, anthropology has held this in apparent monopoly. *We* made the move that took us bodily into alterity;

as fieldworkers we became part of the space we studied, and to which we attributed a dreamlike order. The dream has vanished. The manifest disorder in the world and the discovery of the others' capacity to mime us have made it clear that, while difference remains, the world is one. To explore the epistemological foundation of anthropology at this stage, therefore, serves a different purpose than just providing a lifeboat for a sinking discipline. It serves to remind it about its own constructive ambiguity: in addition to its being a field of knowledge, a *disciplinary* field, it is also a field of action, a *force* field (Scheper-Hughes 1992: 24–25). This book is an attempt to provide an epistemological basis for a practical integration of these two fields, being the arenas for objectivity and solidarity respectively. The present western disorientation seems to be a privileged starting point for anthropology to once again catch up with its time.

THE HORIZON OF ANTHROPOLOGY

The horizon is as far as we can see from where we are. It is not fixed; if we move in space the horizon shifts. What is within one's horizon is subject to revision and expansion. Scholarly anthropology developed from the Age of Discovery, and was founded upon an exploration of unmapped cultural territories. In this vein, anthropology has continued to contribute to the expansion of the western horizon.

The identity of a person, and of a scholarly discipline, is also firmly linked to the horizon within which we are capable of taking a stand (Taylor 1989: 27). It is not a property but a space with unfixed boundaries, perpetually subject to expansion or contraction. It is a moral space which allows us to orient ourselves, and thus to 'become' ourselves in the first place. The notion of a moral space points to the fact that the space within which we orient ourselves is not just a society or a language, but a space within which our grasping the world in terms of values is inseparable from our way of living (Taylor 1989: 67).

This implies that the identity of the anthropological profession is intimately linked to its practice and to its contribution to the cultural and moral horizons by which our lives are bounded. For some, the claim to a particular profession rather than just a perspective may seem superfluous. To me this is a necessary starting point for qualifying the practice as something other than ordinary travelling and subsequent pondering about difference. Anthropology may not be a prototypical member of the category of scholarship, let alone of 'science', yet its import derives from its ability to discover and define reality just as much as linguistics and physics. Its potential stems from its power to question the givens of western culture rather than confirming them. As such, anthropology continues the Romantic reaction against Enlightenment reason (cf. Shweder 1984), and against the sanctification of the natural sciences (Rorty 1991b: 18). The discovery of other worlds is explicitly creative.

The point is not to dethrone natural science for the fun of it alone; its displacement from the centre of the category of sciences is principally a means of understanding the shortcomings of the view – stretching from physics and extending far into analytic philosophy – that scientific thinking essentially consists in clarification, or 'in patiently making explicit what has remained implicit' (Rorty 1991b: 12). Clarification does not make the trick as far as the human sciences are concerned. The interpretation, or the scientific explanation of matters cultural, is not an inherent quality of the object; it is the result of a project of linking and contextualizing defined by a specific purpose. The event of understanding is intertextual in the widest sense of this term. This event is mediated in words that have often belied the demands of the interpretative frame and presented the understanding as if given by the nature of the object. This can never be the case; clarification of objective properties is but one step in a larger process of radical interpretation.

Articulation, evidently, is not the target. All scholarship needs to be articulated to make sense. In spite of the delusive nature of language, proponents of silence are unconvincing (cf. Taylor 1989: 91ff., 98). Articulacy, however, is not a matter of finding words corresponding adequately to the reality beyond them in the hope of finding a final resting-place for thought (Rorty 1991b: 19). There is no such final resting-place, no ultimate, ahistorical reality, to which our vocabularies must be adequate. Clarification recedes to articulation, as a way of making sense. In anthropology, articulacy is a way of explicitly escaping the illusion of fit between words and lived experiences, by demonstrating the lack of fit between different reference schemes.

The mismatch between reference schemes, or cultures, as experienced in fieldwork is conceptually overcome by our shared human capacity of imagination. The range of imaginative power in anthropology is an integral part of its ability to contribute to a liberation of culture from its own obsolete vocabularies by its ability to weave new metaphors into the fabric of common beliefs. Metaphors are not parasites upon reality, they are extensions of it. As such they are forerunners of a new language, stretched to fit new experiences. In short, anthropology is one important source for acknowledging that cognition is not necessarily *re*cognition, and that the acquisition of truth is not a matter of fitting data into a pre-established scheme (cf. Rorty 1991b: 13).

The prime virtue of anthropology lies in the fact that its space is as open-ended as the world to which it belongs. It cannot, therefore, make claims to a particular regime of truth in the Foucauldian sense – implying just another possible epistemic order. The open-endedness of anthropology is owed to its unfailing commitment to exploring different epistemologies, but this does not amount to a claim that all orders are equally possible or equally good. This is where the subjective standpoint is once again insurmountable; as pointed out by Taylor, the

> point of view from which we might constate that all orders are equally arbitrary, in particular that all moral views are equally so, is just not available to us humans. It is a form of self-delusion to think that we do not speak from a moral orientation which we take to be right.
>
> (Taylor 1989: 99)

There is no way of speaking from nowhere in particular, as previously argued, not even for transculturated anthropologists.

So far anthropologists have spoken from an off-centred position within the category of sciences. If this has seemed to marginalize our contribution, I believe that the inherent eccentricity of anthropology *vis-à-vis* the dominant world-view is a source of extreme strength. This, of course, has still to be demonstrated in practice. Trajecting the present horizon of anthropology, as I do in this book, points to the future. In a sense I am trying to 'project back' from some future vantage point to an evaluation of the present. Evaluation is part of knowledge; people – and anthropologists among them – not only learn to think, they also learn to care. If it seems daring thus to stretch the present to its limits it is perfectly in keeping with the anthropological quest: the expansion of the horizon takes place in time as well as space.

Evaluating the present is to make claim to potentiality as well as actuality.

PRACTISING ETHNOGRAPHY

Stressing the need to take off in the present implies an emphasis upon anthropology as practice, that is, a mode of doing and creating. The anthropological practice bifurcates into a field practice and a discursive practice, implicated also in the performative paradox identified above.

The anthropological discourse has been marked by an extensive use of what is known as the 'ethnographic present'.[1] It implies the use of the present tense as the dominant mode of representing the others. The use of tense has been seriously criticized as reflecting a particular relationship of observation and distancing to the object (Fabian 1983: 86). It has been described as a vague and essentially atemporal moment (Stocking 1983: 86), reflecting the ahistoric or synchronic pretense of anthropology (Crapanzano 1986: 51).

The ethnographic present is, evidently, a literary device, and as such it needs to be questioned along with other conventions of representation in anthropology. However, it is not solely an accidental temporal mode loosely linked to the synchronic nature of fieldwork (Marcus and Fischer 1986: 96). Nor is it in any way a simple matter of synchronizing our descriptions. Rather it covers a variety of texual *mise-en-scènes* (Davis 1992a). The ethnographic present is a corollary of the peculiar nature of the anthropological practice as identified in the performative paradox. It is a necessary construction of time, because only the present tense preserves the reality of *anthropological* knowledge. I argue this in full recognition of the critique raised against the earlier ahistoric mode of anthropology. The choice of tense was right but it rested on false assumptions. My contention is that we are now in a position to reassess our assumptions and to reinvent the ethnographic present without previous connotations.

Fieldwork is diacritical in the anthropological practice. While it lasts, it is a radical experience of estrangement and relativism. Afterwards, it becomes memory and the backbone of objectivism. By way of opening this well-known theme I shall present a fragment of my own memories from the field.

Looking back upon my fieldwork in Iceland in 1982–1983 I

recall that I suffered a lot.[2] Although it took place within the
boundaries of the self-declared western civilization, my sufferings
were of a general kind. In addition to the monotonous diet, the
cold, the blizzards, and the inescapable nature to which I was
constantly exposed, I had the not uncommon problems of loneli-
ness, of sexual assaults, loss of identity and offensive enemy
spirits. In spite of all this, one of my greatest shocks in the field
was to be reminded of my own world. Towards the end of my
first year-long stay in Iceland, when I lived and worked in a
fishing village in pitch-dark and ice-cold winter, and where I had
for some time felt completely cut off from the rest of the world,
I once received six letters addressed to Kirsten Hastrup. They
were full of questions like: would I organize a conference?; what
would I like to teach in the spring term?; would I do an Open
University course?; and would it not be wonderful to get back?
That really got me down, and I knew instantly that I would never,
ever go back to that world which had nothing to do with me. I
was infuriated that people assumed that they knew who I was.
They did not, obviously. I was Kristín á Gimli, worked as a fish-
woman, smelled of fish, and shared my incredibly shabby house
with three young and wild fishermen. That was who I wanted to
be, I decided, and threw the letters into a heap of junk.

They remained there, but as readers will have guessed, I myself
returned – at least partly – to the world I had left. In that world
I write articles on the fishermen's violence and the god-forsaken
village. Experience has become memory, and the relics are embel-
lished so as to pass for anthropology (cf. Boon 1986). The anecdote thus serves the immediate purpose of situating fieldwork
between autobiography and anthropology (cf. Hastrup 1992a).

It also illustrates the nature of the ethnographer's presence in
the field. At the time of my inverse culture shock I had in some
sense 'gone native'. Margaret Mead once warned us that although
immersing oneself in local life is good, one should be careful not
to drown; allegedly, one way of maintaining the delicate balance
is to write and receive letters from one's own world (Mead 1977:
7). In my case the letters pushed me even further down into the
native world; I had no choice of degree of immersion. Even
though we now recognize that 'going native' is to enter a world
of one's own creation (Wagner 1975: 9), there is still reason to
stress the radical nature of the fieldwork experience – profoundly
marking the entire anthropological discourse. Whether the indi-

vidual anthropologist goes temporarily native or not, the field-work practice implies that the well-established opposition between subject and object dissolves in anthropology. The ethnographer is not only labelled by the others, she is also named. As named, that is, as an identified subject in the alien discursive space, the ethnographer becomes part of her field. Her presence is the occasion and the locus of the drama that is the source of anthropological reflection (Dumont 1978: 12). There is no absolute perspective from where we can eliminate our own consciousness from our object (Rabinow 1977: 151). By her presence in the field, the ethnographer is actively engaged in the construction of the ethnographic reality or, one might say, of the ethnographic present.

This is where we can begin to see that the practice of fieldwork eliminates both subjectivism and objectivism and posits truth as an intersubjective creation. In this sense, fieldwork is almost like a possession, which by itself is nothing but the collapse of the subject–object relation (Fernandez 1986: 247). Although our results cannot be measured against the requirements of natural scientific verification, we have no choice: anthropology is radical interpretation and cannot, therefore, be *wertfrei* (cf. Taylor 1979: 71). It can be scholarship, of course, and of a kind that may have radical implications for the world. Before that, fieldwork has to be transformed into text. The practice of anthropology implies a writing of ethnography from a particular standpoint of knowing and interpreting – in time.

WRITING CULTURES

Culture is an invention, tied up with the invention of anthropology (Wagner 1975). Unlike earlier generations of anthropologists who thought of culture in essentialist terms, we now realize that it is a creation on our part, and one which may become increasingly poeticized – in fact and in text (cf. Rorty 1991a: 110). Whether construed in the singular, and denoting a philosophical counterpoint to nature, or in the plural, designating sociological entities, we can no longer claim culture to be an objective fact. Cultures materialize in contradistinction to each other; differences are exaggerated in the process. Anthropology has cemented the exaggeration and described the others as everything we were not. Conversely, the others have presented simulacra of themselves in

order to fob off and satisfy our search to understand their speci-
fity (Ardener 1989b: 183).

A primary conclusion is, then, that unlike a society which is an
empirical entity, culture is an analytical implication. The cultural
order is virtual; it is realized only as events of speech and action
(Sahlins 1985: 153). Events are the empirical form of system,
which is, therefore, under constant risk from practice. Ultimately,
that is why we have to *write* cultures in order to perceive them
as wholes.

The invention of culture in anthropological writing must (in
some sense at least) reflect the ways in which cultures invent
themselves if anthropology wants to be faithful to its own aims
(Wagner 1975: 30). Not any piece of writing will do, if we want
to call ourselves anthropologists and not just travel writers. We
have to seriously investigate the lived space, which is the experiential counterpart to the implicational cultural space. I shall term
this experiential space a 'world' (Hastrup 1987c). It will be understood that this is not solely an ideational space, but one that is
made up of people and actions. Indeed, the old dichotomy
between idealism and materialism makes no sense (Ardener 1982:
11). However, the main point here is that the implication of
culture – to pose as an analytical object of anthropology – must
have a lived counterpart in the world. It is this world that the
ethnographers must enter if their writings shall be 'realistic.'

We shall return to realism later (in chapter 9); here I shall sum
up about culture that it is sensed only by way of 'culture shock'
– summing up in dramatic form the exposure to another culture.
In anthropology this implies the ethnographer's deliberately subjecting herself to a world beyond her competence; we cannot
write real cultures without experiences of other worlds. The road
to anthropological knowledge goes via shared social experience
(Hastrup and Hervik 1994). The degree of sharing is often astonishing, as another anecdote from my fieldwork will illustrate.

For some months I lived and worked on an Icelandic farm
where I, to the best of my knowledge, practised participant observation. It implied a particular kind of presence that made me an
object in the Icelanders' discourse; they wrote their culture all
over me. In order to achieve a proper position in the farming
world I had assumed the role of milkmaid and shepherdess.
During my first stay, I had actually been partly responsible for
the milking and tending of some 30 cows. It was gratifying to

achieve new basic skills in itself, but more importantly, my working position also greatly facilitated an actual shift of identity, theoretically implied by participant observation. As an anthropologist one cannot easily get a close relationship to thirty relatively stupid cows, but as milkmaid one is bound to take them seriously. One must surrender to the role in a very direct manner; there is no way of finding oneself between cows handling their udders and still pretending that one is there only for scholarship. For me, the work soon entailed differentiated relations to the cows, which I could no longer deal with as a category but had to deal with as named individuals. I collected their names, of course, for later analysis, but first of all I experienced how some cows were nice and friendly, while others were stupid, and some even hostile. One cow in particular always annoyed me, and once it occasioned a sprained thumb – an injury that is very inconvenient for a milkmaid. I really got to dislike the beast and I am sure it was a mutual feeling.

After a few months I left the farm to go elsewhere, but also to return six months later. On my return I immediately found my old place in the cowshed and went from cow to cow to recall their names. In front of my old enemy I sensed the well-known feeling of anger and murmured: 'So there you still are, you silly old beast.' Next morning, when the farmer and I went into the cowshed to do the morning milking, the beast was lying dead on the floor, for no apparent reason. I was deeply shocked, because I knew that in previous times such occurrences had brought witches to the stake.

The point of this tale is not only to show how the cow recognized me as 'of the Icelandic world' so full of magic and witchcraft, but that even I, the anthropologist disguised as a milkmaid, was prepared to take responsibility for the death of the cow. I had internalized an experiential space where time was another and where the usual patterns of causality were suspended. While undoubtedly in some sense a space of my own creation, the experience was real – and of the kind that makes ethnographers doubt self-evidences.

My own implicit allegation of witchcraft (as against myself) was not a question of belief, and far less of superstition. It was an expression of my experiencing a distinct reality of which I was temporarily part, and which once and for all taught me that we cannot separate materiality and meaning. They are simultaneities in the world in which we live, and as such they write themselves onto the ethnographer who temporarily shares the world of others. It is this simultaneity that makes actual presence in the other world a precondition for the writing of culture, and which transforms the inherent paradox of participant observation into a literary dilemma of 'participant description' (Geertz 1988: 83).

PRESENCE AND REPRESENTATION

Until recently, the ethnographer's presence in the field was the sole stamp of authority needed in the anthropological monograph (cf. Clifford 1983b). Since Malinowski, fieldwork was a strategy of discovery by which the anthropologist could intervene in alien spaces and behave 'like an ideal metering device' (Ardener 1985: 57). The invention of this strategy – of I-witnessing (Geertz 1988) – made a new genre of writing possible, the genre of realism. Within this genre 'the author as fieldworker was always implicitly present; the author as author was always implicitly absent' (Boon 1983: 138). Today, the questioning of the anthropologist's authorial status marks the end of modernism.

Physical presence in the field is no longer the source of absolute authority. The kind of participation needed to identify events and write real cultures cannot be glossed as mere 'being' in the field. It implies a process of 'becoming'. Becoming is a metaphor for a kind of participation that can never be complete and which is no immediate consequence of physical presence. It does not imply that the anthropologist gradually becomes identical with the others. I did not become an Icelandic shepherdess although I participated in sheep-farming and experienced the unreality of shepherdesses in misty mountains (cf. Hastrup 1987a). The concept of becoming implies that one gives in to an alien reality and allows oneself to change in the process. One is not completely absorbed in the other world, but one is also no longer the same. The change often is so fundamental that it is difficult to see how the fieldworker has any identity with her former self. Fieldwork, therefore, escapes our ordinary historical categories. The space discovered has neither a firm future nor a distinct past, because intentions and memories are transformed as definitions, categories and meanings shift. Participant observation today implies an observation of participation itself (cf. Tedlock 1991); it is not self-evident that what we participate in is the real life of the others.

Although part of the anthropologist's life-history and also representing a moment in the course of local history, the experience of the fieldworld as such is outside history (as a particular temporal mode). It is so strongly marked by liminality that the ordinary succession of events is suspended (cf. Turnbull 1990). Furthermore, insight is obtained by a degree of violence; the ethnographer must keep up a certain pressure in order to elicit information (Griaule 1957: 14; cf. also Clifford 1983a). Power differences inform the dialogue and distort history. They also create history, but it is a kind of history that is but a fleeting moment and cannot be spoken about in ordinary historical categories. Hence the ethnographic present. The tense reflects the reality of fieldwork.

The problem is that within realism as a genre, the ethnographic present was thought to represent the reality of the other *society*. For functionalists and consorts, the realist monograph *r*epresented what societies were: timeless, islandlike entities (Boon 1982: 14). However, the critique of realism as genre and of the assumptions behind earlier modes of representation should not make us lose sight of the reality of fieldwork and of 'realism' as quite a respectable epistemology.[3] We must not continue the logical error of mistaking the one for the other, that is, of confounding genre and epistemology.

Fieldwork is outside history quite irrespective of the fact that all societies have histories of their own and are deeply involved in global history as well. The reality of fieldwork is a liminal phase for both subjects and objects, in which the distinction between them is dissolved; at alternating points in the discourse subject and object take on the complementary positions of namer and named (Parkin 1982: xxxiii-xxxiv). History seems to be suspended for both parties. The present is what frames the encounter and lends it meaning. The frame is far from fixed, but somehow fieldwork is stuck within it.

The liminality of fieldwork is one reason why it has been likened to a *rite de passage*, and generally identified as the central ritual of the tribe of anthropologists (Stocking 1983: 70). Now, the meaning of ritual is not its inner essence, but its being part of a wider self-defining social space.[4] Rituals often are among the more remarkable declarations of such spaces. Although the history of anthropological theory tends to belie this, ritual cannot be studied isolated as 'text'; it is a context-marker. So also for the central ritual of anthropology: fieldwork marks the context of anthropology while it does not exhaust its content. The ethnographer's ritual presence in another world, with all that implies of intersubjectivity and intertextuality, has no absolute inner meaning. Something else is meaningless without it: anthropology. As a distinct field of scholarship, anthropology invests itself in the present not only to document cultures but to experience the processes of their making.

In this context we become our own informants on the ethnographic present. The fieldwork ritual implies a particular construction of time; Johannes Fabian has introduced the distinction between the coevalness of fieldwork and the allochronism of writing (Fabian 1983). Fieldwork implies a sharing of time with the other, while writing often implies a temporal distancing. I would suggest that the ethnographic present be re-read as an implication of a shared time. Using the present tense is to speak from the centre of another time-space, which existed only at that fleeting instant when the ethnographer impressed herself upon the world of the others – and changed it. Its implications, however, transcend the Cartesian coordinates of time and space.

Criticizing the split between coevalness and allochronism is relevant only if we conceive of the anthropological endeavour as one of substantive representation, that is, of reproduction and of accurately mapping one space onto another. If, contrarily, we perceive representation as a creative process of evocation and re-enactment (not simply to say: 'description') we have no choice of tense. The ethnographer saw or heard something sometime in an autobiographic past, but the implications must be *presented* to be of relevance as anthropology, and to avoid the imputed loss from fieldwork to writing.[5]

The reality of the encounter is outside ordinary history; it is its own history, if you wish. As discourse it must be realized temporally and in a present (cf. Ricoeur 1979: 74). The ethnographic present reflects the instance of the discourse. In short, the reason for the present tense is located in the dual nature of anthropological practice of fieldwork and writing, or presence and re-creation. The reality of the cultures that we write depends on a particular narrative construction, a discursive present; the realities of other people, of course, have histories that are retold in local language. It is not for anthropology, however, to recast biographies and social histories in full, or for that matter to retell local stories. That is far more convincingly done by those who live them. The hallmark of anthropology is to experience the force of detail in practical life and to recast it in a theoretical mode that transcends it. Life has to be recreated in a separate language in order to be comprehended.

CULTURAL TRANSLATION

We are led towards a reconsideration of cultural translation. This notion has been used as a metaphor for anthropology, especially within British anthropology since Evans-Pritchard. Although lip service has often been paid to the fact that it is not really like linguistic translation, it is only recently that a serious questioning of the metaphor has begun, notably by Ardener (1989b) and Asad (1986).

One example to which Asad draws attention is Godfrey Lienhardt's seminal work on 'Modes of Thought' (1954), in which he writes:

> The problem of describing to others how members of a remote tribe think then begins to appear largely as one of translation, of making the coherence primitive thought has in the languages it really lives in, as clear as possible in our own.
>
> (Lienhardt 1954: 97)

Leach is even more direct when he says that the anthropological problem of coping with cultural difference essentially is one of translation; it may be difficult but a 'tolerably satisfactory translation is always possible' (Leach 1973: 772, quoted in Asad 1986: 142). Behind the idea of cultural translation lies a mode of thinking about anthropological representation as an attempt to reproduce one social space in the discourse of another as accurately as possible. As we have seen, this is an untenable epistemological assumption.

The problem is not merely that some categories can only be rendered by approximation and then only on a considerable, encyclopaedic (or ethnographic) background (Sperber 1985: 44). A much more important source for the unease about the metaphor of translation is the profound asymmetry between languages; the alleged translation takes place between languages that are unequal from the outset (Asad 1986). This is partly due to the lamented legacy of colonialism out of which anthropology grew,

and the related power structure always inherent in the legitimiz-
ation of language (Bourdieu 1991), partly to the nature of the
anthropological discourse. To put it briefly, the discourse in which
one can write *about* somebody for a specific audience is by definition a discourse of englobement. The linguistic inequality is
aggravated by the implicit hierarchy between between literate
and oral forms of knowledge in western culture (cf. Clifford
1988b: 339–341). Dissecting the notion of translation thus leads
back to the point that anthropological knowledge is a symptom
of our own society (Scholte 1980: 66–67). That is a political point
worth repeating.

A theoretical point also worth making is that we cannot properly translate cultures into our own without destroying their specificity. Taken to the extreme, translation implies a transformation
of the unknown into something known, and anthropology would
clearly become absurd if this was taken literally:

> What lies at the end of translation . . . is a kind of entropy of
> the translated system – a total remapping of the other social
> space into entities of the translating one. At our destination
> the terrain would, however, be disappointingly familiar.
>
> (Ardener 1989b: 178)

Thus, at the end of the road of translation, anthropology would
have to start all over again – by re-establishing difference.

Difference always mattered more than similarity in the writing
of cultures. What goes onto the anthropological map is cultural
difference. Any idea of translation from one cultural space to
another is vastly complicated by the symbolic interpenetration of
cultures by which difference is first established. 'Culture' is
already an implication, and in spite of claims to accurate representation, ethnographic texts are inescapably allegorical. The difference is not translated, it is posited and transcended.

Difference is posited through the experience of fieldwork, from
which we know that cultural understanding is about disequation
rather than equation (Ardener 1989b: 183). After the initial
experience of relativism, difference is transcended in writing and
its implied objectivism. This process is not a mechanical process
of translation but a highly complex process of understanding and
re-enactment, in which the anthropologist herself plays a crucial
part, and which is complicated by features of heteroglossia and
muteness.[6]

Once we have realized that anthropology is not about replacing one discourse by another, or about representation or translation, we may return to a consideration of the anthropological practice as a creative process – of *presenting* ethnography. Even if the object of study must be historicized in all sorts of ways, the choice of tense is right; what would the point of anthropology be if its truth had already gone at the moment of writing.

THE PROPHETIC CONDITION

However provisional in a larger historical perspective, the truth carried by the message of the anthropologist must be convincing. This is a problem she shares with Hermes, another trickster (Crapanzano 1986: 52). It is also a problem she shares with the prophet whom I shall now introduce. Both timing and translation are put into perspective by the prophetic condition, as identified by Edwin Ardener (1989a; cf. Hastrup 1989). The prophetic condition is a condition of both structures and individuals who find themselves between two worlds. The prophet gives voice to a new world but belongs to an old one. The voice is not always heard. The words seem incomprehensible beforehand; afterwards they are trivial. When the new world has materialized, the words of the prophet are indistinguishable from ordinary speech. The structural conditions for prophecy can be more or less favourable. A privileged condition obtains when a discontinuity is generally sensed, but when it is still not conceivable in known categories.

The anthropologist is 'like' a prophet, structurally speaking. The two worlds mediated by the anthropologist are more often separated in space than in time, but in principle the anthropologist gives voice to a new world. The prophetic position of the anthropologist is further substantiated when we realize that prophets do not *predict* a future. Predictions are always part of current language and when they prove 'correct' it is because they are essentially repetitions. Predictions always fail when they are most needed, that is, when repetition does not occur. The prophet does not predict the future, he foretells it before it has been incorporated into the collective representations. He gives voice to and in that sense defines the world he has discovered. He expands on the present by telling it to its limits. In other words, the perception of a new world is closely related to an expansion of language. A new reality takes shape as it is conceptualized, in anthropology as well as in prophecy. The 'other' world is discovered and defined simultaneously; observation and theory are one.

There are, of course, realities and histories before and beyond anthropology. But through the dual nature of the anthropological practice, of experiencing and writing, a new world of betweenness is created.[7] It is this betweenness that places the anthropologist in a prophetic position and forces her to speak in the ethnographic present. In spite of recent claims to multiple authorship, it is still the voice of the anthropologist that presents the other world in the text. Like the prophet, the anthropologist offers another language, another space, another time to reality. That is the emergent meaning of the anthropological practice.

I argue, then, that timing in anthropology – seen as an essentially prophetic discourse – involves the use of the ethnographic present. Its inevitability is linked to our ritual presence in the field, without which the context is meaningless as anthropology. The ethnographic present is a narrative construct that clearly does not represent a truth about the timelessness of the others. We know that they are as historical as anybody in all possible ways. But the betweenness implied in fieldwork, and the fact of the ethnographer's sharing the time *of* the others, makes ethnography escape the ordinary historical categories.

The prophetic condition implies that the unspeakable becomes spoken, and that language expands on both sides of the dialogue. Whereas translation presupposes two separate discourses, one of which is the object of the other, prophecy implies intersubjectivity or intertextuality affecting both worlds. To the extent that we are now ready to acknowledge that the ethnographer changes in the field, we should also admit that neither do the informants remain the same. Nor do they remain 'other'. We have to abandon the use, not of the ethnographic present but of the term 'informants' that construes the others as (verbal) pathways to separate worlds. In the newly discovered world between us and them, the illusion of distance is broken.

In the prophetic condition of anthropology there is an implicational truth that is not outlived when the ethnographer leaves the field, and which should not, therefore, be rendered in the past tense. When this is realized, the ethnographic present may lead to many possible futures. As such, the ethnographic present is what potentiates anthropology.

Chapter 2

The language paradox
On the limits of words

The relationship between the language and the world is at the core of epistemology. It has been probed into from various philosophical angles, which have suggested as many ways of seeing it. In this chapter I shall limit my discussion to some areas that have particular pertinence for anthropology. My approach is pragmatic in the sense that I aim at identifying current concerns of anthropology as practice, rather than at tracing the history of anthropological thought about language. This, of course, is related to my wish to expand on the present. My principal focus in this chapter is on local or natural language, but it reflects back upon anthropological language as well.

As indicated by the heading of this chapter, I believe that there are serious limitations on local words and writings as sources of genuine anthropological understanding. The paradox of language to which I refer lies in the fact that while it may indeed sometimes be difficult in real life to determine whether we are dealing with a social or a linguistic phenomenon, because language somehow is to the social as a measuring rod is to the measured, linguistics alone cannot unlock the complexities of social life (Ardener 1989b: 180). Language, spoken or written, measures but does not represent. As measuring rod it imposes its own scale upon the plasticity of the social. This applies to local language as much as scholarly works.

This reflects back upon the understanding of the relationship between language, culture and identity that always had a prominent position on the anthropological agenda. The discussion of this particular item has taken a new turn with the emergence of world-wide literacy, virtually if not actually or statistically. Literacy implies that part of any culture is now stored in writings, ranging from laws to poetry, and the question naturally arises how we should deal with this kind of material. The traditional ethnographic practice of eavesdropping outside the local walls of silence has been supplemented by a reading over broad native shoulders.[1] With reading we are on home ground, and we do not even have to take notes, a practice which has recently been unveiled as cumbersome and loaded with professional frustration (cf. Sanjek 1990). Small wonder that anthropologists have taken such an interest in the multiplicities of native writing as sources of cultural understanding. We might wish to recall that by 'natives' I refer to all of us – in our capacity of being 'at home' in some world or other.

Native words and texts may provide cultural clues and qualify as ethnographic material in all sorts of ways, but I contend that there is an ontological gap between words and social processes that cannot be bridged from within the language itself. To understand this, and to point to a new constructive communion with our principal means of expression I shall explore the relationship between language and the world from a range of perspectives. First, my argument starts from a discussion of categorization as a particular reflection upon the world; the aim is to demonstrate the potential mismatch between the words and the realities they name. Next, I shall deal with the feature of metaphor as a linguistic and literary device allowing people to mean more than they can say, and perhaps also to say more than they mean; the point here is to show the limitations of metaphor as a clue to social action. Third, the argument will make a tour around etymology as an often-used instrument in the reconstruction of social phenomena and meaning. Towards the end of the chapter, I shall make some general points on the relationship between writing and social process and the nature of anthropological understanding. The general idea underlying the argument is that whatever the representational shortcomings of language, and their redoubling in writing, there is nothing to be gained from verbal abstinence. There is no surplus solidarity to be gained from not listening to the natives, nor any extra scholarly reputation to be gained from not writing.

CATEGORY

The nature of categorization is central to any discussion of the relationship between language and the world. In classical linguistic theory, the doctrine held categories to be abstract containers, implying that things were either inside or outside the category, affiliation to which was determined by the sharing of a certain number of properties.[2] As far as identity categories are concerned, this view entailed that all members of a particular category a priori were defined by their shared cultural (and linguistic) identity. No less important, the idea of categories as empty containers had particular implications for the view of *reason* as disembodied and abstract, and of knowledge as essentially objective. As most explicitly specified by Whorf (1956) and his followers, it is language that determines the conceptual system in this particular objectivist view of the world.

The presumed one-to-one correspondence between language and reality has passed for axiomatic truth in philosophy and science for a long time. Accordingly, the scope of scholarship was to formulate those theories or models that best fitted the discovered realities. We have lost our objectivist innocence and the idea of correspondence between language and world, yet we have still to come to terms with a remarkable continuity between words and worlds (Ardener 1982; Hastrup 1987c), which precludes a facile resort to constructionism.

Compared to the old objectivist view of categories as containers of reality, new linguistic theories have turned the world around. Experiment and reasoning have shown that language does not represent the world in any direct fashion; categories cannot be understood independently of a knower or a culturalized subject (Rosch 1978: 29). This implies that categorization is essentially a matter of both human experience and imagination, from which it follows that reason is based on the same factors and cannot be viewed solely in terms of the manipulation of abstract symbols such as categories (Lakoff 1987: 8). Meaning cannot be reduced to reference.

Anthropologists have known this for a long time, of course. In those other cultures that we have been studying we have been met with a kind of reason that did not reflect the western notions of rationality. Many attempts have been made to sort out the relationship between the obvious cultural relativism and the need

for a shared scientific standard. Relativism has been variably
contrasted with universalism, absolutism or objectivism, and if
anything, the endless debates demonstrate the multiplicity of epistemologies even within western scholarship (Hirst 1985). While
the debate has not brought us closer to a final solution, in anthropology it has generally confirmed the point that relativization is
our only road to objectivity, and at least we have been forced to
review our 'strategies for *coping* with the consequences of relativism, accepting that our knowledges lack foundations in independent criteria of validity' (Hirst 1985: 85). One of these strategies
is a renewed reflection upon the nature of cultural categories.

If categories are not empty containers – of identity, for instance
– their significance shifts. They do not simply reflect the world,
they intervene into it, as we have known since Whorf. His insight
about intervention was transformed (by Sapir, who in contrast to
Whorf was a professional linguist) into a doctrine of determination in the Sapir–Whorf hypothesis, leading several generations
of scholars to believe that language not only mediated cultural
perceptions but also determined them. The often-quoted statement by Sapir is quite explicit about this:

> The fact of the matter is that the 'real world' is to a large
> extent unconsciously built up on the language habits of the
> group. No two languages are ever sufficiently similar to be
> considered as representing the same social reality. The worlds
> in which different societies live are distinct worlds, not merely
> the same world with different labels attached.
>
> (Sapir 1951: 162).

In other words, if a people have seven words for snow, they
perceive seven kinds of snow; and if people have no term for
blue, they have no idea of it (cf. Lakoff 1987: 40). Further, if a
particular language has no tenses, its speakers can have no sense
of time – a parallel to the allegation that if anthropologists write
in the present tense they have no idea of history. In anthropology,
this kind of argument has been implicit in the announcement of
'separate realities' to a point of relativistic caricature (Ardener
1989b: 164ff.). In turn, this has spurred equally reductive universalist statements denying any real basis for cultural misunderstanding (e.g. Bloch 1977).

Neither perception nor meaning can be deduced directly from
the category system. The 'properties' of particular categories are

not something that exist objectively in the world independent of particular people; they are what Lakoff calls interactional properties, or 'the result of our interactions as part of our physical and cultural environments given our bodies and our cognitive apparatus' (Lakoff 1987: 51). This firmly locks the meaning of categories into human experience.

This means that even within categories there is no unity and strict symmetry. It is not all members of the category 'bird' that are equally good examples of birds; sparrows are more representative of the category than ostriches, to take just one of Rosch's many examples of what she has called the 'prototype effect' (Rosch 1978; cf. Lakoff 1987: 40ff.). Prototypes reflect clusters of experience, and show how asymmetries prevail within the categories, asymmetries that could neither be predicted nor read from the position of classical linguistic theory, which attributed categories with almost mechanically reflective potential and believed them to be exhaustive. The question of 'Why is the Cassowary not a Bird?' (Bulmer 1967) and thousands of related questions in the anthropology of classification can now be answered by a treatise on how it might be a bird after all, although not prototypical and maybe also something other than a bird.

In anthropology, a striking and independent parallel to the notion of prototype is Ardener's concept of 'semantic density' (Ardener 1982, 1989b: 169). Density is related to frequency, a frequency of association and interaction with reality. Categories contain a statistical feature that is part of their material reality – a kind of materiality foreshadowed by Whorf but often overlooked with the dismissal of his general hypothesis. This feature is the main reason why no reality can ever be exhausted by a set of categories: 'The statistical figure marks irregularities of experience which are flattened by unit categories. This is an important point, accounting as it does for the existence of ways of incorporating experience into the category system' (Ardener 1989b: 169).

The insight into the nature of categories has important implications for our understanding of social stereotypes, where the prototype effect results in a metonymic replacement of the entire category by only part of it (Lakoff 1987: 79f.). Thus the notion of 'working mothers' points to the fact that the category 'mother' is metonymically reduced to 'housewife', to cite one of Lakoff's examples. The prototype effect also highlights the workings of cultural identity categories, which are particularly prone to features of density. One example is provided by the Scottish; the category more often than not evokes an image of the tartan-clad Highlanders, although they are in a numerical minority. In this particular case the 'Gaelic' emphasis seems to have been a product of Romantic poetry in the first place, and only later interpreted as a 'historical' fact (Chapman 1978; cf. also 1982). Similarly, as I myself have shown, not all members of the category of 'Icelanders' are equally 'Icelandic' in the mental image of Icelandicness (Hastrup 1990d).

Considering the prominent position of identity categories in anthropology ('We, the Tikopia', 'The Tallensi', 'The Icelanders'), we begin to understand the implications of the semantic densities, as expressions of the particular continuity between words and worlds. In a discipline dedicated to the study of peoples, the flattening out of unit categories has had particularly unfortunate consequences, sometimes also for the people defined, because their multiplicity was portrayed as unity. Treating identity categories as real and unproblematic reflections of reality has been aggravated in the featuring of 'others' and 'selves', as if they were equal on the map of the world. Because our ideas about categorization in general made no room for asymmetries, we were prevented from realizing the fundamental imbalance between our culture and theirs. From our new vantage point, however, we can see at least one basic asymmetry in this field: 'they' are always more like 'us' than 'we' are like 'them' (cf. Lakoff 1987: 41). Because we are our own prototypes of humans, they are less representative. The eccentric nature of words intervenes in the experience of worlds. This adds an important dimension to the discursive asymmetry inherent in anthropology.

There is no way of understanding natural language independent of social and experiential context. When the ethnographer is engaged in conversation and in participation in social life somewhere, the experiential basis is to some extent shared. Actually, because anthropologists are themselves part of the class of phenomena studied (i.e., people) there is no way of understanding people independent of the more or less shared human experience (Vendler 1984: 201). This does not imply that whenever we share a word with someone we have a clue to his or her inner life; as forcefully demonstrated by Rosaldo, anthropologists themselves are positioned subjects whose particular experiences allow only a selective comprehension (Rosaldo 1984). What is more, 'inner lives' are by definition beyond inspection.

When it comes to writings that are often read at a distance – in time or space – from experience, the experiential space is less accessible, and the results of our reading are potentially distorted to an even higher degree. There is no way of assessing the centres of gravity, that is, prototypes and densities, directly from a text. We have no ways of ascertaining that the structure that we 'find' actually binds together the relevant focal areas of the words (cf. Friedrich 1986: 120). We may construct some abstract conceptual system but we will never learn about the degree of chaos in both language and society.[3] In the period when it was considered appropriate to regard society as 'text' these methodological short-comings did not present themselves as such; today the text metaphor seems exhausted and we can no longer overlook the fact that we cannot 'read' cultures. This particular metaphor died when it became interpreted too literally.

The emergence of native writings does not neutralize this methodological problem; rather, it redoubles it, because writing removes language even further from its immediate referential context (Goody 1987: 292). Literacy has not only facilitated the possibilities of self-distancing in the abstract and general, in the same process it has also facilitated alienation from the sensations of everyday life and reality (Fernandez 1986: 151). Writing is a particular form of representation which may be completely alien to local modes of knowledge. With its stress upon linearity and chronology it suppresses instantaneousness and space. Even if we are able to ascertain that writing actually conforms to local conventions of representation, no native text ever exhausts the full flavour of ethnography. Words of themselves do not reveal the semantic densities of the experiential space. The idea that culture can be exhaustively described as the product of human beings trafficking in signs (cf. e.g. Daniel 1984: 229) must be abandoned. The taste of ethnographic things implies so much more than the sight of signs (Stoller 1989).

METAPHOR

Metaphor is a particular linguistic construction, that has generally been seen to bridge the gaps between categories and to provide a particular kind of insight into the frontiers of the category system. If there are methodological problems in bounding and comprehending ordinary linguistic categories, they appear to multiply with metaphors that were always seen to be parasitical upon language. Also, they have been feared in an empiricist tradition that was generally repressing emotion, imagination and other elements of what was seen as subjectivism (Lakoff and Johnson 1980: 191).

At the heart of western scholarly discourse has been what Whitehead called the search for 'the One in Many'; in anthropology, too, traditional wisdom had it that to discover the meaning of a particular institution the analyst had to uncover the (structured) reality that was obscured by the haze of appearances (Stoller 1989: 133ff.). The search for Platonic truth, i.e., a reality lurking behind appearances, has always been seriously disturbed by such disorderly features of language and behaviour that could not be directly fitted into the image.

> In our fieldnotes there inevitably lurks a certain amount of material that we perceive as 'disorderly', 'illogical', and 'contradictory'. We ponder over such data, feel guilty about their presence, and in the end must make a decision about how we are going to deal with them.
>
> (Overing 1985b: 152)

We have invented 'metaphor' as a safety net; we do not want to attribute our subjects with irrationality, 'but because we do not truly understand them, we construe their rationality as tropic creativity' (ibid.).

By labelling particular forms of language as metaphor or trope, we have firmly placed them outside the system. Chaos could have no part in the classical model of the world, and metaphors were identified as more or less imaginative associations between separate semantic fields, which were really separate. In the words of Lévi-Strauss, metaphor is 'a code which makes it possible to pass from one system to the next' (Lévi-Strauss 1963: 96). A well-known example is the Nuer's insistence that twins are birds, which has led anthropologists to take great trouble in explaining that of course the Nuer do not really believe that twins are birds, because to them – as to us – twins and birds are clearly distinct categories. Language maps reality, while metaphors do not in this vision of the world, which is based upon an idea of the autonomy of language.

This idea that language can be viewed as an isolated, identifiable and objective system, as strongly held by authorities like Saussure, Chomsky and their followers, has been undermined. There is no *langue* or *compétence* independent of practice, no tight system of grammar and syntax that is correct while the rest are just individual and accidental deviations from the rules. Deviation and disorder are not exceptions to the system, they are part of it. Things are what they appear to be: chaotic, paradoxical and inexhaustive.

With the dissolution of the opposition between reality and appearance, chaos has been readmitted to the world and must be accounted for. The details that are left out by the grammatical map ('the exceptions to the rules') constitute what the linguist Lecercle has tentatively named 'the remainder' (Lecercle 1990: 19 *et passim*). The remainder is where poetry, babbling, metaphor and fantasy break through and question the autonomy of language; where silent and unspeakable desires uncover the limits of *la langue*.

The remainder is not extrinsic to proper language; it is an intrinsic and constitutive part of it. Thus, language can never be a simple representation of the world; it is also an intervention within it. (An apparent commonplace, perhaps, for anthropologists used to dealing with verbal practices such as that of Melanesian big men whose power was based in rhetoric or with Inuit drum dancers whose verses made all the difference between war and peace in small local societies.) These examples illustrate the fact that words may exercise power and control in the social space, but the point I want to make here reaches further – to the formative power of words upon mental and moral spaces. In any case, the force of words has to be assessed empirically.

When we turn to texts or other dead stretches of experience, we can still not know the power of the chosen words without studying the wider context of social life. We cannot know whether a particular metaphor is 'dead' (like 'this man is a pig' in our own language), or whether it is part of the creative field of linguistic indeterminacy, where new insight is found, and where the old definitions on everyone's lips are constantly put at risk. Such definitions include definitions of particular identity categories that are subject to a remarkable degree of inconsistency.

The field of linguistic indeterminacy has been studied in depth by the anthropologist-cum-linguist Paul Friedrich (1986). He elevates the poet to particular power: if the individual utterance is unpredictable and imaginative this is precisely where poets and others manifest the 'link between the ascertainable order in language and the intimations of disorder in and beyond language' (ibid.: 5). Far from removing us from reality, the poetic indeterminacy recalls the holy union between definer and defined. Language is not just there as an empty container to be filled with meaning; meaning emerges in the articulation of its potential (cf. Lecercle 1990: 167). This point reinstates the individual contribution to reality, and not just as a 'carrier' of culture and categories. As Friedrich has it:

> The imagination of the unique individual gains particular relevance in the case of poetic language, where the role of the poet or the poetic speaker is more important than the role of the anonymous individual in language structure or in the history of language.
>
> (Friedrich 1986: 3)

Not only is language (as a system) inseparable from its usage, but it is also (and for the same reasons) deeply embedded in the social. In short, and in spite of previous attempts to isolate it, it is non-autonomous. The same applies to the 'structures' referred to in anthropology; structuralism had no theory that could account for the essential unity of structure and action: 'structuralism floats, as it were, attached by an inadequate number of ropes to the old empiricist ground beneath' (Ardener 1989b: 159).

One of the ropes was the identification of metaphors. I have already quoted Lévi-Strauss on the subject. For him, 'metaphor' was still a relatively precise technical term, while it has now become a catchword for almost everything ranging from allegory, through fantasy and conceit, to anything involving some degree of similarity across categories (Friedrich 1986: 30). It has become the target of a new wave of interest; some scholars seem to expand the notion by maintaining that there can no longer be any sharp distinction between the literal and the metaphorical, because metaphors reach far into our daily language use (e.g. Lakoff and Johnson 1980). Others want to restrict the term 'metaphor' to that which is consciously opposed to the literal (e.g. Cooper 1986), or are inclined to abandon the term altogether and replace it with relevant notions of allegory or trope (e.g. Friedrich 1986).

The various linguistic theories of metaphor shall not detain us here, since obviously the field of culture is not coterminous with the field of language. It is important to note, however, that when the imaginative aspects of language are recognized as of primary and not only secondary (or parasitical) value for our understanding of reality, and when reason itself is treated as both embodied and imaginative, metaphors are no longer 'the same'. They are identifiable only with difficulty, because their identification rests on unwarranted assumptions of categories objectively reflecting separate domains of reality. When this stance is abandoned we can see how metaphor, metonomy, allegory and fantasy infiltrate reality. Once the illogical and the chaotic have been acknowledged as part of the world, the literal and the metaphorical dissolve as distinct forms that can be deemed true or false, real or imagined. As the dreamwork of language, metaphor reflects back upon the interpreter as much as the originator (Davidson 1984: 245).

When we talk of metaphors, then, we cannot be sure that they are not perfectly true. Twins may be birds, girls may be chicks, men may be rams, and tapirs may be grandfathers, to mention only a few categories of identity. Before we can distinguish a literal from a metaphoric statement, we must share the relevant knowledge about the world with the speaker (Overing 1985b: 158). Once we share this knowledge, the label becomes less important than the understanding of the social predicates attached to the categories. The understanding of the particular utterances presupposes a comprehension of the experiential spaces of the speaker. In other words, when we have the *knowledge* to accept for instance the Piaroa claim that the tapir is their grandfather, we no longer need to resort to either notions of how the Piaroa 'feel' or 'believe' themselves to be in a mystical relationship with the world, or to the notion that the Piaroa are speaking 'metaphorically' (Overing 1985b: 71). We *know* what they mean. They mean what the words mean in their most literal sense; metaphors cannot be unsuccessful (Davidson 1984: 245).

For an anthropologist, the important thing is to discuss the social consequences of local phrases. One of the missions of metaphor is to give the inchoate pronouns of social life (I, you, he, she, it) an identity by predicating some sign-image upon them.

Before one can become a subject, one must have been an object, according to G. H. Mead (1934). This becoming an object is helped by metaphors (Fernandez 1986: 35 *et passim*). The kind of identity chosen (bull or chick) is not innocent, but induces people to action because it accomplishes affective movement in the pronouns. Thus, the identity label – however metaphorical from our point of view – sets part of the scenario for social action. If you have objectified yourself in terms of a ram (like Icelandic men, cf. Hastrup 1985b), you measure your achievements on a ram-scale. Similarly, if your cultural identity-marker is an untouchable mountain woman (like in Iceland) you are likely to be more than sceptical about mixed marriages between native women and, for example, American soldiers (cf. Björnsdóttir 1989).

This is more than a game of words; the effect of metaphorical thinking stretches far into daily life. Thus, Lakoff has convincingly demonstrated how the high incidence of rape in America might be related to the ways in which anger is conceived as an entity that acts more or less on its own behalf, while lust is seen in terms of sexual hunger ('he is sex-starved'), heat ('he is burning with desire') and warfare ('he makes conquests, she surrenders'). The metaphorical underpinnings of quite ordinary human feelings may make even an atrocity like rape seem an almost 'natural' human reaction under certain circumstances (Lakoff 1987: 406–415).

And this is the point: metaphors are not conceptual puzzles external to social life; they intervene, shape and produce action. The tropes play on real life. If we operate on the distinction between what words mean and what they are used to mean, metaphor belongs to the domain of use (Davidson 1984: 247). It cannot be paraphrased, because it has no meaning outside its use. The usage of a metaphor may intimate something that goes beyond the literal meaning of words, yet intimation is not meaning.

Metaphor has been studied as a literary device *par excellence*. It has been seen as a posit of figurative meaning. We can now see that, while the poetic indeterminacy serves to make us notice what we might not have seen, its meaning is given in the literal meaning of the words. What distinguishes metaphor is its use, whether its use in a particular poem or in a social waltz. This has a particular consequence for the anthropologists' use of literary expressions as sources for their reconstruction of cultural worlds.

Literature is language at work, but when metaphors are frozen in writing, the lack of experiential context makes them a clue to nothing but the anthropologist's vision of the world, whether past or present. The interpreter is the one who fills in the gap between the dreamwork of language and language itself. This implies that however much novels and poetry may give clues to culture, this clue does not belong within the texts themselves. Actual social life cannot be read directly from texts. Understanding the social means comprehending the *use* of words in practice, not solely having the capacity to read them. Just as language can be likened to a measuring rod, so literature introduces its own inherent scale in its measuring of the social. The text, therefore, is a 'source' only in a very specific sense.

What complicates the interpretation of literary metaphors is the fact that there is an imbalance between reference and definition: one can refer before one can define, and speak before one knows what one is talking about. The excess of signifier and the deficiency of signified, so characteristic of metaphor, allows one to say more than one means (in the sense of being able to define), or to mean (in the sense of refer) more than one says (Jenkins 1987: 21). This implies that with metaphors we are beyond description, or paraphrase, as we said earlier. We are in a realm of what may amount to reference without meaning. Metaphor '*says* only what shows on its face' (Davidson 1984: 259). It may be a patent absurdity, but it is the literality of the words used that prompts an insight beyond the words.

To identify the play of tropes in writing, we must first know the world upon which they play. If literary metaphors are clues to the social, they can only be identified as such retrospectively. First, metaphors are *not* about comparison (the comparing of two semantic fields with each other, and identifying their similarity); metaphor only has one subject – which cannot be identified from within it. Second, the anthropological interest in metaphor is located in its relation to social process, but the power of intervention cannot be assessed from the point of view of language itself. Because metaphors are true, we must take them literally.

ETYMOLOGY

Etymology has often been cited by anthropologists as evidence for hidden meaning.[4] The examples are legion, and although they are backed by arguments that often appear convincing, we should be highly sceptical about drawing social or historical inferences from etymology. Languages – and cultures – differ too much between themselves to be treated in the same way.

However, with the idea that language reflected reality went another idea, namely, that etymology reflected the history – not only of words but of worlds. As Lecercle has it: 'Words are the monuments on which our history and our origin are inscribed, and etymology the device that enables us to decipher the inscriptions' (Lecercle 1990: 191).

Etymology has been a separate linguistic discipline since classical times, when the origin of words was first questioned. The word itself derives from a Greek word meaning 'truth'. The point is, however, that the truth about the origin of words does not reflect a straight line from an alleged starting point to a terminal point, as presumed by the early etymologists (Ullmann 1972: 1, 30–31). Etymologists themselves have become aware of this and now describe the aim of etymology as an attempt to 'depeindre la vaste fresque des vicissitudes que le mot a traversé' (Wartburg 1946: 109). From the point of view of etymology, the depiction of the vicissitudes through which the word has passed may come closer to its true history, but the practice of etymology still separates morphology from semantics.

In other words, the history of a particular word need not reflect the history of its meaning. The object-word may remain the same, 'and yet the meaning of its name may change for us if there is any alteration in our awareness of it, our knowledge about it, or our feelings towards it' (Ullmann 1972: 56). The 'atom' is the same as it was fifty years ago, even though we now know that it is not the smallest constituent of matter, as etymology would suggest. The word by itself gives us no clue to present-day feelings about the atom – including the implicit apocalyptic associations. With the concept goes an evaluation that may shift at its own pace.

Etymology, then, is not a direct pathway to the history of meaning. When the remainder is admitted to language we realize that there are no simple signs any more, no simple reflections, only constructedness and putative meanings. In the real world, the social space has logical priority to words, texts and any other system of signs that the definers of that space may evoke to make themselves clear. Thus, etymology – as one branch of linguistics – becomes logically secondary to the branch of semantics. In the words of Wartburg:

> Quiconque veut écrire aujourd'hui l'étymologie d'un mot ne doit pas se contenter de constater la disparition d'une signification ou l'adjonction d'une signification nouvelle. Il doit se demander encore quel mot est l'heureux concurrent, héritier de la signification disparue, ou à quel mot il a ravi sa nouvelle signification. La première condition pour effectuer cette recherche est une exacte compréhension de la sémantique et des conditions dans lesquelles se développe la vie des mots.[5]
>
> (Wartburg 1946: 104)

'La vie des mots', the life of words, is social. This implies that meanings are locally constructed, mocked or transformed. In connection with the history of words this also implies that false etymologies may be invoked in support of particular world views. For example, a male chauvinist world view would argue that women come second because 'female' is derived from 'male', or (worse) because it derives from the Latin *femina* (*fe mina* – 'lesser in faith'), as the (in)famous *Malleus Malificarum* had it (Lecercle 1990: 40).

As we may now understand, 'etymological reduction' is open to various social uses; popular wit and poetic creativity may be accompanied by sinister ideology. Because of the arbitrariness of the linguistic sign (in the Saussurean sense), the life of words has a social logic of its own. Therefore, scientific etymology is possibly of less interest to anthropologists than 'popular' or 'associative' etymology, which is an expression of people's desire to motivate what has become opaque in language (Ullmann 1972: 101–102). As the French linguist Vendryes has said: 'l'étymologie populaire est une réaction contre l'arbitraire du signe. On veut à tout prix expliquer ce dont la langue est bien incapable de fournir l'explication' (quoted in Ullmann 1972: 102).

The latent folk-etymologizing propensity (a diachronic equivalent of the poetic play in the synchronic dimension) radically disturbs the directly reflective potential of etymologies. As we can see from the witch-hunters' claim about women, etymology 'is not only false history or ficticious science, it is also synchronic history – language being appealed to as a monument to the authority of history' (Lecercle 1990: 194).

Folk-etymology is not only a symptom of the remainder or the chaotic part of language, but also the embodiment of its historicity. It is metaphor in the diachronic, established on the basis of homonomy which may in fact only reflect a series of phonetical and historical coincidences. In the western tradition of historical linguistics, the reading backwards to *possible* origins of particular words through standard rules of phonetic development has become fixed as a source of 'canonic' etymology. Putative history has been launched as generative model. Little has been made of the 'surplus historicity' generated by such models, that is, the other *possible* developments of particular categories.

In oral cultures there are no privileged etymologies (Ardener 1971a: lxxii; cf. also 1971b). The point is, that whether a particular 'culture' is written or oral, we never know how or when effects of phonetic change may be bypassed, if semantically unacceptable to people. The values of similar terms cannot be assessed outside context; linguistic ambiguities cannot be read as history. Different temporalities should be taken into account. The temporality of society – as the institutionalized form of culture – may differ significantly from that of language.

Words may store cognitive knowledge, but have a much lesser capacity for storing other kinds of experience, which are embodied and stored in the social habit-memory (Connerton 1989). It is this habit-memory that paves the way for the continuity of the commonplace (the gestures, the social habits, the rules for action), in contrast to the breaks and shifts in the cognitive outlooks of people. The use of etymology as a privileged access to the history of ideas, then, is another instance of western logocentrism. Our lives are so much more than words, however.

LANGUAGE AND SOCIAL PROCESS

By way of concluding this discussion of the paradox of language I shall now address myself to the relationship between language and social process in a general fashion. Through the discussions of category, metaphor and etymology I have argued that there is no one-to-one correspondence between language and the social, either in the synchronic or in the diachronic dimension. They cannot even be viewed as two separate fields; rather, they work themselves into each other's definition – often violently. This clearly undermines any notion of simple correspondence, as well as an equally simple view of reality as constructed in a language of categories.

Language, then, provides no direct way to culture. From forms of language we may construct a structure, even a grammar, but this has no reality outside the analytical space. 'Knowing a language does not mean knowing rules and structures but knowing how to make oneself understood' (Tyler 1978: 120). Similarly, knowing a culture does not imply a knowledge of rules and structures but knowing how to act in a socially meaningful (or meaningless, for that matter) way. This well-known gap between knowledge, which literally can be spelled out, and experience, which cannot, in fact amounts to a major epistemological discrepancy (cf. Sperber 1982: 159).

Concerning cultural identities, the above implies that they can be elicited neither from spoken words nor written forms. The recollection of the 'rules', which makes actions possible, is not stored in texts, or in linguistic categories, but in a social habit-memory. This is not at all like a cognitive memory of rules and codes, but an embodied set of social practices that are transferred through various types of action. If recollection is embodied rather than written, this implies that there can be no cultural identity outside the collective social experience.

Giving privilege to words as clues to identity, history, society or culture is to commit an epistemological error. Identities are stored in practice; it is the 'habitus' of a particular people that is the basis for that intentionless convention of regulated improvisation, that lends some degree of coherence to their world (Bourdieu 1977: 79). Taken by themselves words are only a limited means of entry into this world. We have to observe and analyse how they are put to use, and how their implicit symbolic capital is put into social play.

The limitation of words as unmediated clues to culture is conspicuous in writing, which conveys an even stronger sense of arbitrariness, because it creates a possibility of disjunction between the signifier and the signified (Tyler 1987a: 20). As frozen *forms*, they are potentially like the rhetoric of totalitarian regimes – that is, clusters of words with no bearing on experience. Elisabeth Croll has recently shown how in China, after 30 years of red rhetoric, 'words without clothes had to be reinvented' (Croll 1991: 11). The atrophied language gave no access to sensations; she cites a Chinese writer for noting on the eve of reform: 'Like everyone else I was exited beyond words, I could not remember how to find the words' (ibid.).

Writings are generalized, holistic and outspoken, and as such they tend to mask the fragmentation, plurality and possible silences of social experience. Writings may be reflections upon the worlds, or interventions within them, but to enlarge one particular convention of representation (or historical genre) to the scale of a global one is essentially non-anthropological, I would argue. Without assuming a radical relativist position, one should be prepared to accept different systems of validation (cf. Gellner 1982: 194).

The 'Great Divide' between literate and non-literate societies may have become undermined (Street 1984), but within all societies there are domains of experience that defy our words. Such domains are not codified, but can only be extracted from social practice, which need not be consistent at all. Literacy creates a norm outside custom, which provides a means for stabilization; but this stabilization is the result of an 'institutional underpinning of the *one* outstanding cumulative cognitive style' that has been developed in the West (Gellner 1982: 194). The practice of *some* people generates an illusion of *one* world.

Beyond this illusion, we can see how written forms may be alien to the validation of particular cultures. One example is provided by Joanne Rappaport, whose work on literacy and power in colonial Latin America shows how the introduction of writing transformed native culture, not by its being a new technology but, more importantly, by its coaching a particular ideology and paving the way for the colonial power structure (Rappaport 1990).

By accepting written forms as direct reflections of reality, or tokens of cultural identity, we run the risk of attributing to language a pure observational status that is completely unwarranted. The so-called cultural translation, which was de-masked in the preceding chapter, is not a question of finding the right words for the native observations, but of communicating another way of understanding things, which may be totally alien to the Enlightenment vision of Reason and its modernist descendant: the writer. The greatest challenge to anthropology is not to read other cultures correctly but to recover disappearing epistemologies. Again, translation is not about the equation, but about the disequation of worlds.

To exploit the full force of this paradox, we should beware of the limitations of local language, and of writing in particular. Words create an illusion of fact, which is bound up with our own culture. Beyond it, anthropology should uncover a world of values, a moral universe, if you wish, that cannot be read, but must be experienced; worlds are lived, not written. It is for anthropology to recreate these worlds in a separate language for them to 'speak'.

The gap between words and social processes amounts to an ontological gap that can only be bridged by a personal encounter with the others – in fieldwork. If words and writings create an illusion of authority that sensations deny us, it is because they make us recognize our own world. That is not the point of anthropology's Romantic rebellion against Enlightenment, however. The rebellion is directed precisely at those notions of the world that reduce it to variations upon the theme of Reason – and of the mind being able to appropriate the world wholesale. It is not; beyond the words is a life into which language erupts but which it never exhausts.

Chapter 3

The empirical foundation
On the grounding of worlds

Like philosophy, anthropology is very much like 'a particular language'.[1] It is a discourse upon the world, a way of describing, interpreting or explaining it. It is the shared discursive quality that makes a dialogue between philosophy and anthropology possible; their discourses may even interpenetrate each other. My own references to philosophy are references to the philosophical discourse; and my reverence for individual philosophers is owed in part to the clarity by which they are able to verbally deal with problems that reflect my own interests. After all, theories *are* sentences – which may be transported.

The languagelike quality of philosophy and anthropology poses a question of their reference, which is the more pertinent as we have now demolished any notion of immediate representation. As languages, philosophy and anthropology consist not of representations but of propositions about reality. Propositions are generally formulated in observation sentences – the vehicle of scientific evidence (Quine 1992: 5). The ease by which we can agree to such statements lies not in their clarity, however, but in their ambiguity. The ambiguity is itself linguistic; the words have multiple reference. Proposition, reality, evidence – these terms have no metaphysical meaning, only a contextual one. And 'context' itself may refer to the context of sentences or the context of the world. Consequently, the truth or falsity of particular propositions may be located in the sentences or in the meaning of sentences (Quine 1992: 77).

The methodological point in the present connection is that language may be seen *as* context or *in* context (cf. Duranti and Goodwin 1992). This applies equally to ordinary and to scholarly languages. In an important way, this distinction by contextuality marks an important distinction also between philosophy and anthropology. The former has generally contented itself with viewing language as context; philosophy more often than not has been pure discourse. If *cogito* is seen as the essence of being human, words become both the content and the context of the philosophical language. This, of course, is a simplification. It is an observation sentence that clearly shows us how 'observation' itself is on the edge of language.

Claiming that philosophy is pure discourse is not to disclaim its historicity, of course, even if there is a strong tradition in philosophy to set itself apart from the real lives of people, politicians and other practitioners of history. Philosophy is not detached from particular knowledge interests, and remains a discourse upon the world, even if this world is conceived of only in language. There is no ahistorical reality to which a given philosophical vocabulary may or may not be adequate. Such a reality is an illusion; vocabularies do not simply correspond to reality, they intrude upon it and make appearances. Nevertheless, in philosophy language more often than not has been seen *as* context.

In anthropology, language must be studied also *in* context, as we argued in the previous chapter. In the terms of Kant, there can be no 'pure' knowledge of the world, only an 'empirical' one deriving from (social) experience. The context of language is a self-defining cultural space, in which the language is but one of the vehicles of definition. The identification of the social space, however named, has always granted anthropology an extra-linguistic subject matter. As a scholarly language, anthropology remains obliged to the world beyond the words. The social experience of people, and hence the ethnographic material, is largely non-verbal. Culture is not text, and anthropology is not literature. The world under study is grounded, not in sentences but in the empirical reality on the edge of these sentences, in the ethnography. 'Ethnography is indeed the arena in which notions of a science of anthropology are held accountable in its ability to encompass adequately the detailed reality of motivated, intentional life' (Marcus and Fischer 1986: 165). Even language is practised, and cannot be heard properly outside the reality of motivated life. Anthropology, indeed, may be seen as an empirical philosophy.

In a post-positivist anthropology this calls for a reconsideration of 'the empirical' as the core of the anthropological knowledge interest. Whatever the actual purpose of a particular study, theoretical anthropological knowledge is based in ethnographic material collected by individual anthropologists in the field. This method makes it abundantly clear that the researcher stands between the facts and the analytical results. Over the past decades, the traditional positivist view of hard ethnographic data has been irreversibly replaced by a vision of reality as in some way created through the encounter between the ethnographer and the people under study. In turn, these people have changed status from informants, speaking cultural truths, to participants in a dialogue initiated by the ethnographer.

At the level of dialogue and of the exchange of words in general, both parties are involved in a joint and apparently symmetrical creation of meaning, including the meaning of selfness and otherness, but the ethnographic project systematically violates this symmetry (Dwyer 1977: 147ff.). While possibly enshrined in mutual friendship and even affection, the ethnographic dialogue is twisted by the fact that the ethnographer's questions are unsolicited, and that knowledge of what is systematically hidden can only be obtained by maintaining a degree of pressure. The material elicited through the ethnographer's symbolic violence is, therefore, always in some sense inauthentic. The identities of the interlocutors are mutually implicated (Clifford 1988a: 11).

This leaves anthropology with a problem of credibility. Its empirical foundation seems to explode, and the question is whether we henceforward can speak about 'the empirical' only in quotation marks. What was once believed to be solidly grounded in ethnographic observation now seems to be floating in thin air.

OBSERVATION

Visibility has been one important criterion of veracity in a discipline that has based itself on observation (Hastrup 1986a). The 'seen' has had the stamp of cultural authenticity, and eventually of anthropological authority. This dates back to the Age of Discovery and became blatant in the Enlightenment when vision became omnipotent. Insight became equated with what was in sight. This is the foundation of visualism in anthropology, and the basis of the extensive use of spatial metaphors in its theoretical landscape (cf. Salmond 1982). This is a particular instance of the general ocularcentrism in western intellectual history, and its related 'scopic regimes' (Jay 1993). Evidently there is nothing wrong in the use of metaphors, but if the figurative meaning is taken to be iconic, we reduce meaning to reference (Crick 1976: 129–130). In other words, we eat the menu card instead of the dinner (Bateson 1972: 280).

It was such logical confusion that governed positivist anthropology. Reality was to be observed, and observations were to be mapped in adequate sentences: menu cards had to be made for all societies, so to speak, so as to guide western gourmets of the exotic. I do not intend to ridicule my anthropological ancestors; they did what they could within their conceptual horizon – which was thereby vastly expanded for their successors to explore further. Many early monographs are actually sensitive to the epistemological implications. Yet the observational language used has proved inadequate; no one ever actually *saw* a social relation, a kinship system or a cosmology. What is observed is behaviour, but this is not what is described. *Behaviour*, like (from my own fieldwork) 'walking in rubberboots across the field while yelling at the cattle' is immediately recognized, classified and entered as a meaningful *action* in the field notes: 'fetching the cows for the evening milking'. Inference takes the ethnographer beyond observation, yet empirical her data remain. We note how even the simplest kind of inference from observed behavioural units takes us past the idea of clarification (as discussed above) as the sole guiding principle of the scholarly quest and on to the notion of radical interpretation.

Instead of just seeing for themselves, anthropologists today acknowledge the force of other kinds of sensation. Recently, this was stated by Paul Stoller in the following manner: 'In a radically empirical ethnography devoid of intellectualist presuppositions, the unseen interpenetrates with the seen, the audible fuses with the tactile, and the boundaries of literary genres are blurred' (Stoller 1989: 153). Note how the empirical is still with us, possibly in a more radical fashion than before, even if we can no longer take it at face value, so to speak. We would deceive ourselves if we trusted our sight to be the principal way into culture. Evidently, the notion of the empirical changes as a matter of course.

I am reluctant to discuss this in terms of a blurring of literary genres, however. The so-called literary turn in anthropology has drawn our attention to the limitations inherent in the conventional canons of ethnographic representation (e.g. Clifford and Marcus 1986). Representations have been unveiled as 'social facts' (Rabinow 1986), transforming life into genre (Ardener 1985). Truly, we have mistaken realism for reality, but this does not mean that we only have to discuss literary genres. What we do have to discuss is ethnography, and ways of presenting it, on the assumption that reality is always definitional. This ambiguity relates to the reflexivity inherent in a discursive practice in which speakers and objects belong to the same class of phenomena: people.

REFLEXIVITY

In anthropology, we are witnessing an era of 'reflexivity, relativity, and the rejection of a privileged position for science or scholarship' (Fox 1991b: 4). The question remains, whether we have actually broken loose from the old structures. Sceptics suggest that we have not; old securities may have gone, and postmodernism apparently has provided 'a happy lifeboat' for some, but it still works 'within the structures of the same securities from which they imagined themselves to be sailing free' (McDonald 1989b: 229). From this perspective, and as recently phrased by Trouillot, the postmodernist critique of anthropology remains within the very thematic field that it claims to challenge (Trouillot 1991: 22). By contrast to the authors just cited, I do not take this as an indication of the vagueness of postmodernism; rather I believe it to be a token of the fact that anthropology was never really modern, and that it cannot, therefore, be postmodern either. The experienced continuity in the thematic field is owed to the fact that anthropology always was *non-modern*, if often in spite of itself. Postmodernism in anthropology is a conscious, critical and continuous effort to explore the epistemological implications of this. As such it does not form a new critical tradition. Any notion of a critical tradition should fill us with scepticism; critique cannot be not cumulative as Fabian has recently argued (Fabian 1991: 183). If anything, postmodernism is a condition, not a tradition (cf. Jameson 1991).

In this condition, we realize that reflexivity and relativity are not means of analysis but part of ethnography. The reality of anthropology is constituted in a relationship of continuity between the ethnographer and the world. This is what makes the ethnographic present and what leads to anthropological knowledge. There is no way of understanding people independent of a more or less shared human experience (Vendler 1984: 201). This applies to all human sciences, of course. In anthropology, which is my concern here, this is also where reflexivity starts – not as a particular style of writing but as an inherent element in any empirical ethnography.

Reflexivity in this sense refers to the way in which the accounts and the settings they describe elaborate and modify each other in a back-and-forth process (Watson 1991: 74; 1987; cf. also Woolgar and Ashmore 1988). This implies that accounts that describe a setting are made up of expressions that derive their specific sense from that very setting. It is an essential (rather than instrumental) reflexivity that allows us to take full advantage of the experience of relativism, without destroying our more general aims, i.e., the search for objective knowledge.

Reflexive anthropology places itself between the poles of correspondence theory and constitutive theory, which were both seen as inadequate in the preceding chapter. The first claims to mirror reality; ontology and epistemology are one. The second disclaims this kind of realism and admits to constituting reality. With a truly reflexive anthropology we shall not have to make a choice, but shall be able to live with the paradox of definitional realities.

The fieldworker's experience of different worlds leads her to question the foundations of her own. This questioning is part of her search for a general understanding of how 'worlds' are premissed and produced, and how their inhabitants reach agreement about social action and moral value. In short, her scientific aim lies beyond the detection of a particular culture, in the understanding of the premises for its declaration.

To understand the interplay between social processes and cultural knowledge, the model set by Enlightenment (natural) science is of limited value. The search for an Absolute Truth is at odds with the relativist experience of anthropology. In its turn this does not entail the abandonment of the quest for knowledge. The fact that there is no uniform objective reality does not mean that there are *no* objective realities. The project of Romanticism is 'to dignify subjective experience, not to deny reality; to appreciate imagination, not to disregard reason; to honor our differences, not to underestimate our common humanity', as Richard Shweder puts it (1991: 11).

Clearly, ethnography is based in a social experience that is shared by the ethnographer and 'her people' (a term, which I, incidentally, do not find disturbing, cf. Hastrup 1992a). It is an experience of estrangement – intellectual and sensual – and of a temporary shift of identity; the ethnographer operates as a 'third person' in the field (Hastrup 1987b). This is what allows her to handle different epistemologies. In short, this is what makes her experience-near ethnography a first step towards a recognition of the historical constitution of difference (cf. Wikan 1991: 317). But the work does not stop there. There is more to anthropology than an ethnography of the particular (*pace* Abu-Lughod 1991: 149). Even if we would want to pursue the notion of culture to wherever it takes us, we have to leave it behind before we can talk about it knowingly. This is related to the fact that, generally, 'culture' is not something we talk about but a position we speak from; its 'referential transparency' is implicated in its very self-evidence. Culture is what one *sees with*, but seldom what one *sees* (Quinn and Holland 1987: 14).

Before I embark on a further qualification of anthropological knowledge let me just summarize the implications of my claim that reflexivity and relativity are part of ethnography rather than analysis. If reflexivity is part of ethnography, this means that the anthropologist becomes her own informant. Sharing the social experience of others implies the using of all senses and the suspension of judgement, possibly to a still unprecedented degree, but it does not entail the creation of fiction and thus the undermining of any scientific standard. While we cannot, obviously, experience the world from the perspective of others, we can still share their social experience. In fact, there is no social experience that is not shared. Sharing implies that we are part of the plot, and it is this position that provides us with a unique key to an understanding of worlds, of how they are constituted and transformed, and how positions are assigned to individuals within the plot-space understudy.

Returning now to the initial question of whether we can speak of the empirical except in quotation marks, I would argue that there is no reason at all for this kind of distancing between our project and ourselves. On the contrary, we should realize, and creatively exploit, our intricate implication in the world. Reality is no less real for all our being part of it.

THE REALITY OF EVENTS

Being part of the reality studied means to register 'events' as such, that is, to distinguish them from mere happenings by way of their significance from the point of view of the local world. 'An event becomes such as it is interpreted' (Sahlins 1985: xiv). The ethnographer in the field is tested by her ability to register particular happenings as events, forming the core of her empirical material. This presupposes intimate experiential knowledge. It is the gradual mastering of the local mode of registration that eventually neutralizes the fright inherent in the initial unknowing.

Consider the following episode from my own fieldwork: one November Saturday night in Iceland, I woke up to the sound of screaming and the breaking of bottles and, eventually, the crushing of a table in the room next to mine in the fishermen's barrack. A handful of young people had had their usual party with lots of drinking. I could not help overhearing the loud voices of a village girl and her boyfriend, whom she had come to visit in the barrack. The core of their 'conversation' was the fact that the girl was pregnant and wanted the man to marry her. He was furious, beat her, and repeatedly yelled at her that he wanted to amuse himself and that she was a damned whore, and he was certainly not going to live with her in a family house. She cried, and there was a lot of violence and screaming on both sides, as well as meek other voices hardly taking sides, until he finally, and literally, flung her out of the house down the snow-covered steps. The other girl present left with her, and the remaining young men in the barrack settled down to a mutual and extremely vociferous confirmation of their determination to remain free.

The happening was certainly unique, and I was shocked by the degree of violence. Yet the situation was also in a sense familiar and had so many precedents at a certain level, that it was immediately registered as an 'event'. The incident was linked to other incidents and to a space beyond the barrack. A fight is a fight, of course, but although events do have objective properties it is not these properties as such that give them effect but their significance within a particular cultural scheme.

In the case related, the event bore all the marks of the local cultural scheme embedded in the conceptual opposition between inside and outside in Icelandic culture (Hastrup 1990d). The barrack was conceptually outside, because it was associated with fishing and because it was outside the ordinary authority structure of the village, and it was male (cf. Hastrup 1985b). Women had no part in this space except as free women or 'game'. Clearly, to announce a pregnancy and to propose marriage within the confines of this space was a cultural impossibility. The man had to refuse violently and to clamorously reclaim his freedom. When, on the following day, the girl came back all smiles and told me that she bore no grudge against the man who had had the right to be infuriated, she unknowingly confirmed the ethnographer's apprehension of the 'event'.

The point is that although no events are exact replicas of previous ones, the relationship between a particular happening and a cultural scheme of interpretation generates recognition, and makes registration possible. Although personally shocked by the particular event and the meaningless violence, the ethnographer suffered no culture-shock and experienced no meaninglessness, professionally.

Some social spaces are more event-rich than others. This implies that more happenings are registered as events, and more behaviours immediately interpreted as actions. Event-richness is a feature of 'remote areas' in particular, i.e., social spaces that from the point of view of the defining world are considered peripheral, such as the conceptually marginalized fishing world of Iceland.[2] This makes participant observation both more demanding and more immediately rewarding, because becoming one's own informant under such circumstances implies being eternally caught in a web of social significances. In order to substantiate this claim, and to add more weight to the reality of events as registered in the field, I shall relate another episode from my fieldwork.

Again we are in the fishing village, where my taking up residence in the migrant fishermen's barrack associated me with 'the wild' and made me an ambiguous figure in local eyes. I had moved outside the social order, initially without my knowing it, and from within the controlled social space I was under more or less constant supervision by male members of the community, for whom I was in some sense legitimate game. I worked in the fish factory to gain access to the closed community, and only gradually did people realize that I had a third purpose in addition to earning money and claiming freedom. However, even when they knew, my dwelling marked me as part of an accessible category of women, which I was to experience rather forcefully on several occasions.

Once I had walked some distance from the village to interview an old solitary man. A snowstorm blew up and the weather was prohibitive to going back to the village within the limited time of remaining daylight. The old man invited me to stay overnight, but the tone of the invitation made me strongly want to decline it, and in spite of the snowstorm I prepared myself to take leave from my friendly informant. All of a sudden a car stopped outside the house with glaring lights and a man from the village whom I knew well came in. He said he had come to fetch me in his four-wheel-driven car equipped with snow chains. He explained that he had feared that I would start walking home, which could easily have been fatal. Under the Arctic conditions this was absolutely true, even if I had been prepared to overlook the fact only minutes earlier. I wondered, however, how the man knew where I had gone.

It kept intriguing me and once we had set off in the car, leaving the somewhat crestfallen older man behind, I enquired about my friendly driver's motive. He then volunteered the information that he always knew where I was, allegedly because my 'lone wanderer' was so conspicuous in the physical as well as the social landscape that everyone noticed it. He added that he, personally, had so strongly resented my staying overnight in the old man's house that he had no choice but to come and fetch me even though he was risking his own comfort. Somehow he wanted to reclaim me from disorder, but not necessarily for the sake of order.

It so happened that we missed the road and slid down a rather steep slope, and we were absolutely stuck in the snow-storm. My naive suggestion that we should start walking was immediately turned down. There is no way of orienting oneself in weather like that; in the rugged landscape one is likely to fall down a cliff or walk directly into the sea, or die from the cold before one ever knows where one is. So we had no choice but to wait patiently in the lopsided car that became increasingly covered by the snow while the cold began to make itself felt – and *seen*, in the ice in the man's beard and in the glow (of fear?) in his eyes. After endless hours in the dark, car-lights emerged on the road above our heads. The village rescue team had come to find us, and we were saved. Because of my frozen condition I could hardly speak, and I did not ask how the team had known where to find us. However, once we were in the rescue vehicle, a radio message was sent back to the village to the effect that the (named) man and the (unnamed) Danish woman had been found safe. Everybody heard this, and the message had some significant sequels.

Thus, the next day when I had thawed and returned to my own quarters after having been taken care of by my driver's wife, I was told by a friend that had I become pregnant under the circumstances, no one would have blamed me or the man (even though both of us were married), because we had been stuck *úti* (outside) and not on our own account. As a piece of completely unelicited information, this single statement was major evidence of the semantics of the 'outside', associating it with uncontrolled sexuality, among other things. To begin with I was completely taken aback by the bluntness of the statement and its implications, but when I later heard that the leader of the rescue team had composed a song about 'the blacksmith and the Danish lass', which played very much on the probability of something having actually happened between us in that snowstorm, events fell into a distinctive pattern. Living the outside and unknowingly emphasizing it through my uncontrolled wanderings in the untamed nature around me I was marked by the wild. In turn, it was this marking that made me one of my main informants – as an objectified figure in the Icelanders' discourse upon their world.

It is this world, which forms the experiential space of culture, that the anthropologist discovers and defines through her becoming part and parcel of it. And it is this world that frames and identifies 'events' as ethnographic data – of significance. In the singular instance of fieldwork the materiality of the local world is experienced rather than elicited by questioning and noting the answers. It is this experience, and the gradual ability to sort out events, that grants reality to the anthropological task.

THE REALITY OF KNOWLEDGE

Fieldwork may even result in an acute awareness of the reality of what in a different world may be deemed 'unreal' (Hastrup 1987a). By sensing the total and complex texture of events, be they rituals, payments of bridewealth, bull fights or the taste of one's own tears, the anthropologist experiences a space that cannot simply be seen. As I have exemplified above, my own fieldwork experience in Iceland taught me that the texture of cultural events evades the clinical gaze, yet may leave sensational marks in recollection; the meagre fieldnotes in the language of observation are complemented by rich headnotes that defy our alphabetical prose yet provide us with contextual clues.[3] I myself got to know the hidden people, the magic and the emotions that filled the air in Iceland but which could not be photographed (Hastrup 1992b). The sensitive ethnographer comes to *know* reality.

In order to truly *understand* it she must cut herself loose, however, and discuss how local knowledge (including her own) is premissed and exploited. In the process from 'knowing' to 'understanding' the shared reality of social experience is transformed from a largely implicit local knowledge to an explicit and external understanding which subsumes and transforms local knowledge. Individual sensations and subjective viewpoints are generalized and presented as objective (scientific) knowledge. The personal symmetry between subjects in the dialogue is transformed into a logical hierarchy, in which one category embraces another.

The hierarchical distinction between anthropologists and others is a logical corollary of the process of knowledge construction in anthropology. Far from being just an ethnographic account, anthropological knowledge is 'about' or 'of' some people. The people and their conditions must be historized in all sorts of ways, and full admission must be given to the inherent processes of reflexivity and relativization, but anthropological knowledge transcends the particular instance. This is one reason why the ethnographic present has to be reinvented, as I have argued in chapter 1.

Recently, it has been suggested by Louis Dumont that there are only two ways of recognizing *alter*: hierarchy or conflict (Dumont 1986: 267). In so far as anthropology makes a point of documenting truly alternative epistemologies, we have a choice to make between these two strategies. To recognize other worlds as alternative implies either disclaiming them by way of allegations of irrationality or incomprehensibility, or hierarchically embracing them in a discursive space that may span them all. While there is no pure observational language that will bridge the gaps between different worlds (Barnes and Bloor 1982:

39–40), there is still a discursive space in which equally reasonable ways of talking about the environment may be meaningfully juxtaposed. Experiential relativity does not entail absolute incommensurability. After all, humanity is united by the fact that we are imaginable to one another (cf. Shweder 1991: 18). This is where reflexivity takes root.

The shift from a realist to a reflexive anthropology redirects our strategies of contextualization. Realist ethnography contextualized social phenomena with reference to a totality in the form of a geographically situated community or a positioned semiotic code; this conventional concept of context is denied the reflexive anthropology, in which the fragments of life are connected through reflections of the experiential space of the ethnographer. Place has become replaced by space – which is but 'practiced place' (de Certeau 1984: 117). In this perspective, the notion of context itself cannot be formally defined, but must be invoked through analytical practice (Duranti and Goodwin 1992: 2). The practised place of necessity incorporates the ethnographer; in an important sense, she herself is the ritual context-marker. She does not construct reality, even if it is never uncontaminated by her knowledge interests. She is part of the defining consciousness of the space.

In spite of this continuity, a distinction between cultural and anthropological knowledge remains. The latter is of value, precisely because it may overcome the distance between worlds – if surely not in an observational language – and generalize about the global human condition in which the worlds are assigned different positions. While cultural knowledge is essentially practical, anthropological knowledge is theoretical. This is why generalizations cannot and should not be avoided, even if they do not convey the details of social experience. Thus, when it is argued that generalizations are best abandoned (e.g. by Abu-Lughod 1991: 153ff.), it is based on a confusion of experience and anthropological knowledge. Experience is what makes ethnography or, if you wish, cultural knowledge. However, knowing a culture does not imply that one knows how culture is actually premissed and constituted. This is anthropological knowledge.

When we shift from cultural to anthropological knowledge, the referent changes as a matter of consequence. Reference is about absences, and is, therefore, essentially reflexive. The referents of culture and of anthropology are not the same, but they are equally real. It is the scale that has changed. When moving between implicit cultural knowledge and explicit anthropological understanding, reality is displaced, so to speak. From sensing the social imperatives to identifying the cultural thematicity in the social spaces we study there is a shift, but not a leap out of reality (cf. Quinn and Holland 1987: 10). The explicating of the points of orientation in any one culture, that is, points where values or meanings have a directive force, is not part of ordinary cultural knowledge. It could, however, be an important part of anthropological knowledge.

We realize, of course, that 'knowledge is a social achievement: it consists of meanings that have "made it" ' (Crick 1982: 28). The production of knowledge is partly a result of someone being able to objectify their own notions of reality. An awareness of the asymmetrical relationships of discursive power must be incorporated into a thoroughly reflexive anthropology, even if at the cost of western logocentrism.

THE HYPOTHETICAL

Implicit in the previous argument is a view of science as a search for 'explanation' – here taken to include radical interpretation.[4] Explanations of necessity belong to a register that is different from the phenomena explained. The politics of explanation may vary widely, as may the range of phenomena explained, but any idea of explanation implies *distance* between the things explained and the explanation (Latour 1988). The *raison d'être* of scholarship lies in its ability to exploit this distance on the one hand, and to overcome it on the other.

The shift of register implied is not a shift from the real to the unreal, from practice to structure, or from the concrete to the abstract. Each field contains its own reality, its own practice, its own concreteness and, indeed, their opposites. The switch involved is better seen as a switch from the manifest to the hypothetical. They do not part company along any lines between reality and representation, or between the real world and speculation. No such line can be drawn, not even a dotted one. Rather than forming a dichotomy or a symmetrical dualism, the polarity is asymmetrical, and of a concentric kind. Depending on our perspective, either the manifest or the hypothecical can be seen as contextualizing the other. Our object of study, and the results of our analyses are eternally and essentially reflexive.

In spite of the distance implied in the change of register, there is always a fundamental continuity between the world and the science about it. Anthropological theories are social phenomena (Herzfeld 1987: 3). This continuity has scared off a number of anthropologists from claiming anything but partial knowledge and led them to abstain from any attempt at generalization. While certainly there are solid reasons for questioning the nature of generalization and the possible hegemony of science, there seems to be no epistemological grounds for abandoning anthropology. The fear of being partial is pathetically related to old Enlightenment visions of scientific omnipotence and absolute truths. Knowledge is so self-evidently partial that the label is meaningless.

Partiality is not only a result of the unavoidable perspectival relativity and of positioned human subjects. More profoundly it is the consequence also of the nature of scientific pursuit itself, that is, the process implied by the change of register from phenomena to be explained to some kind of explanation. Whatever the politics of explanation, this process of explaining is inherently reductive; it is impossible to transport the totality of phenomena from the field-world to the field of scholarship. The distance between the two cannot be overcome by simple reproduction elsewhere. Reduction in this sense is seen as a necessary condensation of social facts in order to move them across the distance between the lived world and the world of anthropological knowledge. By its nature anthropological knowledge is, therefore, partial and reductive.

My argument is this: anthropological knowledge starts in the sharing of social experience and in the documentation of another definitional reality. But it does not end there. The world has to be explained in words; this always involves an element of reduction. It also implies a certain degree of distortion, because reality is lived, not talked or written. While experience cannot be spelled out, anthropological knowledge must be communicated through writing; 'the text, unlike discourse, can travel' (Clifford 1988a: 39). Theories are sentences – ensnaring silences as well as words.

Rephrasing the anthropological endeavour as one of stating the hypothetical helps us realize that there is absolutely no need to dismiss scholarship. Quite the contrary; by formulating new hypotheses about the nature of social life and human understanding, anthropology contributes to the creating of new historical possiblities in a spirit of solidarity.

The hypothetical in anthropology has been given a number of names, among which 'culture' and 'society' have been the most vital and still can hardly be dispensed with, even if a whole range of counter-propositions have been put forward in denouncement of the misplaced concreteness of the old terms (e.g. the notion of 'ethnoscape' in Appadurai 1991). Whether one prefers to redefine old terms or to invent new ones, 'the hypothetical' in anthropology is of a particular collective kind. Since Durkheim, the object of investigation has been some kind of collectivity that transcended the sum of individuals. This has been part of the anthropological politics of explanation, if you wish. It still is. The search for some kind of truth at the level of the collectively hypothetical is epistemologically complicated as it stands, but it is further complicated methodologically by the fact that the anthropologist herself belongs to the class of phenomena studied. This means that the anthropologist studying social relations, actions and imaginations in an important way must draw upon her own experience of being human. As practising anthropologists we are invariably part of the plot; our discoveries of the collectively hypothetical enter into their definition.

To summarize, in spite of the strategic distance between the manifest and the hypothetical, there is a profound ontological continuity between them. It is this continuity that lies at the heart of subjectivity, relativity and reflexivity in anthropology. It is not an obstacle to science but its starting point. The ethnographer epitomizes the continuity in the field where she shares the social experience of others by no longer being herself.

Although redefined, the empirical foundation of anthropology is as pertinent as ever. The anthropological discourse is intimately linked with a reality beyond itself, about which it conveys an evocative message. If 'like' a language, anthropology remains grounded in a world of actual and shifting experiences that continually challenge the current vocabulary.

Chapter 4

The anthropological imagination
On the making of sense

The passage from the manifest to the hypothetical is made by way of imagination. In the process, language is stretched to match manifest yet unprecedented experiences. The empirical is condensed and made ready for travel. By its attempt to incorporate cultural remainders in a global scheme of comprehension, anthropology takes Donald Davidson's notion of radical interpretation to its full effect (e.g. Davidson 1984: 128). Radical interpretation of alien sentences and lifeways hinges upon the ability to set up particular truth-conditions for these manifestations in a separate language; only then can we claim to know what they mean. This is what anthropological theory amounts to: a set of hypothetical truth-conditions for the variety of cultural expressions.

This is not a matter of simple translation from one language or idiom to another; it is a process of transformation, which is governed by its own rules of clarity and ecomomy of expression. In a discussion of Davidson's tenet, Hilary Putnam propounds the view that an idea of 'one' language of interpretation is untenable or at least at odds with the notion of conceptual relativity: the meanings of conceptual alternatives will be reproduced at the meta-linguistic level (Putnam 1990: 104). The shift from a linguistic to a cultural idiom transforms the problem, but Putnam's point is worth keeping in mind. The manifest conceptual relativity in the world, i.e., the fact that people live by different epistemologies, is likely to reproduce itself in theory. The examples are legion; medicine 'means' different things to different peoples, as does motherhood, sorcery, cattle, love and the rest. Consequently, anthropology has made various theories to accommodate the differences. But note here that theories of that kind – or such hypothetical relativities – concern only meaning in a narrow linguistic sense and presuppose a distinct meaning of holism. This is not the sole objective of anthropology; there is a wider sense of purpose than establishing meaning within a particular (cultural) reference scheme. Semantic understanding is only a first step towards the anthropological making of sense, which is based in a thorough knowledge of manifold meanings, but which transcends them all in its concern with questions of how meanings are pre-missed and produced at all. This is where we may still seek for 'a' language of interpretation, in which meaning is emergent rather than given by a pre-established theoretical scheme.

Emergence points to a latent change of meaning; the making of sense implies that the language of anthropological theory cannot be stable. In contrast to earlier Objectivist propositions we can no longer entertain the comforting view that science is really progressing toward *the* correct description of reality (cf. Johnson 1987: 197). Knowledge expands with language; the confrontations with worlds and experiences beyond western notions of rationality and logocentrism make an extensive use of metaphors inescapable in anthropology; they are seen as prime instruments for conceptual change; as will be recalled, metaphors are forerunners of insight that cannot as yet be incorporated in preconceived categories. As '*every* observation report has some component which could be described as "inferential" ' (Putnam 1981: 183), we cannot possibly adhere to a belief in a transparent language of observation. The desire for fixed standards fades in the view of language being able to incorporate 'the unlikely' only by way of the linguistic remainder: metaphor.

Metaphor hinges on the use of language, rather than the meaning of language, as we have seen. By way of a literal use of words, metaphor makes us see *as* rather than see *that*. 'Metaphor makes us see one thing as another by making some literal statement that inspires or prompts the insight' (Davidson 1984: 263). Metaphor is not a wastebin for the not understood. Rather, it is a prime element in our structuring of experience; it is a pervasive mode of understanding by way of projecting particular patterns or connections onto the unprecedented (Johnson 1987: xiv *et passim*). The frightening indeterminacy of experience is transformed to a temporary making of sense.

Consequently, all theory-building is in some sense metaphorical; but I want to carry the argument further than to state this simple descriptive point. The implications are much more profound, because 'the metaphoric sentence expresses a proposition; but the *seeing as* response that it inspires is not a propositional attitude' (Cavell 1986: 495). Briefly, in Davidson's terms, 'words are the wrong currency to exchange for a picture' (Davidson 1984: 263). Even theories in some important sense have to get beyond their own words.

The 'dreamwork' of metaphor, evoked by Davidson, implicitly points to a feature of condensation and displacement inherent also in Freud's analysis of dreamwork (Cavell 1986). Condensation and displacement, or in the words used before, reduction and dislocation, are prominent features of establishing the hypothetical in anthropology. In the process, anthropology makes use of imagination as a capacity for understanding unprecedented experience; it is part and parcel of any rationality that we might claim. Even innovation is a rule-governed behaviour; 'the work of imagination does not come out of nowhere' (Ricoeur 1991: 25). The theoretical phrasings that we arrive at must connect to the anthropological tradition.

My aim in this chapter is to discuss the nature of the anthropological imagination, and to show that however much anthropological knowledge rests upon the investment of individual anthropologists' imaginative powers, this does not subvert the empirical foundation.[1] Rather, it makes room for novel connections that come out of experience.

In keeping with the topic of this chapter I shall start with a parable in the shape of one of Hans Christian Andersen's fairy tales, which actually has very little to do with fairies. It is 'The Story of a Mother'.[2]

THE STORY OF A MOTHER

A mother sat by her little child: she was very sorrowful, and feared that it would die. Its little face was pale, and its eyes were closed. The child drew its breath with difficulty, and sometimes so deeply as if it were sighing; and then the mother looked more sorrowfully than before on the little creature.

Then there was a knock at the door, and a poor old man came in, wrapped up in something that looked like a great horse-cloth, for that keeps warm; and he required it for it was cold winter. Without, everything was covered with ice and snow, and the wind blew so sharply that it cut one's face.

Here the harsh northern scene is set; the frosty weather, the wind, the horse-cloth. And no sooner had the mother put some beer in a pot on the stove to warm for the stranger, confessed her worry to him, and fallen asleep for a minute, than Death, because that was the old man, escaped with her dear child.

When she awoke to the empty cradle, the mother set out to pursue the stranger and rescue the child. She met all kinds of difficuties, but the major obstacle is met by the shores of a lake:

The Lake was not frozen enough to carry her, nor sufficiently open to allow her to wade through, and yet she must cross it if she was to find her child. Then she laid herself down to drink the Lake; and that was impossible for any one to do. But the sorrowing mother thought that perhaps a miracle might be wrought.

'No, that can never succeed,' said the Lake. 'Let us rather see how we can agree. I'm fond of collecting pearls, and your eyes are the two clearest I have ever seen: if you will weep them out into me I will carry you over into the great green-house, where Death lives and cultivates flowers and trees; each one of these is a human life.'

'Oh, what would I not give to get my child!' said the afflicted mother; and she wept yet more, and her eyes fell into the depths of the lake, and became two costly pearls. But the lake lifted her up, as if she sat in a swing, and she was wafted to the oppposite shore.

The problem now, of course, is that she cannot see what is there, and is even more dependent upon others to direct her. Among other things she has to pay her beautiful hair to the old woman gardener of Death for her to show the way to the greenhouse. She senses the life all around her, and believes herself capable of identifying her own child by its heart-beat. In fact she is unable to distinguish the various plants or human lives from one another. Only Death can tell them apart, and he has not yet arrived.

Death finally comes, and expresses his surprise at seeing the Mother there. On his way he had collected her pearly eyes from the bottom of the lake. He gives them back to her, 'clearer now than before', so that she may see the variety of possible destinies.

She realizes that however much she loved her child she could not have known what was in store for it. She then resigns her quest, and lets Death take away her child to the unknown land.

This story belongs to my own most dreadful childhood readings. Like so many other of Hans Christian Andersen's fairy tales, this one is not really meant for children. Most of his stories were written for grown-ups as allegories of life and with various edifying purposes. I, too, want to use his sad story of the mother as a parable of what I want to say about the anthropological imagination.

The Mother, of course, is Anthropology, who seems to have lost its innocent child: the empirical object. It was stolen by the dreaded Death of Postmodernism, sometimes invoked as the end not only of anthropology but of science in general. The monster carried away the child to the hothouse of a thousand exotic flowers, representing the fragmented world.

In the attempt to reclaim its object, Anthropology was even prepared to weep out its own eyes at a certain stage, that is, to abandon the idea of empirical observation. In the world that she eventually sensed, however, Anthropology became acutely aware that the variety of flowers could not be known without empirical observation. Deception was likely to follow, were she only to judge the flowers by their heartbeat. It seemed as if there were no standards for scholarly judgement, no canons of professional success or failure, yet also no choice of returning to innocence. Small wonder that fright ensued.

The aim of this chapter is not to reclaim the child-object of Anthropology, but to comfort the Mother and contribute to her confidence in her own vision of the world, 'clearer now than before'. Confronted with the gap between this side of the world and the other, Objectivism provides no lifeboat. The ocean that separates and, indeed, connects selves and others can be traversed only by way of the anthropological imagination.

SOME SOCIOLOGICAL PREDECESSORS

Addressing the theme of anthropological imagination naturally brings the work of C. Wright Mills to mind. His book *The Sociological Imagination* (1959) was once (rightly) thought to be highly provocative, and it is interesting briefly to retrace his main points.

In Wright Mills' terms, the sociological imagination is a particular quality of mind that 'enables its possessor to understand the larger historical scene in terms of its meaning for the inner life and the external career of a variety of individuals' (Mills 1959: 5). The sociological imagination, and the social science that embodies it, enable us 'to grasp history and biography and the relations between the two within society' (ibid.: 6). The message is clear: the task and the promise of the sociological imagination is to make intelligible the interrelatedness of what Wright Mills calls 'the personal troubles of milieu' and 'the public issues of social structure' (ibid.: 8).

With the book, Wright Mills wanted to alert social scientists to the new significance of the social sciences for the cultural tasks of the time, prophesying that the sociological imagination was to become the major common denominator in the intellectual and social life of the time to come, replacing the domination of the natural sciences.

Retrospectively, his programme was at least partly successful. The relationship between the individual and the structural has been on the agenda ever since in the social sciences. I would be prepared to argue that the present anthropological concern about the relationship between the local and the global is a late variant of the same idea. In many ways this particular issue is little more than a rephrasing of the by now commonsensical requirement of seeing ethnography in its historical context. Anthropology cannot take scale for granted, however, and the 'local' and the 'global' cannot be studied as ontological entities, interfacing somewhere in space. Scale has to be questioned along with any ethnographic description. The dualism between local and global is, I would contend, not only theoretically impotent but also epistemologically untenable. There is no way to separate these two dimensions experientially.

The central tenet of Wright Mills was the *craft* of sociology; the kind of imagination called for implied an establishment of empirical links between various contexts, and was a methodological means of unearthing the hidden connections. With no intent of discovering hidden meanings that are already 'in' the object, and with no assumption of a transparent language of pure observation, anthropology today has a different sense of purpose. The empirical of whatever scale provides the basis for hypothetical reflections that may expand the field of significance for anthropology. This also implies that we have to reconsider the nature of the anthropological imagination in other than methodological terms. Our concern is not primarily with the craft of anthropology but with its epistemology.

This, again, means that the scope of this chapter is different from Paul Atkinson's recent volume on *The Ethnographic Imagination*, concentrating on one aspect of the intellectual craftmanship in sociology, namely, how sociological texts and arguments are constructed (Atkinson 1990: 3). In Atkinson's view, ethnography is a particular genre within sociology, and imagination is invoked as a pathway to the textual construction of reality. As such, it echoes another sociological predecessor, namely, the work of Berger and Luckman (1967) on the interpersonal construction of social reality. With their focus on craftsmanship and the idea of hidden connections, all of these works remain within rather narrow Enlightenment concerns and fail to explore the Romantic view of creative imagination as 'a creation which reveals, or as a revelation which at the same time defines and completes what it makes manifest' (Taylor 1989: 419).

For Kant, the Enlightenment was 'a way out' of immaturity. It was the immaturity of Reason, correlated with a weakness of will, that made people readily give in to authorities, sometimes against better judgement. Because of this immaturity of Reason, people also lacked the courage to alter their situation. In this version, Enlightenment was to be understood both as an individual and a collective project towards freedom. The work of Wright Mills clearly belongs to this tradition.

There is no for or against Enlightenment in this; after all, the Enlightenment position may be re-read as a particular scholarly attitude, an ethos 'in which the critique of what we are is at one and the same time the historical analysis of the limits that are imposed on us and an experiment with the possibility of going beyond them' (Foucault 1984: 50). In the experiment lies a Romanticist strategy, which in principle straddles the gap between reason and imagination. The identification of what we cannot yet know, given present knowledge conditions, rests on an imaginative investment that is rarely acknowledged, however.

A CENTRAL MYTH

Generally, the historical changes attributed to the Enlightenment gave rise to a central myth of our time, i.e., the myth of the great divide in our intellectual history between 'before' and 'after' Enlightenment, later projected onto space as a radical distinction between 'them' and 'us'. Before, or with them, people were intellectually confused; they could not tell the difference between fact and value, truth and convention, nature and custom (see e.g. Shweder 1991: 2). The Enlightenment made such distinctions possible, and the road to progress was open. After, or with us, rational knowledge projects were set in motion, exploring the facts of nature and leaving behind the conventional wisdom of the premodern people. The goal of science was to liberate these people from superstition as well as from false authorities. In short, reason had to be liberated from imagination.

For Descartes, writing in the seventeenth century, the process of becoming modern implied a separation of intellect from imagination, even if both of these faculties were important elements in the construction of knowledge.

> Where knowledge of things is concerned, only two factors need to be considered: ourselves, the knowing subjects, and the things which are the objects of knowledge. As for ourselves, there are only four faculties which we can use for this purpose, *viz*. intellect, imagination, sense-perception and memory. It is of course only the intellect that is capable of perceiving the truth, but it has to be assisted by imagination, sense-perception and memory if we are not to omit anything which lies within our power.
>
> (Descartes 1988: 12).

The supremacy of the intellect in perceiving the truth was based also in a firm distinction of mind from body, rationality from intuition, and science from rhetoric. As demonstrated by Ernest Gellner, Reason in the Cartesian sense was closely connected to individualism, and contrasted with culture (Gellner 1992). Reason was a kind of thinking that was purified from the collective errors of culture. Deep into the postmodern condition, we have realized that there are other stories to be told about these matters. We have cleared the vision – if not the object. The anthropological project is, as we have noted before, not a matter of clarifying what is already there, but of making new sense. In this way also, anthropology parts company from Cartesianism, in which the visionary power was to be taken literally; since sight was deemed the noblest among the senses, inventions such as the telescope were of utmost importance: 'Carrying our vision much further than our forebears could normally extend their imagination, these telescopes seem to have opened the way for us to attain a knowledge of nature much greater and more perfect than they possessed' (Descartes 1988: 57). But evidently this is so, if by knowledge we refer only to registration by way of the senses, and understanding by way of intellect. We note in passing that vision supplants imagination in this view. The scopic regime of modernity as located by Descartes in the telescope was further cemented in the intellectual world by the increasing circulation of printed works.[3]

Visionary metaphors are prominent in communicating understanding between persons or cultures; we *see* what other people mean. Visualism is on the wane, of course, yet the metaphors remain and thus inadvertently keep fusing energy into an outmoded dichotomy between realism, in which images aim at a faithful reflection of the world, and rhetoric, in which images evaluate the world as they portray it (Comaroff and Comaroff 1992: 158). Rhetoric is the bed-fellow of imagination; it is the ability to draw hypothetical connections that are in some way persuasive. Any theory is made within a particular context of persuasion (Atkinson 1990: 2). This is diacritical within anthropology, as based in an ethnography that 'surely extends beyond the range of the empirical eye; its inquisitive spirit calls upon us to ground subjective, culturally configured action in society and history – and vice versa – wherever the task may take us' (Comaroff and Comaroff 1992: 11). That spirit takes us right into the idea of human imagination as a collective, social phenomenon (Le Goff 1988: 5), and it will not allow an a priori separation of rationality from superstition. If superstition has social effect, it belongs to the empirical, and people's reactions cannot be deemed irrational.

To give an example: during my fieldwork in Iceland in the 1980s I kept stumbling upon references to 'the hidden people' (*huldufólkiD*, a people of elf-like features). They had played a prominent part in folk tale and legend during the centuries, and they were known to me and to my interlocutors as such. It was part of the rhetoric of collective imagination, or of the poetics of history, and as such we all knew it to be patently unreal. The unreality would be emphasized in conversation: direct questions would invariably yield answers in terms of past belief. Only an increasing intimacy with the people who had allowed me into their world finally made me realize that 'the past' was still very much with us. Once, when the hidden people were again half-jokingly mentioned over coffee as the cause of disappearing ustensils, I simply asked my friends when they had last encountered these people directly. Some internal debate on local chronologies and events yielded the answers of 'ten years ago', and I was given an elaborate account of where and how. Further conversation yielded more details, and there was no question whatsoever that *huldufólk* had an experiential reality within living memory. As an ethnographer I had no choice but to take the information as an empirical fact. The hidden people had a historical reality in the Icelandic world, and who was I to relegate local history to superstition, or to label my highly knowledgable friends premodern irrationals, bent on imagination for lack of reason. No way. Having unearthed the hidden people in the present, my task was to understand their manifest presence in theoretical terms. Without questioning local faculties of reasoning, the anthropologist has to cultivate her own powers of imagination in order to incorporate conceptual alternatives into a coherent vision of the world.

The making of sense in anthropology is based on an exploration of the potentiality of the present. Imagination becomes an active force in the construction of theories, that are in many ways no more and no less than metaphors intimating a particular world.

THE CENTRED SELF

Sense is not an inherent quality of social facts; it is attributed on the basis of experience. Empirical studies and recent epistemological reconsiderations have pointed to a fundamental moral, as phrased by Mark Johnson: 'any adequate account of meaning and rationality must give a central place to embodied and imaginative structures of understanding by which we grasp our world' (Johnson 1987: xiii).

The embodied attention to the world points to a centrality of the self, which has been curiously absent in the age of individualism. The absence is rooted in the Copernican revolution that initially decentred the world. Humans were displaced from the centre of the universe, and the road towards a mechanical view of the cosmos was open. Copernicus demonstrated how the Sun and not the Earth was the cosmological centre; the result was a mechanical model that alienated human experience from learned cosmology (cf. Merchant 1980). Later on, Darwin contributed the idea that the human species was but a temporary result of inter-action between fortuitous environmental pressure and random mutation. The world had no purpose; life was not of itself edify-ing. The image of what it meant to be human changed vastly as a matter of course. The self was displaced from cosmos to mind.[4]

In the early twentieth century, when the tradition of pro-fessional anthropology as based in fieldwork was invented, the decentred nature of human beings was further substantiated by Freud. He discovered, or claimed, that the ego is not master in its own house, and he likens his discovery to the previous reali-zation that the Earth is not the centre of the universe (Rorty 1991b: 143–144). The person is as fragmented as the solar system. There is no single reason governing the 'self', even if some kind of reason was often engaged in a virulent battle against unreason-able passions or brute bodily cravings. According to the Gospel of Sigmund, the self is ruled by an internal dialogue between conscious and uncounscious conversational partners. I believe that at some level this model provided the rationale for seeking the meaning of 'other worlds' in unconscious collective represen-tations rather than in practice. Meaning became transferred to the implicit; nothing was to be taken at face value.

While one could possibly claim that 'Freud democratized genius by giving everyone a creative unconscious' (Rieff, quoted in Rorty 1991b: 149), it can also be claimed that democratization in this sense diluted the idea of responsibility that was still embodied in the enlightened view of reason, permanently engaged in fighting irrational brutes. With the alleged fact of fragmentation went a sense of irresponsibility that made people lose sight of the good as a directive force; morality was displaced. From then on, people *reacted*; they did not *respond* to circumstance.

There is a need to recentre the human world if we are to overcome the pessimist view in anthropology – and elsewhere. The mechanical view of cosmos and the idea of the fragmented self reached a peak with the many claims to postmodernism that are, and for that reason, but a continuation of the modern view of the world. A radical break with the decentred self takes us squarely past the demand for a therapy that aims only at self-fulfilment. In the particular cultural turn that promotes individual therapy as instrumental advice against meaninglessness, the reintegration of the self has turned into parody. 'A total and fully consistent subjectivism would tend towards emptiness: nothing would count as a fulfilment in a world in which literally nothing was important but self-fulfilment' (Taylor 1989: 507).

The integrity of experience has to be acknowledged. For all the conversation that may go on in the heads of individuals they are still responsible for their actions as whole persons. Responsibility presupposes a subject. The denouncement of the individual subject as a 'curious entity from which many of us have grown to latterly distance ourselves' (Taussig 1992: 1) seems to me to be a short cut, past the real challenge to anthropology. The badly needed revision of the modern view of the rational and disengaged self does not entail selling out any idea of the subject. It means revising the notion of the subject, of course, and reclaiming an understanding of self-realization that presupposes 'that some things are important beyond the self; that there are some goods or purposes the furthering of which has significance for us and which hence can provide the significance of fulfilling life needs' (Taylor 1989: 507).

If it is true 'that knowing is giving onself over to a phenomenon rather than thinking about it from above' (Taussig 1992: 10), knowing the world presupposes a subject that is willing to go beyond its own internal conversation between intellects. Whether our knowledge project in a particular world is of a practical or a theoretical nature, we can only engage in it by way of ourselves. We respond to the world as subjects, who are responsible. This, I believe, is to carry the reflexive mode of anthropology to its logical conclusion. The anthropologists' inward-bound reflection has been both necessary and fertile, but there is now more to be gained by reverting the process. Self-reflexivity may be redirected out into the world once 'they' have been recognized as of 'us'; the heightened sensitivity and awareness of the relationship between anthropology as radical other and the world itself opens for a new kind of insight into reality.

Somewhat paradoxically the recentring of the self makes a new outward-bound expansion of knowledge possible because it allows us to project our imaginative powers out into the world.

BEYOND REASON

To fruitfully approach the methodological problem awaiting us, we need first to recognize that the apparently insurmountable problem of reuniting the dualisms created in the wake of Enlightenment is itself constituted within the specific discourse that separated them in the first place. This implies that we do not necessarily have a serious epistemological obstacle, but simply a problem of terminology. The words that we are currently using are in many ways outmoded. If the belief in reason is nothing but superstition, both terms lose sense. On this account, too, there is an acute need for acitivating the anthropological imagination, so that the words may not only catch up with, but possibly also redirect present concerns.

My aim is not to find another 'way out' of the impasse created by immature Reason and weakness of will. Instead, I would like to explore the alleged weakness as a stronghold of genuine insight in human life. As we know from so many field-worlds, people's actions are not governed solely by will or rational calculation. Attempts have been made to demonstrate that they are just governed by different rationalities. But why adhere to such notions, when people manifestly are engaged in what philosophers call 'incontinent actions', i.e., actions that go against better judgement, as it were (Davidson 1980: 21ff.). Incontinent actions imply weakness of will; as such they have been repressed and relegated to the non-scholarly universe of anecdote and joke. Their real significance as conveyors of unprecedented insight in the workings of culture and scholarship has been overlooked. From fieldwork we know that the experience of not being able even to understand oneself is crucial to the understanding of the limitations of western reason. Reason invariably gets stuck; that is, when we need imagination and emotion to break the tie (cf. de Sousa 1990: 16). Neither the label of irrationality nor the invocation of a different kind of rationality is of any help here.

Actions done intentionally but 'against one's better judgement', are done for a reason, and are therefore rational, yet there were better reasons for doing something else, and the actions are therefore also irrational. The relative saliency of the two opposed arguments or possible actions is determined by a motivational force that disconnects the 'better' judgement from the course of action, and that cannot be referred to Pure Reason in the Enlightenment sense.

This is where Romanticism enters as an important supplement to the Enlightenment heritage in anthropology. Romanticism and creative imagination have more often been associated with artistic creativity and fantasy than with scientific discovery and discursive novelty in a broader sense. In anthropology it gave rise to new, and rather blurred, genres of ethnographic writing, legitimized by postmodern ideas of social constructionism and the 'writing of culture'. The perplexing idea of constructionism made all anthropological writing seem as if made in water.

The redemption of imagination as an important means to knowledge is not to abide with constructionism, however. The notion of 'social construction' – of this and that and the other – is at best a preamble to further investigation. Claiming that gender, race, society or whatever is a social construction has far too often been converted into a conclusion (Taussig 1993: xvi). A conclusion, moreover, that does not transcend the obvious. Constructionism begs the question of the very process of social construction, which is a key issue in anthropology. Or, as Taussig has it: 'With good reason postmodernism has relentlessly instructed us that reality is artifice yet, so it seems to me, not enough surprise has been expressed as to how we nevertheless get on with living, pretending – thanks to the mimetic faculty – that we live facts not fictions' (Taussig 1993: xv).

One way of expressing and exploring this surprise is to unfold the notion of the anthropological imagination in Romantic terms while not necessarily discarding the Enlightenment ethos. The act of reasoning itself implies imagining within a social and cultural context. Understanding is an *event*. We 'intimate' unprecedented incidents or other worlds by means of imaginative projections from previous experience. As related above, a theory of imagination is an important ingredient in any theory of rationality. Once we have abandoned the demand for a disembodied rationality, imagination need no longer be excluded from our vision of the processes of understanding. While so far, a logic of creativity seems to have been a contradiction in terms, we can now see that even novel connections come out of past experience. Imagination provides the metonymical and metaphorical links between previous experience and unprecedented events and wordings. The logic of imaginative creativity is not distinct from the logic of reasoning; they are aspects of the same capacity for intimation, which is part of our being 'cultural'. Imagination is both constitutive and creative. It is a process, central to any event of understanding.

And this is the point: to acknowledge and to advocate an anthropological imagination is not to replace the scholarly standard of ethnographic presentation with a demand for creative writing. It is to explore the human potential for novelty in the real world. Anthropological knowledge is a creation that reveals. In so far as it is also a revelation that defines and completes what it makes manifest, we need new criteria for the acceptability of the anthropological revelations. The notion of interpretation as correlation with objects in themselves is no longer prominent. As pointed out by Hilary Putnam, this notion of interpretation is not the only notion available to us, however. We can still seek to correlate discourse with discourse, or constitute a meaningful commentary on one discourse in another (Putnam 1990: 122). Whatever practices of interpretation we have in anthropology, and however much they are context-sensitive and interest-relative, there is still such a thing as 'getting it right'. We can live with degrees of professional success and failure, but we cannot survive without implicit scales for making such judgements.

The conceptual relativism inherent in anthropological practice should not be mistaken for an ontological relativism.[5] It is this confusion that has marred any debate about universalism and relativism in anthropology. The conceptual relativity inherent in solid ethnography and amounting to a locally meaningful whole is no impediment to the achievement of a more general understanding or of the context of understanding itself. Anthropology must reject the idea of incommensurability, and admit to some criteria of rational acceptability of particular interpretations. We have to accept standards for scholarly 'emplotment', to invoke Ricoeur's notion of the mechanism that serves to make one story out of multiple incidents (Ricoeur 1991: 21). In the language of anthropological theory, the truth conditions must be made explicit. The intellectual craftsmanship of anthropology is not a matter of linking contexts of different scales, but of convincing the world that new kinds of shared knowledge are imaginable.

By way of concluding this edifying tale, I would like to return to the story of Mother Anthropology standing by the lake between this world and the other. I have been wanting to say that in order to traverse the gap, Anthropology has neither to drink the lake nor sacrifice her eyes. The miracle of being able to empty the lake and thus to level the world will not happen; local differences will remain. But by blinding ourselves we can make nothing of them.

If there is anything common to humanity, it is that we are imaginable to one another (Shweder 1991: 18). To perceive and understand different worlds of whatever scale, we must extend our imaginative powers as far as possible, and make more events of understanding happen. Exploring the imaginative character of anthropological reason may be both unsettling and liberating (cf. Johnson 1993: 1), just like anticipation may turn out to be disabling as well as potentiating (cf. Strathern 1992: 178ff.). We have no choice, however, but to explore the prophetic condition of anthropology: it is in this perspective that the anthropological imagination makes sense.

Chapter 5

The motivated body
On the locus of agency

> Berkeley stood up in front of his chair to speak, and so active
> was the uprightness of his slight small figure that the old people
> got to their feet, one by one, and stood facing him, their eyes
> in his, gravely.
>
> (Karen Blixen, *Out of Africa*)[1]

Some kinds of personal presence exert an almost physical force
upon others. Conversely, the affected people seem to react in a
manner that gives preeminence to the body over the mind.
Together, these manifestations of embodied energy point to a
field of social action that still has to be explored by anthropologists. It is a field of embodied motivation.

In this chapter, my aim is to encircle this field in an effort to
confront the problem of agency in culture from a particular angle.
The perspective is related to recent attempts to investigate the
relationship between reality, experience and expression (Turner
and Bruner 1986). Supplementing the effort to comprehend
'experience' as such, my ambition is to explore the bodily locus
of agency with a focus not only on the expression or action itself
but also its motivation. The assumption is that motivation forms
an important link between culture and action (D'Andrade 1992:
41), a link, moreover, that makes the distinction between culture
and action obsolete: action is deeply enculturated, and culture
exists only in practice.

In the process of my general anthropological exploration I shall
draw upon insights from philosophy and theatre anthropology.[2]
The former contributes new perspectives on rationality, the latter
provides a key to bodily performance. Both supply important
comments on the anthropological attempt to come to grips with

the motivated body. I want to add a dynamic dimension to the notion of 'the mindful body' (Scheper-Hughes and Lock 1987), and to discuss how it is that the body is not only a vehicle for collective social memory but also, potentially at least, for creative action and cultural transformation.

The ordinary enculturation to which the human body is subject for the most part takes place implicitly, by way of analogy, if you wish. Our living presence in society is a means to learn to act socially by way of an experience which is continuous with daily life. By contrast, the learning of particular performance techniques represents a kind of explicit socialization, or acculturation, namely, the internalization of a new set of rules for action (cf. Barba and Savarese 1991: 189). The actors have to learn a new kind of presence, drawing upon experiences that are not continuous with the performative space. Presence is here the end, not the means to the end; the means to dramatic presence is the technique of the performer, which again is based in training (cf. Barba and Savarese 1991: 246). In theatre anthropology this difference has been related to a distinction between the ordinary body of people in general and the extra-ordinary body of the performer, sometimes cast as the real and the fictive body.

Obviously, there is a qualitative difference between theatrical and social performances – the one designed to realize presence by way of illusion, the other illuding reality by way of presence – yet taking the performing body as the point of departure allows us to conflate the two. From the perspective of the acting body there is a profound continuity between acting on stage and living in the world; if nothing else then because of the dialectic between performing and learning identified by Victor Turner: 'One learns through performing, then performs the understandings so gained' (Turner 1982b: 94). From the ringside of the theatre, Constantin Stanislavski warned the actor: 'Always act in your own person. . . . You can never get away from yourself. The moment you lose yourself on the stage marks the departure from truly living your part and the beginning of exaggerated, false acting' (Stanislavski 1963: 91). And from the ringside of general anthropology, ordinary and extraordinary experiences are perforce seen within the range of the normal (cf. Abrahams 1986). Even if theatre produces an experience of 'heightened vitality' (Turner 1986b: 43), this vitality is apprehensible only through a continuity with lived experience in general. This will be substantiated in the following section and suffice it to emphasize that instead of operating with an a priori distinction between ordinary and extraordinary bodily experiences and expressions, I take both to be within the range of normal capacities for 'dilation' (cf. Barba 1985), if of different degrees and with different effects. In my investigation I shall, therefore, draw freely from both the field of cultural and of theatrical performances.

LIVED EXPERIENCE

In anthropology, the notion of experience has received increasing attention over the past few years. It has been acclaimed as the starting point for all ethnography, both in the sense that 'lived experience', comprising thoughts and desires, words and images, is declared 'the primary reality' (Bruner 1986a: 5), and in the sense that the ethnographer's shared social experience in the field is hailed as the initial step towards anthropological knowledge (Hastrup and Hervik 1994). Whatever the alleged reason for privileging experience, a privilege that has actually been strongly contested in some quarters, the attempts to make of this fuzzy category an analytical term points to a breakdown of traditional views of culture as a tight logical system, and people as passive bearers of that culture. Instead, people are reinstated as active agents in the reproduction as well as the transformation of culture. Even reproduction takes an effort (cf. Sahlins 1985; Moore 1987)!

Again, we sense a continuity between theatre and anthropology, both abandoning the petrified view of their object. As Antonin Artaud has it in a critique of traditional theatre: 'Our petrified idea of the theater is connected with our petrified idea of a culture without shadows, where, no matter which way it turns, our mind (*esprit*) encounters only emptiness, though space is full' (Artaud 1958: 12). The theatre is particularly forceful in stirring up shadows, left out by referential language, yet to move the spectators these shadows must connect to their own experience of the unspeakable.

The emphasis on human agency should not let us fall back on the classical transactionalist notions of society simply as the cumulative result of rational individual choices. Nor do we subscribe to the 'fax-model' of the internalization of culture, implying that the individual simply copies a set of shared notions about the world, and reducing socialization to a process of getting the original through the fax machine (Strauss 1992: 9; Strauss and Quinn 1993). Yet we still have to face the fact that some notions are shared, and that *social* practice cannot be studied with reference to individual choice or creativity alone. There are certain ways of learning to learn by way of experience that make their imprint. This is where a clarification of the concept of experience becomes absolutely vital.

Approaching society or culture through 'experience' immediately takes off in an ego-centred view of the world. There is no experience beyond the experiencing subject – the recentred self. People are seen as active agents in the world rather than passive reproducers of the systematic aspects of culture (Bruner 1986a: 12). This implies that, far from being static and predetermined by a particular semantic structure, meaning is always emergent. This is the first absolutely vital point to keep in mind. There are no givens in culture. Or, in other words, culture provides no fixed set of coordinates for meaning and action that can be identified from outside. At the same time, however, there are limits to creativity and choice, and there are learned dispositions that cannot easily be unlearned. But social actions are not rule-governed in any simple way. Actions are, actually, 'acts', allowing for improvisation as well as shared comprehension.

Actions in this sense do not necessarily imply actual movement in space or talking aloud. Action is everywhere in life. As Stanislavski has it for the actor: 'On the stage you must always be enacting something; action, motion is the basis of the art . . . of the actor; . . . even external immobility . . . does not imply passiveness. You may sit without motion and at the same time be in full action' (Stanislavski 1963: 7–8). The person as bodily presence is the locus – and the pre-text – of action. Action is not conceivable as a mental category; it is materialized, expressed by a 'body-in-life' – evidently so much more than a body merely alive (Barba 1985: 13). Like language, the body serves as a depository of deferred thoughts 'that can be triggered off at a distance in space and time by the simple effect of re-placing the body in an overall posture which *recalls* the associated thoughts and feelings, in one of the inductive states of the body which, as actors know, give rise to states of mind' (Bourdieu 1990: 69).

Nevertheless, the body has been curiously absent in anthropology, in spite of the fact that the people under study invariably have bodies. This is excactly the point: the view of people *having* bodies has made these disappear from analysis. The biological bodies are everywhere alike, and their very self-evidence has paradoxically obstructed our view of the centrality of the body in social experience. At most, the body has been interesting to anthropology as culturally conceptualized (e.g. Blacking 1977) or as a metaphor for society (e.g. Douglas 1970). One of my aims in this chapter is to dismantle the implicit notions of the body as a passive carrier or container of thought, and of a hierarchical relationship between mind and body, the former being the locus of the subject, the latter being merely an object.

The idea that agency is not merely located in the mind, and that expressions of inner experiences are not reserved for words, connects my propositions with certain parts of performative anthropology. When the notion of performative anthropology was first suggested, it was with a specific view of the anthropological object as being social dramas, 'erupting', as it were, from the fairly even surfaces of continuous social life (e.g. Turner 1982b: 9). The social drama has a 'protoaesthetic' form in its unfolding and therefore lends itself to analysis in theatrical terms (Turner 1986b: 39). The interrelationship between stage drama and social drama may take the shape of an inversion, each drawing upon the other's implicit social processes for their overt performances (Turner 1990: 17). Yet the continuity between them is always presupposed. Both reflect upon a shared social experience. It is in that that the ethnographer may adopt the role of ethnodramaturg (Turner 1982b: 100).

Furthermore, the ethnographer in the field is comparable to the actor on stage: the ethnographer, too, has to acculturate her body to new patterns of appropriate action. Fieldwork itself can be seen as a second enculturation. That is, after all, its *raison d'être*. As for the 'third theatre' so also for anthropological field-work; 'In the third theatre there is no difference between a personal and a professional life, since how theatre is made takes precedence over what is produced' (Watson 1993: 21). And again, both the actor's and the ethnographer's enterprise critically involve reflexivity: both have to reflect upon their reflections, or to be aware of their awareness – even if with the purpose of letting go of it (cf. Bruner 1986a: 22–23).

Today, the notion of performative anthropology has been taken a bit further on epistemological (rather than sociological) grounds. A shift from informative to performative ethnography is taking place, in the broad sense of replacing the kind of ethnography where the ethnographer determines the questions and notes the answers, with a kind of ethnographic communication where 'the ethnographer does not call the tune but plays along' (Fabian 1990: 19).

While previously, performative anthropology gave preeminence to cultural and social expressions, or eruptions, and made us keenly aware of the dramatic representations of culture, Fabian wants to draw our attention to the fact that 'about large areas and important aspects of culture no one, not even the native, has information that can simply be called up and expressed in discursive statements' (Fabian 1990: 6). In other words, most cultural knowledge is stored in action rather than words. The methodological consequence is that we cannot hope for a coherent logical structure determining the meaningful in any one culture but have to comprehend meaning as it emerges in practice. In ethnography as in culture there is no external standpoint of knowing. Knowledge is inherently reflexive.

Reflexivity in this sense does not imply that the knowing subject is lost in his or her own self-referential musings, even if the culture of Narcissism, identified by Lasch (1978), is still prominent in our world. Quite the contrary; reflexivity implies an awareness of self as both subject and object (Myerhoff and Ruby 1982: 2). This applies on both sides of the ethnographic encounter; the 'others' can no longer be de-subjectified in anthropological analysis. The problem remains, of course, of how we can avoid a professional transformation of the experiencing subject into a dehumanized object, 'a caricature of experience' (Kleinman and Kleinman 1991: 276).

So far the anthropology of experience and of performance have been unsatisfying at precisely this point: the experience has been read – literally – as narrative (e.g. by Bruner 1986b); while certainly experience is often *expressed* in narrative, like illness narratives for instance (Kleinman 1988), the very literality of the notion of narrative has blurred its referent. That is one reason why we must now direct our search towards the field of embodied motivation. This search is governed by a methodological paradox: it is only by abandoning the idea of the clinical gaze, as descibed by Foucault (1963), that we get access to the living bodies of social agents as well as the directive force of cultural models. It is characteristic for the performative anthropology of Victor Turner that it was still very much based on a classical, observationist view of anthropology. Hence, the focus on the expressions of experience rather than the experience itself. The idea of the clinical gaze related directly to the ocular and experimental view of science, modelled upon the opening and curious inspection of a dead body. One of the results was the splitting apart of body and mind that we have had to straddle. Realizing the impossibility of equating lived experience with dead bodies, anthropologists face a methodological problem of acknowledging the living body as a locus of experience.

The point is not to individualize experience or culture, but to locate the centre for 'the making of sense' as discussed in the preceding chapter. Events make sense, not in terms of propositions, but in their coherence with our own experience. While we are bound to use propositional language to describe both experience and understanding, we must not mistake our mode of description for the things described. As Mark Johnson has it: 'propositional content is possible only by virtue of a complex web of nonpropositional schematic structures that emerge from our bodily experience' (Johnson 1987: 5).

We share a good deal of this experience cross-culturally; this is one reason why we remain imaginable to one another. Imagination springs from the body as well as from the mind. Johnson, for instance, shows convincingly how the fact of our walking upright so to speak 'naturalizes' certain cultural models based on the distinction between up and down. Embodied patterns of experience become shared cultural models (Johnson 1987: 14). This also applies to the experience of performers from different traditions, and it forms the rationale for theatre anthropology: 'Different performances, at different places and times and in spite of the stylistic forms specific to their tradition have shared common principles. The first task of theatre anthropology is to trace these recurrent principles' (Barba and Savarese 1991: 8).

While, certainly, theatre anthropology is a particular mode of research focusing on universal performative principles rather than relative conceptual schemes, the distance to general anthropology is not insurmountable. In both cases, the theoretical project leads beyond the sociologically manifest and into a general field – of the hypothetical. In theatre anthropology, one hypothesis of embodied creativity has been proposed in terms of the actor's dilated presence (Barba 1985; Barba and Savarese 1991). The dilated body of the actor is what takes the spectator into the unknown lands *of his own experience*. The actor can reveal only what is already true, if belonging to the unknown side of things (Grotowski 1969: 194–195).

One consequence of acknowledging the dialectic between experience and learning alluded to above, and of realizing that experience is not open for autopsy yet still may be studied, is a twisting of the notion of experience itself. In the terms of Edward Bruner (1986a), the 'lived experience' of people needs attention as a corrective to previous notions of a cultural grammar, and regulated social action. The key thing is the physical manifestation of life; the lived experience is the actual series of lived-through events. I shall propose a notion of 'social experience' as a replace-ment of the lived (yet methodologically killed) experience. As I see it, 'experience' is always mediated by interpretation, which again is always socially based. We acquire social wisdom 'not by abstract solitary thought, but by participation immediately or vicariously through the performative genres in sociocultural dramas' (Turner 1986a: 84). Not only is experience always anchored in a collectivity, but true human *agency* is also incon-ceivable outside the continuing conversation of a community, from where the background distinctions and evaluations neces-sary for making choices of actions spring (Taylor 1985a: 8).

In some respects this echoes the distinction between 'experi-ence' and 'an experience' made by Dilthey and further explored by Victor Turner. 'Mere experience is simply the passive endur-ance and acceptance of events. *An* experience, like a rock in a zen sand garden, stands out from the evenness of passing hours and years and forms what Dilthey called a "structure of experi-ence' (Turner 1986b: 35). In other words, while all of us have experiences all the time, *an* experience is cut loose from the chronological stream in a non-arbitrary fashion. By submitting to the drive towards expression, the socially effervescent experience is processed, socialized and ultimately transformed, if nothing else then because it is allotted an initiation and a consummation – a beginning and an end – that cannot be granted 'mere' experi-ence. The theatre – like the plague – qualifies as *an* experience *par excellence*: 'Like the plague, the theater is a formidable call to the forces that impel the mind by example to the source of its conflicts' (Artaud 1958: 30). Both carry with them the power of revelation, of comprehension, and thus of contagious experience.

In contrast to a phenomenology of experience that reflects 'an experience which, by definition, does not reflect itself' (Bourdieu 1990: 25), anthropology must always question the conditions for experience and explore 'the coincidence of the objective structures and the internalized structures which provides the illusion of immediate understanding, characteristic of practical experience of the familiar universe' (ibid.: 26). In short, in so far as anthropology takes off in the real social experience of people, it cannot continue to accept a radical discontinuity between mind and body, culture and action.

THE ABSENT BODY

Given the forceful argument about the bodily locus of experience, it becomes all the more curious that the propositional distinction between body and mind has remained so tenacious in our worldview. To understand this we must start by tracking the origin of this distinction, not solely in the history of ideas, but also and more importantly in the nature of the human body itself.[3]

The shift in scientific theory pioneered by Galileo and to which Cartesian Reason was intimately linked, transformed the idea of a unified cosmos embodying the ideas of the world, and of which humans were but fractions (and representations). Instead the world became recast in mechanistic terms; moral virtue and self-mastery were transformed in the process (Taylor 1989: 144). The mechanistic approach dissociated humans from nature, as it were. This dislocation also implied a uniformation of time that dissonated with the ordinary experience of uneven periods of event density or emptiness. During the seventeenth century, reality was recast as a machine, a precise clockwork, rather than an arhythmic living body. This paved the way for the domination of nature and of 'primitives'.

It also redirected people's quest for self-understanding. Reflection had been inward bound for centuries, reaching a crescendo in Augustine's 'radical reflexivity'; in contrast to earlier thinkers, Augustine adopted a first-person standpoint (Taylor 1989: 130). Knowledge or awareness became that of an agent. This is not solely the matter of musing upon own experience, making it an object of contemplation. 'Radical reflexivity brings to the fore a kind of presence to oneself which is inseparable from one's being the agent of that experience' (ibid.: 131). This is what makes one a being that can speak of itself in the first person, and what made the language of inwardness irresistible. 'I think' somehow became an action outside the world, inside the self.

We are now in a position to resituate thinking in the world. Not only is our historical position different from Augustine's, however, our project is also another. His project was still defined in theological terms, being one of establishing 'God' as part and parcel of the person. Self-knowledge was instrumental to knowing God; the moral resources were still located in God, if the route to the high now passed within (Taylor 1989: 139). In more general terms it meant that moral perfection required a personal commitment to the good. This implied that 'will' became essential in the early modern period, and 'weakness of will' became the ultimate personal failure, as we have seen.

With Descartes the moral resources became firmly placed within ourselves; outer points of orientation evaded, and the entire inner/outer dichotomy took on a new meaning. Scientific explanation was cut loose from moral vision; the former became a question of correct representation, the latter of individual firmness of will. The very notion of 'idea' migrated from cosmos to person; its ontic sense was translocated to an intra-psychic world. The idea became something one had 'in the mind' (Taylor 1989: 144). There, it became a means for objectifying the world, including the body. The distinction made by Descartes between *res cogitans* and *res extensa* was the basis for the model of a sharp distinction between mind and body to which we have become accustomed. And it is this metaphysical dualism that has ever since been reflected in the subject–object dichotomy as basic for our knowledge of the world (Bernstein 1983: 115–116).

This violates both the classical ontology and the ordinary experience of embodied understanding. To understand, for Descartes, involved disengagement from our own material selves, those uncontrolled sources of error and moral vice. To achieve pure knowledge one first had to achieve self-purification; self-mastery became a matter of controlling the bodily source of error. This demand for instrumental control is implicitly rejected by performative anthropology in the sense defined above. The body is acknowledged as a source of revelation instead of error. There is a need for dissolving the 'Cartesian anxiety', that is the fear of not having a fixed and stable foundation for knowledge, a grounding of reference (cf. Varela, Thompson and Rosch 1992: 140). There is also a need for dissolving Kant's distinction between pure and empirical knowledge, the former being independent of experience, the latter only obtainable through it (Kant 1991: 25–26). Generally, anthropology must reject the mind–body dualism as ontology, and cannot but read it as a particular western ideology of the mind as superior to the body. As pointed out by Jerzy Grotowski, to be cerebral and discursive has become a token of civilization:

> Therefore we play a double game of intellect and instinct, thought and emotion; we try to divide ourselves artificially into body and soul. When we try to liberate ourselves from it we start to shout and stamp, we convulse to the rhythm of music. In our search for liberation we reach biological chaos. We suffer most from a lack of totality, throwing ourselves away, squandering ourselves.
>
> (Grotowski 1969: 211)

Grotowski goes on to suggest that theatre, through the actor's technique, provides an opportunity for integration, and for the revelation of true substance. The implication is that spectators discard their own masks by way of the vicarious experience of wholeness. Again, I think that there is no need to single out the actor in terms of bodily motivation; while certainly there are differences of technical mastery and of deliberateness in motion, vicarious experience is possible only on the basis of resonance between performer and spectator, a resonance that is established via shared experiences of the body as a locus of action.

If such wholeness is in some way part and parcel of human experience, there is all the more reason to pause and ponder over the grip upon our sense of reality held by the dualism of body and mind. As convincingly demonstrated by Drew Leder (1990), the Cartesian dualism seems to echo important aspects of human experience. While it is true that human experience is incarnated, it is no less true that the body tends to disappear from our awareness of *how* we experience. This is owed to the dual nature of the body: ecstasy and recessiveness, in the terms proposed by Leder. The ecstatic body consists of the senses by which we reach out for the world and which are, therefore, prominent in shaping our experiential field, while the recessive body points to all those invisible and unknowable processes that make sensations possible at all, and keep us alive as humans.

The ecstatic functions of the body, and not least the power of the gaze, are most prominent in shaping the experiential field, and are, therefore, 'natural' candidates for the Prize of Perception – first awarded by Descartes. In theatre, the gaze is explicitly exploited in the shaping of the field of action. The recessive qualities, by contrast, give rise to no projective field, and are therefore easily overlooked in the phenomenology of experience. This has been true also for the phenomenolgy of fieldwork. In fieldwork we are heavily dependent on the ecstatic powers. We go beyond ourselves and reach out towards the new world by all our senses; we take in the differences. The other culture becomes incorporated; we consume it, literally, by way of eating: 'in taste, the experience of world and body are perhaps most closely inter-woven' (Leder 1990: 15; cf. Okely 1994). Metaphorically, we also internalize unknown sensations of magic and ritual anxiety, by our corporeal being in the world of others.

Generally, the incorporation of culture implies a process of sedimentation; more and more cultural models are taken for granted (Leder 1990: 31–32). In a manner of speaking, the sedi-mented culture becomes part of the recessive or hidden faculties of the self. The process of incorporation is unending in principle; learning in the sense of enculturation never stops. Yet for some people, the original enculturation is followed by one or more later, and separate, processes of bodily sedimentation of patterns of acting. It has been suggested that we might call such secondary processes for acculturation, on the assumption that they are some-how external to the original culture as sedimented. This new or extra-daily pattern of performative capacity has led to a distinc-tion between the actor's acculturated body and the ordinary enculturated body (e.g. Barba and Savarese 1991: 189ff.). From the point of view of the performing body taken here, the actor's training, however specialized and sophisticated, need not be set apart from other processes of bodily sedimentation of perform-ative patterns. For craftsmen, skilled manual labourers, house-wives and anthropologists alike, certain skills become 'second nature' at some stage beyond childhood; there is no way of distinguishing ontologically between the daily techniques of ordinary people and the extra-daily techniques of actors. There may be different senses of purpose, and different degrees of awareness involved in the training processes, but whether daily or extra-daily, both kinds of bodily technique are centred in the body-in-life; what is second nature, of course, always is incorporated culture. Collectively, it becomes a shared 'habitus': 'The *habitus* – embodied history, internalized as a second nature and so forgotten as history – is the active presence of the whole past of which it is the product' (Bourdieu 1990: 56). Learning always implies change (Bateson 1972: 283). The training of actors incorporates this change.

The degree to which this change is embodied has been ignored in general anthropology, however. Sedimentation implies a degree of solidification of the world as incorporated, which will gradually make the person experience a reshaping of the body's actual ability (Leder 1990: 34). This is a prominent feature of fieldwork, notably when actual participation in local work processes takes place – as in my own milking of cattle and rounding up sheep in Iceland. In fieldwork, too, culture becomes 'naturalized' in socialization and experience. The crux of the matter is not a difference in kind between the actor's acquired bodily and performative capacities and ordinary faculties, but a difference in the degree of awareness of the body techniques as such.

This difference is related to the varying projective fields of the actor's and others' bodies. While the lack of a projective field from the material body itself has generally led to an almost complete disappearance of the body from our vision of thinking, for the actor there is always a projective space: the audience, whether actually present or not. Somewhat paradoxicallly, this points to the absolute centrality of the body. Normally, it is so much taken for granted that it may disappear. Only when in pain does the body become unbearingly manifest and demands attention; the self must act upon a telic demand to redress the situation of absence (Leder 1990: 72). Pain, and by consequence bodily presence, becomes an emotionally loaded state, defined as temporary and unnatural. As such it is a universal human experience, even if the state it defines and loads has varying cultural expressions (Good *et al.* 1992). In other words, and as strongly suggested by recent works in medical anthropology, the 'presence' of the body is culturally mediated.

What we share cross-culturally is the *absence* of the body. In the relatively emotionless state of reasoning, the body tends to experientially disappear; this is what makes the Cartesian epistemology a motivated misreading. The dualism is based in lived experience, and then fallaciously interpreted as ontology.

THEATRES OF SELF

To re-present the body as the locus of action, we must first realize that the art of performing, dramatically or culturally, cannot be studied independently of the performing body. One does not *have* a body, one *is* a body. There is no manifestation of the self outside the body, even if our senses and words help us project ourselves outward. Motivated agents create theatres of self. They stage themselves and meaning emerges in the process.

Culture is meaningful only to someone in particular. In so far as it exists, it is both in the world and in people's minds (Strauss and Quinn 1993: 28). There is a centre of knowing that has remained obscure, partly due to the apparent naturalness of the lived space, and partly owing to the lack of any projective field arising from the material body itself. The naturalness of the lived space is related to 'the way our own body is, as the vehicle, the stage, and the object of experience at the same time' (Hanks 1990: 5). Through our daily activities we define and redefine a corporeal field that sediments and resonates with the recessive or self-concealing aspects of the living body. In theatre anthropology this has led to a dismantling of the fiction of duality, that is, the idea that the body is the performer's instrument. The performer does not 'use' his body; if this were the case, then who is the performer, and where is his will to using the body located? There is only one person, combining bodily and mental images in a unified performance. So also with social performances. There are no loose bodies that can be used or put into play by dislocated minds. Will is situated; body and mind are confused.

For any one action, be it aimed at ensnaring an audience into an illusory world or a mundane task such as fetching water, the point of departure, literally, is always a mindful body – an enculturated self. Enculturation implies internalization of local concepts, values, and gestures. In the process 'cultural givens' sink down below awareness.

In theatre anthropology, there is an assumption of a 'pre-expressive' level of all performance; it is a basic level of performative organization common to all performers irrespective of culture (Barba and Savarese 1991: 186ff.). The temporal implication of the term points to a feature of the training, not of the actual performance; during the training, the actor may work on different parts of the body in isolation, pre-casting, as it were, single elements of what will later be performed as a whole. The pre-expressive techniques for controlling bodily energy will eventually provide a coherent and rhythmic presence. In actual action, be it theatrical or social, there is only simultaneity; there is no meaning prior to the act itself. Meaning is always emergent, as previously stressed. There is no structure, no system of principles existing outside, beyond or somehow prior to the manifestations.

The dimension of time marks performance in another way, however. As pointed out by Victor Turner, 'acting' itself is an ambiguous term, pointing to doing things in everyday life and within ordinary time, or to performing on a stage in a time that is extra-ordinary (Turner 1982b: 102). In the present argument, this ambiguity is seen as a reflection of the paradox of the experienced absence of the body in ordinary social performance. I shall not, therefore, separate theatrical from other cultural performances, but deal with all of them as variations of those 'theatres of self', in which the motivated bodies act.

Already in 1959 Erving Goffman discussed the presentation of self in terms of staging, and introduced a major distinction between front and back stage. He separated the self as character and the self as performer; the self that appears to others is a performed character, a public self paying lip-service to standardized social obligations while concealing its true desires (Goffman 1959; cf. also Burkitt 1991: 57–60). Today, the primary concern is not to explain deception, but rather to comprehend why deception is impossible. There is no way to hide the enculturated body from one's action; the body is the locus, the rationale, and the manifestation of the act. There is no acting apart from the self, ontologically fused of body and mind. Even on stage the performer and the character are one, if we are to believe Stanislavski: 'the actor ceases to act, he begins to live the life of the play' (1963: 121). Whatever the stage, people have no choice but to live their part.

In my perspective, what is interesting about the self is not that it is constructed in culture but that it acts on its own behalf, as it were. The theatre of self has no front or back stage. It is a unified space, with no boundaries. It only has a centre: the performing self. Just as there is no language independent of acts of speaking, no knowledge without a knower, so there can be no culture without performers. The presentation of self is always a performance to be taken at face value. There is no compartmentalization of human presence.

Nor is the presentation of self just the end-result of other people's designations, as implied by Goffman's work on asylums (Goffman 1961). In this work, it is presumed that the role of mental patients sticks to people who have become so designated by the expectancies of others. One is forced to perform as mentally sick, against one's character. I do not believe this to be possible. It is the self who engages in social role-playing; not necessarily a self who is totally aware of what is going on, of course, since so many acts have been preformed during the process of enculturation.

While language has informed us that the script-writer is called *I*, psychoanalysis has taught us that many scenarios were written years before the 'I' was identified. The self plays out roles from the past in its own secret theatre: the 'psychic plays may be performed in the theatre of our own minds or that of our bodies or may take place in the external world, sometimes using other people's minds and bodies, or even social institutions, as their stage' (McDougall 1986: 4).

While there is much to be said for at least some of the psychoanalytical claims, it has to be stressed that the scenarios of the self need be neither neurotic nor psychotic; the acting out of preformed scripts may in fact be little more than the performing of enculturated motives. In other words, beyond the 'psychic theatre' analysed in psychoanalytical terms is a comprehensive cultural context that implies that the theatres of self under scrutiny here cannot be understood as 'psychic', in the sense of being individual, or private. They are deeply enculturated and socially premissed; the self becomes manifest within a collectivity.

If psychoanalysis is an enterprise of decoding inner dramas of the individual analysand by way of the analyst and the process of transference, performative anthropology is a study of social actions in a context of which the ethnographer is part. Thus, in contrast to psychoanalysis, anthropology is not concerned with capturing the lost and wandering characters in want of a stage on which to perform (cf. McDougall 1986: 286), but by demonstrating how characters and performers are always one – a person in body.

While Freud's decentring of the self may have been a democratization, it was not really a dislocation; the multiple self was still in the mind. The self was no longer seen as a one-stranded rational person, but as a set of mental interlocutors. While the burden was thus lifted from the *rational* mind, the mind itself was still not freed from its floating position. The fictive duality of mind and body remained. By the end of Freud's century, we still have to replace the Cartesian tension between mind and body *within* the self with a view of a unified self as the horizon where real actions meet the imagined space of beyond, always in the process of being conquered.

In culture, 'imagined worlds become not only theatricalized but factualized as religious axiom and social custom. Illusions thus serve the cause of belief, if not truth, thanks to the magical series of transfers between theater and reality held in place by mimetic art and the public secret' (Taussig 1993: 86). By way of experience, cultural messages literally and metaphorically get under people's skin. The master-motives may vary from one culture to the next (which is why we may isolate them analytically in the first place), yet the motivational link between culture and action is a general feature of the practical knowledge of the world – as opposed to the theoretical project of anthropology.

Practical mastery implies constructive use of the body's ecstatic faculties, resonating on the board of the recessive body. So also for the mastery of the dramatic act; by way of its integrative power it has been compared to 'an act of the most deeply rooted, genuine love between two human beings' (Grotowski 1969: 212). In love, one transcends one self; by accepting the passionate objectification by the beloved, ecstasy becomes a vehicle for mutual incorporation, and thus for enlarging the world (Hastrup 1993c). More generally, the ecstatic powers of the body reach a climax in the sexual attraction to another, while certainly the desire itself springs from unknown sources; sexuality exhibits the chasm between ecstasy and recessiveness in pure form (Leder 1990: 137). It also emphasizes the force of bodily agency. Thus, in theatre as well as in love, passion and compassion melt into one. Motion and emotion are barely distinguishable in the theatres of self.

CORPOREAL FIELDS

To recapitulate: the body is never simple presence. In its ecstatic qualities it expands beyond itself and projects itself outwards; one experiences the field through the senses. In its recessive qualities the body tends toward self-concealment; even the ethnographer in the field remains curiously unaware of the degree to which the experience is incarnated. The almost mythological status of fieldnotes as recorded observations has obscured the pertinence of the highly emotionally loaded 'headnotes', the unwritten recollections. This has echoed the view of intentionality as located in a disembodied mind, and a view of agency as the outcome of cognitive rationality alone.

This is a peculiar western view of agency, and of the modern self. In this view, the general concept of person has a reflexive element: 'A person is an agent who has an understanding of self as an agent, and can make plans for his/her own life' (Taylor 1985b: 263). But we should not let ourselves be deceived by this notion, since 'understanding' and 'planning' is only part of our apprehension of the world, and of time. Causation, in biography as well as in history, cannot be reduced to the explicit level of intentionality (Hastrup 1990f). Beyond intention and the indi- vidual rationalization of particular actions lie deeper motives that do not belong to the explicit and empirical but to the implicit and receding order of incorporated culture. Intentions and motives must be distinguished (Pettit 1976); the former point to efficient causes, the latter to final causes. In a recentred perform- ative anthropology, the acting person is not only a rational, inten- tional 'person' but a deeply motivated body-in-life.

The reason for action is not located in the mind alone. Practical mastery of the world has a more complex rationale, including incorporated experience. Ethnographers themselves often experi- ence how in the field (and elsewhere, of course), they are caught in a web of apparently 'irrational' behaviour. They act as if 'out of their mind', or as if they were not really 'themselves'. They hear their own voices utter absolutely unreasonable words and arguments; they, too, engage in incontinent actions, the rationale for which is anchored in a set of emotions. Emotions are part of social practice, not outside it (cf. Lutz and Abu-Lughod 1990). The affective registers may vary from one culture or one situation to the next, but emotion as such is located in a community, not in the individual (cf. Irvine 1990). Emotion is a relation, not a substance. Theatre moves because of its skilful manipulation of the emotional relation between actor and spectator.

Will is imbued with hidden motivational force: common sense incarnate. The incarnation of common sense implies that the body cannot be treated as pure object, or as a designified and passive bearer of the mind, solitarily attending to the world as subject. We cannot understand the texture of the perceptual field without reference to the body; the body *is* the self, not just its carrier. The body is a nodal point in our attention to the world. As suggested by Merleau-Ponty, one's own body is a 'third term', always tacitly implied in any figure-ground construction (Merleau-Ponty 1962: 101). The body is the zero-point of perception, the centre from which the senses project themselves out into the world, and defines the horizon of the self. As zero-point it has remained absent from view; not unlike the ethnographer who has been a 'third-person' in the cultural encounter in the field, discursively absent as a locus of perception (Hastrup 1987b).

Clearly, the world is not experienced through the fixed coordinates of a semantic space. The world is always experienced from a particular point in a social space. Moreover, the point from which we experience the world is in constant motion. As the person moves about in social space, the perspective shifts. There is no seeing the world from above, and thus no fixed coordinates of a semantic space that we can just objectively map. There is simply no referential practice outside a corporeal setting, in which the individual agent is situated.

This amounts to a recentring of social performance in the corporeal fields of people. By 'corporeal field' I refer to that larger space with which every individual is inextricably linked by way of the physical, sensing and moving body (Hanks 1990: 92ff.). The implied shift to an ego-centric approach to referentiality is a shift from a semantic to a pragmatic view of culture. The agent of social action is a living person, not just a mind. This reformulates the lived body as a path of access, rather than a thing. To understand the nature of this path within the corporeal field of lived experience means to acknowledge the degree to which culture is incorporated, yet at the same time is open for improvisation. Internalizing culture does not imply a passive copying because the individual processes of naturalization take place within separate corporeal fields and motivations are, therefore, transmitted unevenly. In the tension between shared models and individual motivations cultural transformation becomes possible. This is fully explored in radical theatre, where one of the driving forces, or motivations, has been seen as its power to transform. The politics of performance has sometimes been phrased in terms of a radical intervention in society (e.g. Kershaw 1992). I would contend that theatre is but a concentrated form of a general power to improvise while also abiding to the principles of incarnation. Reproduction and transformation are indistinguishable in practice; all experience is 'new'. Nothing has ever happened before, yet by a process of assimilation, it may become incorporated into the familiar universe. Conversely, the 'world' may change as a result of the alternative process of accomodation.[4]

From the centre of the corporeal field, energy may be projected outwards and bring forth motion.

MOVING PEOPLE

In the quotation from *Out of Africa* that opens this chapter, Berkeley moves people. His presence is so powerful that his audience cannot but respond in action. The energy bound in his person stirs people out of their immobility and between them an active space is created, underscored by their mutual gazing. In the preceding pages I have attempted to encircle the general quality of this field of embodied motivation, which has its highest vitality in theatre. Time is ripe for recentring the argument.

Lest there be any misunderstanding, let me emphasize that the recentring of anthropology in the body is a far cry from a return to a natural science of action. There is no return to the reductive views held by behaviourism, or to any other objectified reduction of human agency as essentially mechanistic. Acting, as an expression of agency, can never be reduced to common principles or natural laws. It always takes place in a particular space and within a particular corporeal field.

The point is that even when the body is 'decided', it also always 'decides'.[5] Culture, like theatre, may be regulated improvisation, yet improvisation it remains. Each instance is singular, and decisions must be made accordingly. Decisions are made with reference to evaluations, which form the background of our understanding ourselves as persons. Neutrality in decision-making is an illusion; facts are imbued with value (Putnam 1981: 127ff.). The procedural rationality implied by Objectivism rests on an ideal of disengagement, that can no longer be sustained (Taylor 1985a: 6).

In other words, social acting implies a kind of agency that is of necessity governed by a sense of worth; there is no human motivation without an implicit morality. The quintessential feature of human agency is the power to evaluate and rank desires and satisfactions (Taylor 1885a: 17), not simply the power to act upon desires and redress sensations of pain. People respond rather than just react. Their motivations are inextricably linked with their self-understanding (Quinn 1992).

In so far as we see theatrical performances as telescoped social performances, this qualification of agency applies equally to both. Theatre provides a social drama of heightened vitality because it condenses the agent's energy, not because it transforms it. Agents, whether actors on stage or in life, must be seen as self-interpreting and reflexive humans, for whom motivation is governed as much by implicit moral evaluations as by disengaged minds.

In a view of culture that allows for shadows and corporeal depth, instead of reducing it to a unilineal narrative, agency is to respond to motivation, not simply to act intentionally. Motivation is a symbolic capital that moves. Symbolic capital is a means to transubstantiate real relations of power, and to produce real effects without any apparent expenditure of energy (Bourdieu 1991: 170). Motivation informs the hidden dance and transforms embodied energy into action. This is what dilates the performer's presence and potentiates him.

In theatre, of course, the motivation must become visible; the hidden dance must be consciously explored. Or, if you wish, motivation and intention must conflate. Just like poetry explores the language parallax to the highest degree and effect (Friedrich 1986), so theatre must explore what I would like to call the 'performative parallax' to its most radical conclusion. In poetry as well as dramatic performance, the practitioneers deliberately enter the dynamic zone of poetic or performative indeterminacy, that is, a zone where the emotions and motives of the agents are significantly beyond the scope of exhaustive verbal description and accurate prediction. As poetry may have its master tropes, so theatre may have its key expressions. In both cases, the limits

– of language or of ordinary bodily action – are explored and altered. This is true creativity, a creativity that reveals.

In the general theatre of self, agency is likewise centred in a corporeal field in which meaning is always emergent or inscribed, never given or prescribed. The parallactic potential is always latent in performance, because the sub-text of all performance is nothing but the unprecedented act itself. There is no pre-text for action outside the motivated body inhabiting the ethnographic present.

Chapter 6

The inarticulate mind
On the point of awareness

> Time past and time future
> Allow but a little consciousness.
> To be conscious is not to be in time
> But only in time can the moment in the rose-garden,
> The moment in the arbour where the rain beat,
> The moment in the draughty church at smokefall
> Be remembered; involved with past and future.
> Only through time time is conquered.

(T. S. Eliot 1935)[1]

Having identified the living and acting body as the locus of cultural agency, we are left with a question of awareness. If the subject is not a mind sticking blindly to alleys of practical reason but a living person constantly reformulating her whole being through her doings, we are forced to reconsider our notions of consciousness.[2] We have to 'remind' ourselves about our inarticulacy, as it were. Even if it is axiomatic that humans are self-interpreting beings, we are left with a question of the limits to this self-interpretation, and – not less important from the point of view of the student of culture – the limits of expression and the significance of silence.

With consciousness we approach a field in which questions of ontology and methodology merge: how do people think and how do we know? How do we, as anthropologists, get access to those forms of consciousness that relate directly to the social space, by being both defined by it and being its defining capacity? There is no way in which we can fully grasp other people as subjects, but through structured imagining – often named intuition – we may still infer part of their implicit reasoning from its various expressions. In the logocentric vision of the world one has often envisaged knowledge as directly, and exclusively, expressed in words. Taking the point of departure in experience rather than words and, by consequence, in the recentred self rather than the floating mind, knowledge itself becomes relocated accordingly. It is largely tacit and stored in the habit-memory, not solely in the brain. This implies a degree of inarticulacy on the part of human agents, even if still conscious of the environment of which they are part.

Questions of consciousness entail endless other questions, and to address them one enters an indeterminate field of enquiry. Indeterminacy is no reason to sidestep any question, however, but provides a particular challenge to find one's own way in the hope that it leads through places of general interest. The ambition, of course, is to eventually reach a clearing where one may rest and remember the moments of insight. The route I have chosen in this chapter passes from everyday violence in present-day Brazil to long-term misery in the Iceland of bygone centuries. This unlikely itinerary eventually makes some considerations on the ethics of inarticulacy apposite.

In her thought-provoking work on Brazil, Nancy Scheper-Hughes (1992) is concerned with the silence of the poor inhabitants of a shanty town, and their apparent resistance to articulating their sufferings. Her narrative provides a kind of parable for the inarticulate mind with which I am concerned. I am not trying to reduce a painful reality to an allegory of a new version of a metaphysical reality. Rather, I am seeking to combine a powerful ethnography with an argument on collective consciousness, exploring at least a figment of the relationship between human agency and linguistic articulation, so eloquently dealt with by Charles Taylor within philosophy (e.g. 1985a, 1985b). In order to 'anthropologize' this agenda, I ground my exposition in a particular social reality. The empirical is still within reach.

My second example will be somewhat more elaborate and deals with a particular historical development in Iceland in a long time perspective; the idea is to substantiate the point that agency may be motivated by cultural models that are in many ways obsolete, and to show how the collective self-consciousness of a people may effectively block their awareness of a changing environment. The Icelanders of the period I am dealing with here were highly conscious of their cultural models, yet they cannot make claims to awareness of the interrelationship between these models and history. Thus, in the course of my discussion, the focus of my argument sharpens on the place of awareness in social action.

With such terms as 'consciousness' and 'awareness' we are on slippery ground. We are still squarely within social reality, of course; if we cannot meaningfully explain people's actions without reference to such notions, then these are of course features of the real world (cf. Taylor 1989: 69). They may still call for conceptual clarification, however, even if in the form of *ad hoc* definitions. I would suggest that one operative distinction between awareness and consciousness can be made in terms of relative explicitness: awareness refers to an explicit understanding, while consciousness is largely an implicit vector of comprehension. Explicitness is what makes awareness social, rather than individual, since explicating something, if only to oneself, of necessity involves particular cultural schemes and values. There is no explication outside a conversational community, whether this is actually addressed or not in the particular instance. While meaning is certainly always emergent rather than prior to events or phenomena, it must still in some sense be shared. 'Mad' acts cannot, by definition, be understood (Vendler 1984: 209). The semantic features of language are public features: 'What no one can, in the nature of the case, figure out from the totality of the relevant evidence cannot be part of meaning' (Davidson 1984: 235). Meaning is collectively established even when it is individually elicited.

The emergent nature of meaning implies that it cannot be deduced from a pre-established code, nor is it accountable for in terms of directly observable features. This feature is shared with agency, which is also not derivative from the observable, physical features of the world (Vendler 1984: 207). For both meaning and agency this further implies that they are not directly explicable in words, even if awareness still belongs to the explicate, shared world.

Another distinction between the notions of awareness and consciousness can be made in terms of temporality. As suggested by T. S. Eliot in the lines quoted on p. 99, one may claim that to be conscious is not to be in time. In other words, consciousness belongs to a timeless dimension of (partly) knowing – the world and the self. I would suggest that, by contrast, awareness is in time. It relates to the historically specific moment, whether in the rose garden or in the shanty town.

In order to clarify this distinction we may liken it to the relationship between recollection and memory, following Søren Kierkegaard. Recollections are outside time, eternally present in one's life; their imprint cannot be erased. Memories, on the other hand, are placed in time; they are remembered, narrated, reinterpreted, sometimes rejected and often forgotten. Recollections are unmediated experiences. Memory makes a critical difference to these: in being remembered, an experience 'becomes "a memory", with all that this entails, not merely of the consistent, the enduring, the reliable, but also of the fragile, the errant, the confabulated' (Casey 1987: xii).

Similarly, I suggest that we regard consciousness as indistinguishable from our permanent being between time past and time future. Awareness cuts us loose from this; just like narrative punctuates experience, awareness constantly arrests the flow of consciousness – to make room for action, as it were. Relating awareness to agency is to seek a theoretical understanding of motivation, constituting the link between culture and action. Motivation is the moving force between these (analytical) entities; as such it is timeless in itself, but by inducing movement it spills over into time and informs history.

DELIRIOUS EXPERIENCE: A CASE FROM BRAZIL

Nancy Scheper-Hughes has written an ethnography on the violence of everyday life in Brazil (1992).[3] It is called *Death Without Weeping*, thus immediately drawing our attention to an apparent silence in face of massive suffering. The people studied are shanty town dwellers in north-eastern Brazil, living in the shadow of sugar cane, and of a feudal structure. The poverty of these people is immense, and among other things it results in a child mortality rate that makes one shiver.

In this community there are two generative themes in everyday talk: thirst and hunger. People see their lives as doubly cursed by drought and famine, both of which are the virulent consequences of the encroaching sugar cane fields (Scheper-Hughes 1992: 69). Thirst and hunger seem to be master-motives in the local hierarchy of motivation. Most daily activities are related to the motive of relieving hunger. It is a conscious motive, outside time. It is ever present and serves as an experiential framework of almost any activity. Even the highly praised sexual vigour of the people is interpreted in relation to this scheme. Says one woman: 'Sure I'm hungry. Almost everyday my house is without food. My compensation is screwing. You asked me if I take pleasure in sex? Of course I do! How else am I going to know that I'm alive if I don't screw? At least in sex I can feel my flesh moving around and I know that hunger hasn't killed me yet' (Scheper-Hughes 1992: 165). The delirious experience of hunger resonates with the sensuous experience of sex.

A common symptom and, indeed, a folk-diagnosis is *delírio de fome*, madness from hunger. It is the end result of prolonged starvation, the climax of the lived experience of hunger. The experience of starvation and the ethno-medical discourse fit together. *Delírio de fome* is a state of being that is part of the shared social experience, and to which no numbers, no calculations apply. The facts of starvation in the shanty town are unmeasurable; yet their hardness is witnessed and felt by the people, for whom they become part of the collective consciousness.

Deaths from undernourishment and dehydration among infants and children can be counted, of course, at least to the extent that they are reported. (For fear of organ thefts, parents often hasten to bury their children with only a minimum of bureaucratic intervention.) But the degree to which the shanty town dwellers are conscious of the omnipresent perishment from starvation is not a feature of numbers; it is a feature of experience and as such it is a theme that infiltrates any conversation. Even young children are often sadly aware of their living in a limbo between life and death. Once seven-year-old Edilson's mother told the anthropologist that the boy would probably soon join his dead siblings; the anthropologist advised her not to talk like that in front of Edilson, but the boy shut her up in defence of his mother: 'Hush, Mãe, hush. I'm not afraid; I'm ready to go there' (Scheper-Hughes 1992: 142). The readiness stems from a flow of lived experience with death.

The never-ending story of starvation still frames local life; yet a new kind of narrative intervention has become increasingly pertinent during the twenty-odd years that Scheper-Hughes has been involved with the shanty town. It is a narrative intervention that punctuates experience in a new and different way as a result of the impact of western medical science. The medical discourse is causal and curative and deals with bodies and minds as if separate entities. The result is that with the gradual medication of Brazilian society the centre of gravity in the madness from hunger is being displaced. Starvation cannot be cured, but madness may be relieved; with medication 'mad' acts have required a new public meaning. *Delírio de fome* gradually collapses with the folk-concept of *nervos*, and ailments are sought to relieve this. Hunger is still part of experience, but the narrative focus is on the theme of madness.

> The madness, the *delírio de fome*, once understood as the terrifying end point in the experience of angry and collective starvation, is transformed into a personal and 'psychological' problem, one that requires medication. In this way hunger is isolated and denied, and an individualized discourse on sickness comes to replace a more radical and socialized discourse on hunger.
>
> (Scheper-Hughes 1992: 169).

A new illness narrative is constructed that breaks asunder social experience. Or, in the terms of the present argument, an awareness of individual 'nervousness' supplants the traditional and collective consciousness of hunger. This consciousness was outside time; it was an all-pervasive recollection, inescapably marking people's lives. Hunger was always a generative theme in the social talk, yet the stories never arrested the flow of that experience. They motivated no hope of relief. By contrast, the new medical awareness gives promise of curing, and people seize the opportunity to take fate in their own hands. The buying of useless medicines that leaves even less money for food than before has become an individual strategy to conquer the collective misery, however futile.

THE HABITUATED PERSON

To understand the specific impact of the western medical discourse upon the Brazilian awareness of their suffering it is necessary to study its derivation. The medical discourse derives from a particular world view, focusing on the individual and separating body and mind. With the insights gained – also from within medical science itself – scholars now seek to reunite analytically what was never ontologically separate. The body is in the mind; or, it is in itself mindful, as we have seen. Yet, the distinction between body and mind still seems all-pervasive in the medical wisdom on 'selves', and in natural language, because of its sustained experiential fit. It will be recalled how, with the development of the first-person standpoint in western philosophy, knowledge or awareness became that of an individual agent. Thinking became internalized, and will became located in the mind. This, therefore, became the locus of rational agency. As we saw in the previous chapter, this gave rise to an ontological fallacy. It also violates the ordinary experience of embodied understanding so vigorously demonstrated by the notion of *delírio de fome.*

To understand, for Descartes, involved disengagement from our own material selves, those uncontrolled sources of error and moral vice. To achieve pure knowledge one first had to achieve self-purification; self-mastery became a matter of controlling bodily sources of error, rationality became a matter of instrumental control. The medical discourse epitomizes this. The shanty town dwellers seek to fulfil the demand for instrumental control by subjecting themselves to medication; their 'will' has taken the shape of a pill.

It is a decidedly modern refraction that the mind can be seen as independent of society, and consciousness as disengaged from cultural values. In this view of the world, the 'self' operates on a notion of actual autonomy, and on an internal scale of good and bad. By consequence, agency is conceived of as a feature of the disengaged mind suggesting the right course of action. This is an essentially utilitarian view of agency that seems incompatible with anthropological insight. There is no practical utility defining the correct course of social action independent of symbolic schemes and cultural values (cf. Sahlins 1976).

For the people of the shanty town, the notion of a disengaged self makes no sense. There are no selves engaging in objective discourses on utility; there are persons experiencing unbounded material and social misery. They act, not on the basis of an individual and detached Reason, but on the basis of a process of collective and experiential reasoning. They, like other people, are agents all the same. Agency cannot be reduced to an individual disengaged mind; it is deeply enculturated and as such it has become sedimented in the body. 'Outside of the continuing conversation of community, which provides the language by which we draw our background distinctions, human agency . . . would be not just impossible, but inconceivable' (Taylor 1985a: 8). As we have seen, the conversation in the shanty town is firmly grounded in shared bodily experience of hunger and in the consciousness of madness deriving from it. This is where agency takes off.

The anthropological concern with agency must break away from the naturalism and behaviourism implied in the utilitarian perspective. To be a competent human agent is to exist in a space defined by distinctions of worth, not only by words and practical reason (Taylor 1985a: 3). Such distinctions are socially and historically constructed, and become part of the habitus of people. The disengaged self must yield to the habituated person. As observed also by Scheper-Hughes, the displacement of the experience of hunger is not sufficiently explained by 'false consciousness' or metaphorical delirium. It rather points to a new form of embodiment, or body praxis. 'Embodiment concerns the ways that people come to "inhabit" their bodies so that these become in every sense of the term "habituated" ' (Scheper-Hughes 1992: 184). The people of the shanty town have inhabited famished bodies for a long time; their minds embody this experience. The consciousness of hunger has become part of culture – as incorporated.

The incorporation of culture implies a process of sedimentation during which cultural models and values become part of the hidden, or recessive, faculties of the self. In this sense, culture becomes naturalized by way of experience. Our habits are formed in the process:

> The phenomenon of *habit formation* sorts out the ideas which survive repeated use and puts them in a more or less separate category. These trusted ideas then become available for immediate use without thoughtful inspection, while the more flexible parts of the mind can be saved for use in newer matters.
> (Bateson 1972: 501)

The lived space of the shanty town people has become naturalized as one of starvation. The naturalness of the lived space is related to 'the way our own body is the vehicle, the stage, and the object of experience at the same time' (Hanks 1990: 5). The body is motivated by this experience, and as such it is the locus of agency. It allows for little flexibility; the consciousness of hunger in the shanty town has sedimented and is available for immediate understanding.

When the experience is mediated by words, it is transsubstantiated as nervousness. The delirious experience has solidified while a language of psychological distress has free play on the surface. This language follows its own course, adorning reality with particular arabesques, and intervening into the social by arresting consciousness in a blind alley.

ICELANDIC SOCIAL EXPERIENCE

People are habituated by culture, sometimes to a destructive degree. In this section I shall substantiate this claim by referring to evidence from my own extensive analysis of Icelandic history over a millennium.[4] One of the important lessons from historical anthropology is that the modes of producing 'history' differ from one context to the next. There are obvious differences in environment, economy and social organization. But the making of history is also in part determined by local ways of thinking about history, or by kinds of awareness of change. The conceptual and the material form a simultaneity in the experience of the world. This implies that there is more to time and causation than chronology and sequence. It also implies that a single society may construe its history in a way that seems to blur the western historical genre.

These points have been extensively substantiated by the history of Iceland. This history displays a remarkable long-term vacillation between a highly structured, well-organized autonomous society in the Middle Ages and a disintegrated, dependent and crisis-prone condition in the centuries 1400–1800. Paradoxically, the shift between flourishment and abatement and the correlated distinctive periods in the social history of the islanders appears to cover an equally remarkable conceptual continuity. Through the centuries there is a conspicuous coherence and unity in the image of 'Icelandicness' which, and this is the point, has had a decisive influence upon the actual course of history in this North Atlantic community. Evidently, part of the framework was already given; we cannot and should not overlook the role played by such objective features as subarctic climatic conditions, geographical isolation and political submission. But even such features are subject to a particular local interpretation and a social reaction that transmutes objectivity into relativity. The irreversible is not the same as the inevitable, and the sequential is not coterminous with the causal.

In Iceland in the period 1400–1800, there seems to have been a remarkable discrepancy between social experience and local awareness. A key example is provided by the development of the modes of livelihood of which there were always two supplementary kinds in Iceland, farming and fishing. As formulated in 1786 by Skúli Magnússon, a renowned Enlightenment reformer, 'the Icelandic economy is founded on only two gifts of nature: cattle-breeding and fishing, holding out their hands towards one another, since the latter gets life and power from the former, which again is supported by the latter' (Magnússon, 1944b: 37). There is no doubt that these reports reflect an actual complementarity between farming and fishing at the level of subsistence: the two support each other. The Icelandic annals provide additional evidence that both economic activities were absolutely vital to the Icelanders. If failure occurred within one of the domains, hunger was likely; if both failed, the consequences were fatal to the population. Each individual household was founded on the dual economic pattern, which seems to form a structure of *la longue durée*. Although recognized as complementary at the level of consumption, farming and fishing as two distinct systems of production did not occupy equal positions in the minds of the Icelanders. They were never simply alternative ways of making a living, because they held asymmetrical positions in the (social) system of classification. This undoubtedly contributed to the misery of the Icelanders during the period of main concern here.

The domestic unit had been based on farming ever since the first settlements in the ninth century, when Norse immigrants took land on the virgin island. Land rights were specified in detail, and distinctions between infields, outfields and commons were strictly adhered to. There was a fine balance to maintain between arable and stock farming; grain was grown in the early period, but mostly hay, the latter being vital for the livestock. Natural grazing was adequate only from June to September; for the rest of the year, the animals had to be kept at the farmstead on stored hay. The balance between animal numbers and labour input in the fields was, therefore, delicate. Grain-growing was soon abandoned, however; it is mentioned for the last time by Oddur Einarsson in 1589, when it is reduced to a rare occurrence in a small corner of the island (Einarsson 1971: 126). With it disappeared the plough. This means that during the period 1400–1800, farming was principally a matter of hay-growing and animal husbandry at a simple level of technology.

At the time of the settlements in the late ninth and early tenth centuries Iceland was covered with a primary forest of low birch. Although only one-tenth of the Icelandic soil was actually arable, land appeared abundant and rich to the Norse settlers, who were allowed to claim as much land as they could encircle on horseback from sunrise to sunset – according to legend. As population pressure increased, land became more scarce. Large tracts were laid waste, partly due to soil erosion. The erosion was owed both to the grazing animals and the cutting down of the vulnerable primary forest. The wood was used in house construction and for fuel. Soon the houses had to be almost entirely constructed from stone and turf, and animal dung replaced the firewood. In turn, this made manure for the fields a scarcity, and the delicate balance between the numbers of people and animals on the one hand and the size of the manured fields on the other was under permanent threat. In turn, this made the Icelanders more dependent on another natural resource: the sea.

Fish had always been plentiful, and provided an additional resource for the farming households. During the fourteenth century fishing became a necessity; it also became favoured by new external markets. The Hanseatic League replaced Norway as Iceland's main trading partner, and a new market for dried fish opened in Europe. The net result was an economic upswing that again favoured a separate development of fishing. The old trading ports, which were nothing but temporary landing places, now turned into tiny villages, and a category of 'professional' fishermen emerged. While earlier there had been no specialist groups at all, the late fourteenth century witnessed an incipient division of labour between farmers and fishermen.

In 1404, *fiskimenn* (fishermen) appear for the first time in the documents. Significantly, it is also the last. The Black Death had ravaged Iceland from 1402 to 1404, reducing the population by some 40 per cent (Kristín Bjarnadóttir 1986). Farm labour had become scarce. This was the reason behind a law of compulsory farm service being passed in 1404, obliging *fiskimenn* and workers to settle at a farm and work for a landowner. If they refused, they were to be exiled (*Lovsamling for Island*, vol. I: 34–35). Thus, when fishermen are first mentioned as a distinct group, they are immediately subsumed under the farming structure. This is one of the first hints of the conceptual asymmetry between farming and fishing in the local definition of 'Icelandicness'.

Fishing continued, of course, out of sheer necessity, but fishermen vanished from the records. They became subsumed under the general category of *vinnuhjú* (servants) defined by their position within a *bú* (household) headed by a landowner or a well-to-do tenant on Church or Crown property. Generally, fishing and fishing rights were defined in terms of land rights, which were apparently always given conceptual priority.

This can be inferred also from the fact that farmhands engaging in seasonal fishing were to return for the hay harvest, quite irrespective of the catch at the shore. During the fifteenth century, when the Icelanders still had a clear recollection of the potential surplus created by fishing, the local court passed one law after another that was designed to make fishing less attractive to people. Thus, fishing with more than one hook on the line was banned, explicitly on account of the farmers who feared that fishing, if returns increased, would be too attractive to their servants (*Alþingisbækur Íslands*, vol. I: 432–434; vol. V: 122). Sinker lines were likewise banned, and a prohibition on using worms as bait was issued. It was not until 1699 that part of these restrictions were lifted, when sinker lines with several hooks were again allowed, but still only during the season: outside this period it was prohibited because of its allegedly damaging effects on farming (*Lovsamling for Island*, vol. I: 564–567). By then, the Icelanders seemed to have lost the motivation, however; a century later, in 1785, the afore-mentioned Skúli Magnússon noted how lines with just one hook almost reigned supreme, and he made a strong case for the reintroduction of sinker lines with up to 30 hooks, giving a detailed description of how to make them (Magnússon 1944a: 55–56). Generally, he complains about the conspicuous deterioration of Icelandic fishing (Magnússon 1944b).

The decline of fishing technology had a parallel in farming, where a collective loss of skills can also be documented. We have noted how the plough fell into disuse, and we can add how the fences separating the infields from the wilderness disintegrated. Fences were compulsory to protect the precious infields against stray animals; the laws of fencing had always reflected the farming interests, but the peasants nevertheless failed to keep up with the requirements. In the eighteenth century this became a major issue in the redressment of the Icelandic conditions of living, having reached an absolute rock-bottom by then. In 1776 an ordinance was issued by the Danish king demanding of the Icelanders that they reconstruct their fences, offering the threat of fines and also a promise of rewards (*Lovsamling for Island*, vol. IV: 278ff.). Judging from later decrees it was not an easy task to convince the Icelanders of the necessity of the restoration. It was even suggested that exemplary fences be built in all regions for the people to study (ibid., vol. IV: 426). The old technology was apparently forgotten, while the material (stone) had remained plentiful.

The collective loss of memory is witnessed also in the fact that hay-barns went out of use. In medieval Icelandic society, hay was stored in barns, as archaeological evidence shows. In the later period, hay was just stacked out-of-doors and subject to rather moist conditions. The result of these developments was a lesser yield from the scarce fields, and a greater vulnerability to just one bad winter. We know from the Icelandic annals that of the 400-year period under main concern here at least one-fourth must be classified as lean years by their entailing famine and death (Finnsson 1970).

In short, one of the salient features of Icelandic society in the period 1400–1800 was a failure to keep up with the implicit requirements of social reproduction. The failure to exploit the fishing potential, allegedly to protect farming, entailed increasing material poverty. This was correlated with a remarkable degree of collective amnesia as far as local technological skills were concerned. The result was that the Icelanders became increasingly prone to forces beyond their control. As time wore on, the experience of the Icelanders was one of increasing impotence in all domains of the social; survival had replaced influence as the most important item on the agenda. The idea of human causation in history, as embedded in old notions of fate, faded and gave way to ideas of external and largely uncontrollable causes of all changes. The economy deteriorated, the merchants exploited and the distant Danish king subdued the people. 'The wild' approached from all corners, as the fencing of Icelandic society disintegrated.

To understand how this could happen, since it is by no means an immediate consequence of material factors, we must look into the Icelandic way of thinking about history.

UCHRONIC VISIONS: REALITY IN PAST TENSE

If the production of history is related to the thinking about history
there is all the more reason to explore the local notions of change
and tradition in Iceland.

First of all we note that no conceptual distinction between
history and story was made. The notion of *saga* referred to anything that was 'said' of history; as such, it contained its own claim
to truth (Hastrup 1986b). In this particular case a one-to-one
relationship between the words and the world was claimed. When
the main corpus of Icelandic sagas was written in the twelfth and
thirteenth centuries, their objective was to tell Icelandic history.
Although certainly literary products, they were perceived as history proper. This was true also for the reconstruction of the ninth-
and tenth- century events and characters in the *Íslendingasögur*,
'stories of the Icelanders'. In these sagas, which have rightfully
remained famous, the pre-Christian past of Icelandic society is
recast in the shape of a *Freiheits-Mythos* (Weber 1981). The
original 'free state' of Iceland is celebrated, and the entire literary
activity of the thirteenth century may in fact be seen as an attempt
to raise local consciousness about the Icelandic achievements in
terra nova (Schier 1975). Freedom and the taking of new land
are tokens of original Icelandicness.

One of the consequences of the particular Icelandic conflation
of story and history on the one hand and of the peculiar atomistic
social structure on the other is a remarkable conflation also of
individual and collective history. As observed by one scholar:
'There is no sense of those impersonal forces, those nameless
multitudes, that make history a different thing from biography in
other lands. All history in Iceland shaped itself as biography or
as drama, and there was no large crowd at the back of the stage'
(Ker 1923: 315).

If the individual Icelander was unable to control his own fate
during the 'dark' centuries, he was equally unable to influence the
larger history of Icelandic society. The actual history originated in
a space beyond control, while at the same time the Icelandic
dream was recreated in an Icelandic Uchronia.

Uchronia is nowhere in time. If Utopia is a parallel universe,
Uchronia is a separate history. It is a history out of time, so to
speak. In Iceland, Uchronic visions were part of the collective

representations of the world, and as such they deeply influenced the response of society to its own history.

With modernity, a vision of history as linear growth emerged in Europe; this was to remain the distinctive feature of the western historical genre, and the (largely illusory) basis for the comparison between 'Europe and the peoples without history' (Wolf 1982). In contrast to the old view of a qualitatively defined time-space, the new chronology and linearity implied that any stage in history was temporary. These features also indirectly sustained the idea that history could not go absolutely wrong because it had its own directional logic. Iceland resisted modernity until recently, and the development of Icelandic society teaches us that the vision of history as linear growth was alien to the Icelanders. Even in modern Europe this vision remained elitist for a long time, and may actually still alienate the rank and file from history in more ways than one.

The conceptual discrepancy between two views of history, if not actually between two histories, makes room for Uchronic imagination on the part of the people. Where this is found, and certainly where it achieves the proportions of the Icelandic case, it reveals a feeling of incapacity to influence actual history. It also points, however, to a failure on the part of the dominant historical discourse to incorporate the experience of ordinary people. The gap between the two histories leaves people in a void.

In Iceland, this observation is acutely relevant. With no experience of a progressive history, the Icelanders knew that history could go wrong; the degree of misery that it entailed locally had no logic. In the fight between fire and ice, or between the hot and the cold conditions of history – to invoke Lévi-Strauss – the Icelanders retreated to an imaginary time when history was 'right'. This gave rise to Uchronic visions that were at odds with present social experiences. Uchronia had its own reality, of course, but from our point of view this reality was hypothetical.

We cannot ask the Icelanders of bygone centuries about their imaginations, but we can infer them from a whole range of historical evidence. As a vision of another time, Uchronia connects otherwise disconnected elements and adds a level of comprehension to our historical narrative. The history out of time entertained by the Icelanders was informed by their view of the past. The past was over, yet in narrative form it was continuously reproduced and invoked by the Icelanders, in search of meaning in the void between two histories.

The reproduction of the old images of Icelandicness consisted in a strong literary tradition dating back to the Middle Ages being continually renewed. Young people learned to read from the old lawbook, and the saga literature was consumed during the institution known as *sagnaskemmtan* – saga entertainment – which was a reading aloud of the old stories as a general evening pastime on the farms (Pálsson 1962; Gíslason 1977). As we have seen, the individual farmsteads represented society in miniature; there was no distinction between elite and popular culture as elsewhere in Europe (Burke 1978), no urban populations set apart from peasant culture. Although mass literacy was not achieved until some time around 1800 (which is still relatively early by comparative European standards), there is strong evidence that at most farms at least one person was actually able to read (Guttormsson 1983). What is more, the stories of sagas also formed the core of the *rímur*, popular verses, that were orally transmitted for centuries. The old images were thus continually reproduced by a recasting of the old myths of creation and of the past virtues of men. Through this recasting, the Icelanders were perpetually confronted with an ideal order nowhere in time.

One could even argue, that while other peoples invented traditions to match new historical situations (Hobsbawn and Ranger 1983), the Icelanders reproduced the images of the past to invent themselves.

The Uchronic imagination was concurrently sustained by this invocation of the past. Because the Icelanders had no real 'others' to identify 'themselves' against, the mirror-image of themselves in the past tense had major social repercussions. Living in the imaginary world of Uchronia, the Icelanders had no symbolic exchange with others, and no way of obtaining a position from where they could see themselves and their situation in realistic terms. Due to their virtual isolation in the North Atlantic, the Icelanders lacked a contemporary comparative reality against which they could measure their own culture (cf. Boon 1982). Paradoxically, this meant that the present escaped them; they felt this and stuck even more firmly to Uchronia, which at least preserved a sense of injustice in the existing world.

The Icelanders lived between two histories, or between an empirical and experienced history of decline and decay on the one hand and an imagined Uchronia implying permanence and antiquity on the other. Rather than defining a new reality and shaping it in language, the Icelanders defined the present in terms of a past of which only the language remained real. Experience itself was discarded as anomalous because it no longer fitted the old language. Whatever creative skills the people possessed were directed towards a recollection and a continuation of 'proper' history – as story – at the expense of a comprehension of present realities.

Uchronia represented a structured world nowhere in time that strongly contrasted with the experiential space. Uchronia was a dream about a primodial society, and about a timeless history when man was fully human.

CULTURAL ECCENTRICITY

Culture is the implicational space that gives meaning to social experience. By way of closing the argument on historical awareness, I shall here briefly discuss Icelandic culture in the period 1400–1800, since this is what gives consistency to the disparate realities of society and Uchronia.

The disintegrating fences around the infields provide an apt metaphor of the actual development in this period. Nature encroached relentlessly, diminishing the socially controlled space. The cosmological centre had always been locally represented in the *bú*, the household, which was society writ small and concretized in the landscape. The controlled central space was inhabited by free, sedentary farmers. On the periphery the uncontrolled forces reigned. In the classical period, a concentric cosmological dualism firmly distinguished between an 'inside' and an 'outside' world. Inside, humans were in control; outside the wild forces reigned. As time wore on, more and more humans were alienated from the centre and merged with the wild – because of poverty, vagrancy or fishing. An increasing proportion of reality was beyond control.

'History' itself became split into two: an externally induced and uncontrolled succession of movements, and an internally emphasized repetition of traditional values. The repetition owed its force to the reproduction of past images in a discourse that mirrored the negativities inherent in the contemporary Icelandic world. With no symbolic exchange with real others the Icelanders could engage in no relationship of identification other than with themselves in the past tense. In a manner of speaking, they became 'others' themselves. As such, they were alienated from the larger history – and ultimately from their own present.

This alienation was correlated with a particular pattern of event-registration. As we know, events are happenings that are registered as significant according to a particular cultural scheme, which is constantly subjected to risk by social action. But in Iceland the scheme persisted in a remarkable degree of cultural self-consciousness. The Uchronic vision was intimately linked to the reproduction of the past – in voice and in action. The literary image of the free farmer was proudly read out to everyone, and the image was confirmed in action by the Althing's decisions to concentrate energy in the reproduction of the farming households, at the expense of industrious fishing among other things. Due to the reproduction of an outdated cultural scheme, actions became anachronistic, and contemporary happenings failed to register as events. In contrast to the event-richness of the past – as collectively memorized in history as conventionalized in the local genre – the present appeared event-poor.

Some social spaces or some periods always seem to generate more social events than others. As we know, this is not primarily a mensurational feature, but a feature of registration: for events to be registered as such, they have to be significant from the point of view of the definer. The Icelandic world of our period did not single out many happenings as significant social events. The social space was event-poor; movement, change and innovation were relegated to a non-social space where events did not register. In the period 1400–1800 Iceland was in a state of event-poverty. By comparison to the event-richness of the previous period, contemporary reality was marked by absences. While the Icelanders certainly *had* a history during the event-poor centuries, they only indirectly *produced* it. Poverty was both material and symbolic; the two levels merged in the experience of the people.

Event-richness is a feature of space, and it is identified in the synchronic dimension. In the diachronic dimension, relative event-richness is transformed into relative historical density (Ardener 1989c). In the representation of history, historical density is a measure of the relative memorability of particular events. For events to be memorized and to become part of 'history' they must have been experienced as culturally significant.

This apparently self-evident point covers a fundamental truth: the structuring of history, and the selective memory, are not solely imposed retrospectively. Contemporary event-registration always serves as the baseline for the trace of experience left in history.

For Iceland this implies that the event-rich period of the early and high Middle Ages was matched by a historical density in this period. This contrasts with the unmarked reality of the later period. The continuous attention paid to past events made the present seem insignificant. The comparative historical density of the past also made the present look like not history at all. The reproduction of culture impeded the production of history. Inadvertently, the Icelanders themselves contributed to the destructive course taken by the development. 'History' had become 'myth' – and therefore beyond influence. What we are witnessing here, in fact, may be read as yet another instance of the inherent antipathy between history and systems of classification (Lévi-Strauss 1966: 232).

If culture, generally, encompasses the existentially unique in the conceptually familiar (Sahlins 1985: 146), this had a particular truth in Iceland. The strength of the conceptual scheme actually entailed a failure to register the uniqueness of present existential conditions. In other words, if 'culture' is an organization of current situations in terms of the past (ibid.: 155), in Iceland the 'current situation' hardly registered, because the 'terms of the past' were so vigorous. Having lost control of their own social reproduction, the people were left without a proper historical appreciation of the main cultural categories. The unreflexive mastery of the traditional cultural system made the Icelandic 'habitus' the basis for an intentionless invention of regulated improvisation that was quite out of time (cf. Bourdieu 1977: 79; Sahlins 1985: 51).

The strength of the traditional language entrapped the Icelanders in a state of refracted vision. Their world view was focused on another time, on another history. Their culture became increasingly eccentric due to their Uchronic vision. The cultural eccentricity was instrumental in the permanent crisis of Icelandic society. The particular way of thinking about history influenced its actual course; causation in history conflates the material and the conceptual.

THE DESIRABLE ORDER

Motivation is not found in the disengaged mind or in utilitarianism, as we have seen. The hunger-stricken shanty town dwellers and the misery-prone Icelanders teach us that instrumental reasoning cannot explain the actions taken. In both cases there was a high degree of consciousness of the state of affairs, yet for the shanty town people there was nothing to be said that could alter it, and in the case of the Icelanders, they were caught in a web of illusions about themselves that was actually counterproductive to social reproduction. The cultural models motivated action but somehow obstructed an awareness of the deteriorating social conditions.

We should distinguish between motives and intentions, as we have noted before; the former are largely implicit frameworks for action, the latter explicit rationalizations of it. Intentions and motives relate to what Taylor has called first- and second-order desires (Taylor 1985a: 15). What makes us fully human is our power to evaluate our first-order desires, and thus to act on the basis of relative worth. This introduces a distinction between weak and strong evaluation. With weak evaluations we are concerned with outcomes, while strong evaluations define the quality of our motivation.

There are no selves beyond a particular social context. Phrased differently, identity is intimately linked to orientation in a moral space (Taylor 1989: 28ff.). This implies that 'social actors not only acquire a sense of what is natural, they also acquire strongly motivating senses of what is desirable. They not only know, they also care' (Strauss and Quinn 1993: 3). In practical life, knowledge, so often isolated as cognition in theory, is not independent of emotion and evaluation. In Iceland, people knew themselves as farmers, even while fishing, because of the uneven values attached to these categories.

Evaluation, or the sense of relative worth, infiltrates social action. Facts and values are two sides of the same coin (Putnam 1990: 135ff.). 'Facts' cannot be identified without an implicit scale of evaluation. Taking this a step further, we realize that experience and description are bound together in a constitutive relation that admits causal influences in both directions: 'it can sometimes allow us to alter experience by coming to fresh insight; but more fundamentally it circumscribes insight through the deeply embedded shape of experience for us' (Taylor 1985a:37). The lived experience of the famished circumscribes their insight in their powerlessness. The dislocated medical description of their delirium does not allow for an alteration of experience.

> Because of this constitutive relation, our descriptions of our motivations, and our attempts to formulate what we hold important, are not simple descriptions in that their objects are not fully independent. And yet they are not simply arbitrary either, such that anything goes. There are more or less adequate, more or less truthful, more self-clairvoyant or self-deluding interpretations. Because of this double fact, because an articulation can be *wrong*, and yet it shapes what it is wrong about, we sometimes see erroneous articulations as involving a distortion of the reality concerned. We do not just speak of error but frequently also of illusion or delusion.
>
> (Taylor 1985a: 37–38)

Illusion or delusion may be the result of failure to revise the givens of culture: when too much is taken for granted, flexibility is at risk. Significance becomes distorted as meanings fossilize. This is one major reason for the disintegration of Icelandic society in the period 1400–1800.

It may also be offered as a reason for silence in the face of death in the shanty town. There is no meaningful way to articulate the continuous experience of starvation. The desire to eat is a first-order desire pervading the daily concern with the practical outcome of action. The second-order desire of ranking is completely conflated within this. If it is generally true that 'the strong evaluator has articulacy and depth which the simpler weigher lacks' (Taylor 1985a: 26), the absence of articulation points not to a lack of consciousness of the values or desires implied but to a lack of means to act upon them; in the face of enduring misery and practical impotence, an awareness of particular desires cannot be allowed to arrest the consciousness of the general order of the desirable.

All people are aware of some environment, and offer articulations of it. In so doing, however, they lay out different features of the world and of human action in some perspicuous order. Awareness, like memory, makes room for error or illusion; the experience of hunger may be confabulated as a psychological problem, and the desire to overcome it may be relieved by way of medication. By contrast, consciousness cannot be manipulated: like recollection it is inerasable and cannot be wrong. The desirable order of things is collectively sensed, even when silence prevails and part of the embodied knowledge is overheard. It is one of the tasks of anthropology to reinstall the areas of silence as an integral part of human agency.

THE ETHICS OF INARTICULACY

It remains to be discussed why it is that anthropology can make a claim to a kind of higher-order understanding than can local knowledge. One way of evaluating different schemes for understanding is by their relative position to achieve more or less perspicuous orders of comprehension. A claim of this kind can, according to Charles Taylor, be made by theoretical cultures against atheoretical ones (Taylor 1985b: 150). The former invariably catch the attention of the latter when they meet. The success of western scientific culture is a case in point, but certainly not the only one. If we replace 'cultures' with 'schemes' of a more general kind, we have a way of assessing the force of the anthropological argument in relation to local knowledge.

This is not a correlate of objective or absolute understanding versus subjective or relative knowledge. I agree with Bourdieu when he claims that this distinction is the most ruinous to social science (Bourdieu 1990: 25). Whether cast as objectivism or subjectivism, both are theoretical modes of knowledge, 'equally opposed to the practical mode of knowledge which is the basis of ordinary experience of the social world' (ibid.).[5]

A prerequisite for theorizing in this sense is a degree of self-reflection which amounts to St Augustine's 'radical reflexivity' mentioned earlier, or perhaps to Paulo Freire's 'critical consciousness'. Theoretical knowledge implies an understanding of its own condition, as well as its possible impact upon practical knowledge. This is how anthropology may be said to have a dual legitimacy, as a field of knowledge and as a field of action. Awareness and force are intimately linked in anthropology as well as in culture; knowledge by itself has no power, while an argument may. The *raison d'être* of anthropology lies precisely in its being theoretically aware of the context of local awareness, and its intricate relationship to social agency. This includes a profound theoretical awareness of the fact that the self is not fixed but an ever-emergent being, whose identity is at stake in moments of choice and deliberation. At times this staking of the self may be too threatening and the deliberations repressed, as in the shanty town, or subjected to eccentric notions of reality, as in Iceland – with fatal consequences for individuals. In both cases, what is articulated is neither a utilitarian self, governed by practical reason and instrumental rationality, nor an irrational mind, governed by bodily cravings and weak will. What is expressed is a collective lack of awareness of the degree to which cultural models are obsolete and block out the flexibility necessary to radically alter the miserable situation. This is not to blame the victim, but to demand of anthropology that it takes its share of the global responsibility.

If able to deal convincingly with this complex situation, anthropology may become a site of resistance. Giving voice to silent memories is neither to force people to speak, nor is it a matter of replacing 'false' consciousnesses with correct ones. It is to respect local silence and provide a theoretical context, including the historical situatedness, of whatever awareness people may have of their own situation. This may, then, be offered for the inspection of the people involved.

The anthropological interpretation may arrest the collective consciousness and place it squarely in time; a new awareness may result. People are never just victims of social forms, because social forms owe their shape partly to the fact that they are inhabited by people thinking about social forms (Hollis 1985: 232). And, as said before, thinking implies caring. Moral deliberation is an integral part of self-understanding and self-formation (Johnson 1993: 148).

Transculturally, there is equity as far as awareness and rationality are concerned; or, in other words, people have equal reasons for assuming the correctness of their view of the world. This is no plea for a mindless relativism. There are claims to relative truth to be made; transcultural insight precisely provides a basis for judgement, which blind ethnocentricity *and* relativism both negate. This is one, potentially controversial, reason for pursuing anthropology as a theoretical mode of global awareness.

Likewise, it is the basis for refusing to accept moral relativism as the net result of the anthropological involvement with people. The ethics of inarticulacy implies that anthropology should seek to re-articulate the strong evaluations that have been silenced by

unfortunate social circumstances or hegemonic historical positions, but which are, nevertheless, integral parts of local consciousness and motivation. Re-articulation in this sense means giving
'momentum' to consciousness by reinstating it in time:

'Only through time time is conquered'

Chapter 7

The symbolic violence
On the loss of self

Silence is packed with meaning and, in many ways, to respect it seems at odds with the anthropological task of reaching people's self-understanding as a first step towards the theoretical comprehension of its context and premises. In the domain of human misery, which was used to illustrate the limits of articulacy in the previous chapter, the ethnographer's probing and insistence is particularly painful. The starving may rightfully turn his back to the inquisitor; she, in turn, must realize that solidarity sometimes means silence on her part as well.

It is part of the performative paradox of anthropology, however, to pursue a knowledge project that in an important sense transcends the lives of individuals. In any fieldwork this means keeping up a certain pressure on the 'informants' to have them say what they think. The imposed articulacy may for ever alter their own awareness of the social space of which they are part. In short, we should not too hastily demand articulation; people have their own reasons for evading the words that may explicate their consciousness and thus intervene in their lives. To illustrate this, I shall relate a personal account, by way of which I want to rehearse the play between the ethnographer and the informant from the point of view of the latter.[1]

TALABOT

In September 1988, the Danish theatre group, Odin Teatret, showed *Talabot* for the first time.[2] *Talabot* is a play about the last 40 years of world history told through the biography of a woman anthropologist born in 1948. She is Danish, with an international professional training, fieldwork experience in India and, especially, Iceland, and a relatively successful career. The dramas in her life are reflections of the historical dramas around her. All the wars, killings, and suppressions following World War II form the sonorous background of her generation's history, and of the performance. Living with women's liberation and the global oppression of the weak, her choice to become an anthropologist reflects a fundamental choice between violence and science in a world in crisis.

The scenes draw on her biography down to such minute details as exchanges of words between her and her father, recollections of fears and hopes in her childhood and youth, and of the acute pain during and after fieldwork, when she no longer knew who she was. Woven into the fabric of world history, the play features the anthropologist as a child, as a youth and as an adult woman, the mother of four children pursuing a professional life. The performance shows how her private life informs her public image, or how her person and her profession cannot really be separated. From her childhood dream of becoming a Polar explorer to the painful return from fieldwork in Iceland and the ensuing break-up of her marriage, the personal and the professional dimensions of her life are intimately linked. They are, furthermore, connected to world history in many subtle ways.

My aim here is not to review the play or to assess the significance of this particular performance in relation to the intellectual history of the West over the past 40 years, however much I would like to. My point of departure is the fact that I am the woman anthropologist portrayed in *Talabot*.

This chapter is a personal account of the process implied in my theatrical experience from my first encounter with Odin Teatret's director, Eugenio Barba, through the various meetings and writings, and on to the rehearsals and the final performance. My narrative is personal and informed by my peculiar presence in the play, but my aim lies beyond a simple narration of the process of transformation from autobiography to performance. I intend to analyse the general implications of the anthropologist becoming an object of study and representation. Through the personal account of how my autobiography was turned into a life history that was the contextualized by somebody else, we may learn something more general about being anthropologists in this world.

The account is based on notes I made in the process, on retrospection, and on a certain element of introspective investigation into my own reactions to the play in its various stages. There is, therefore, no way of concealing the author's 'I' in this case. Furthermore, my experiences will be related in story form, which has normally been displaced in scientific analysis where the flow of lived experience has had no place (Rose 1982: 272–273). In so far as one's lived experience enables or inhibits particular kinds of insight, however, the analysis of experience is a legitimate framework for our observations and reflections towards a more general scope of understanding. In the present case, the scope can be identified as the implication of being an 'informant' in somebody else's story, which is a key issue in anthropology in general.

In the following pages, I shall tell the story of my changing position in relation to the theatre and the performance. In the first part of the chapter I shall describe the process from *being* myself, through *writing* myself, to *seeing* myself on stage. In the second part, I add an analytical dimension and discuss the nature of myth and history, of representation, and of authority on the basis of my experience. In both parts, the personal and the anthropological dimensions of the drama are deeply integrated in spite of the shifting emphasis.

I: THE PROCESS

My first acquaintance with Odin Teatret was in 1986, when I attended a conference on 'The Female Role' held by the International School of Theatre Anthropology (ISTA) in Denmark. The organizer was Eugenio Barba. As a novice in the field of both theatre and theatre anthropology, I was fascinated by the implicit search for universals in the variegated performance traditions of Asia and Europe. One concept that appealed to me in particular was the notion of the actor's 'presence' on stage, being much more than a matter of physical presence. It referred to the way in which the actor administered his energy and impressed himself upon the audience. In a subtle way, the discussion of this concept at ISTA contributed to my own perception of the anthropologist's presence in the field, a topic that had been discussed for some years. At the time, I had not been able to pursue the parallels, but it was with a sense of shared interests that I accepted an invitation from Barba the following summer, in 1987, to come and see him at the theatre.

First stage: being myself

Barba had read some of my articles on, or deriving from, field-work (notably Hastrup 1987a, 1987b, 1987c), and he wanted to discuss them with me. I imagined that our meeting would entail purely academic discussion of anthropology as a field of common interest. Very soon I was made to understand that this was only part of it, however. My encounter with Barba on this occasion was to have quite unanticipated consequences. A creative process leading to a performance had started, and with it another process leading to a temporary destruction of my 'self' had also begun.

Processes are difficult to describe, and ordinarily we are satis-fied with the description of sequences that are but time-slices cut out of a world of simultaneities and continuities. Narrations, after all, are constructions playing on time. Sequences, however, belong to a different logical type from the process that integrates them into a whole of different order. A process such as the one I am dealing with here cannot, therefore, be reduced to its sequences, although the narrative requirements force us to start from this reduction.

It is only in language that we can determine when a process starts. To claim that the process to *Talabot* started with my encounter with Barba in June 1987 is not the whole truth. Before that, a series of ethnographic experiences and anthropological reflections had given my academic articles the degree of life that made the theatre director stumble. On his part, the stumbling was related to a series of antecedent thoughts of which I knew nothing.

Our meeting was long, and when the first round of questions and answers were over, Barba revealed his wish to make a per-formance on the basis of my history. I was taken aback. He wanted to stage a play about an anthropologist who encountered 'the unreal' during fieldwork, and he wanted to understand what kind of person it was that became an anthropologist in the first place. And, as he said, 'When we have such a person at hand who is, furthermore, a woman, it is natural to choose her as a central character.'

It was not until much later that I understood what it meant to be a 'central character'. I knew what it was to be a woman anthropologist, and I was surprised that my personal history was thought to be interesting enough for a group of actors to work with for a year to come. To me there was nothing exceptional in being either a woman or an anthropologist, even if the combination perhaps made it statistically improbable that I had, in fact, become a professor. Later, Barba revealed that, to him, the category 'anthropologist' had always been male, quite irrespective of the fact that he knew of many women anthropologists. After my experience with *Talabot*, and having now also edited a book on the nature of 'participation' in anthropological fieldwork (Hastrup and Ramløv 1988), I tend to believe that there is perhaps more to the sex of the anthropologist than the (by now) obvious fact that knowledge is always 'en-gendered' (cf. Caplan 1988). I cannot explore this theme in detail here, only note that because of the cultural construction of gender in western society, women are more 'allowed' to use intuition in their search for knowledge. Like men, they have to 'rationalize' to produce science, but they are not socialized exclusively towards rationality. Unlike most other sciences, anthropology seems to explicitly dissolve the opposition between intuition and rationality. Certainly, in fieldwork both are required, thus mirroring the paradox inherent in the cultural definition of the female gender, including the double socialization to object and subject.

Quite apart from that, I believe that what had caught Barba's imagination in particular was my shift between separate realities, and my negotiations with different I's in the field. Briefly, as a fieldworker I had shared the reality and the time of the Icelanders, and I had met the 'hidden people' of the Icelandic landscape. These 'hidden people' were to play a prominent, if to some extent implicit, part in *Talabot*. Barba was intrigued by their presence in my texts, not as belief but as reality, and was acutely aware of the academic risk I took in revealing my experience – as experience.

In my writings I had attempted to resolve the anthropological dilemma of participation and observation in a particular way. We have reached the point in anthropology where we can see that the problem of participant observation, which implies two antithetical strategies, perhaps is not so much a problem of research method as it is a literary dilemma of 'participant description' (Geertz

1988: 83). The central problem is to represent the complexity of the research process in the anthropological text. More often than not, the experience of a shared reality in the exotic world is concealed in the objectified world of the monograph. Coevalness, or the sharing of time in the field, is replaced by allochronism, or temporal distancing in the text (Fabian 1983). My textual resolution implied an admission of the experience of the unreal, and it entailed a recognition of the anthropologist becoming her own informant, which we have discussed before. The question arises, what will become of 'science' if this is accepted?

There was one further reason for Barba's interest. On the surface of it, Iceland is a very modern society as well as one of the Nordic countries. Thus, to Barba, anthropological fieldwork in Iceland almost appeared a contradiction in terms. Nevertheless, in accordance with the anthropological goal in general, my writings on Iceland had made an explicitly known culture appear implicitly exotic. There is no culture that is beyond anthropological interest, as my venture into the Icelandic world had confirmed.

The first sequence of the progress toward *Talabot*, as here described, took the shape of an exchange of words between Barba and me. At another level, the process touched deeper than this. During our meeting, the words took us beyond academic matters, which of themselves were no topic for a stage performance. After all, it is not the purpose of the theatre to solve scientific dilemmas. As the exchange of words continued, and the implicit question of why I had chosen anthropology as my existential basis became more and more explicit, I was forced to leave my professional 'I' behind and to speak from the position of a much more vulnerable, personal 'I'. Questions were asked about my private life, my fears and my hopes, and answers beyond my normal boundaries for conversation between professional strangers were produced. The nature of the enquiry already changed me.

As the day passed, I became increasingly exhausted. Clearly, Barba's energy exceeded mine; I did not know the theatrical context and I hardly knew the man who made me talk. He had an immense 'presence', which somehow paradoxically made me fade away. As I spoke and related more details from my life and work, I became increasingly uncertain as to who I was. Why was I so interesting anyway? I was not, of course, but 'I' was becoming an object of study, implicitly interesting and exotic. Although I did not realize it then, Barba had started doing fieldwork on me, and I had assumed the wearisome role of informant.

Later, I was reminded about Leiris, who – as early as 1934 – had written an extensive account of the fatiguing experience of ethnographic field practices, which sometimes result in the ethnographer's extreme irritation and the informant's silence. When probing into a particular healing ritual conducted by an old woman, Leiris noted, 'La vieille femme ne dit à peu près rien. Elle sourit malicieusement, déjoue toutes les questions' (Leiris 1988: 95). He went away, irritated, and only later did he understand that the woman's silence was owed to the implicit power relationship between them.

Barba's interest in my story had put me in the old woman's position. Instead of smiling maliciously and keeping silent, I 'chose' to talk. Such was Barba's power that the unspoken was now to be said, and the hidden was to become visible. I was to change radically in the process.

Being myself was not easy under these circumstances. Under the inquisitor's gaze, I lost part of my sense of 'self', and became akin to the witches burned at the stake in previous centuries for their admission that they did not know who they were. Why not a witch, then, or an anthropologist taking part in an unreal communion?

Eugenio Barba provided a dramatic pretext for inventing myself.

Second stage: writing myself

The feeling of a gradually changing concept of self was to increase at the next stage of the process, when I had to write my autobiography. Before that, I had a meeting with the actors, who were to be active in the transformation of my story into a performance. Odin Teatret is a group theatre in the sense that performances are always made collectively and built up from scratch rather than from a preconceived scenario. The director guides the process, but the actors actively contribute to the play.

My meeting with the entire group was an important turning point for my conception of my own part in the process, and for the transition from being myself to writing myself. I felt naked when I entered the room and sat down in the circle of heteroglot actors. Normally, I could hide behind a paper or a prepared speech, but on this occasion I just had to be myself and give the group a part in my life. There was no hiding place, and also no smoke-screen to cover their scepticism about the project and – for some of them, at least – about me.

They were prepared in the sense that they had read my articles and doubtlessly perceived a measure of the drama inherent in doing fieldwork. It was difficult, however, for them to see the 'real' drama in the life history of this inconspicuous and slightly worn woman. One of the difficulties, as far as I was concerned, was that only a few of the actors were actually very 'verbal', at least in comparison with Eugenio's highly intellectual style of speech. Evidently, the expertise of the actors was action rather than argument.

I told them more about fieldwork and about being a professional stranger, and for the first time it occurred to me that the exchange between us had a likeness to fieldwork. The culture studied was embodied in a single individual, and the fieldworker was a plural person, but the situation was somehow familiar. Initially, both parts seemed 'out of context', but gradually we established a common space and a shared language where we could start conducting a meaningful dialoguing and not just talking. The group listened carefully and took notes on the exoticism of the woman anthropologist.

Elsewhere I have discussed how the anthropologist in the field becomes a third-person character in the discourse of her informants. They can converse with her only by insisting on her being a well-defined 'she' in their world. In this way, subject and object constantly change place, as was also my experience on this particular occasion. While speaking of my subjective experience, I became an object of their professional interest. Fieldwork is only one remove from cannibalism, and in my position as object, I sometimes felt consumed – as have innumerable informants before me. The story of Minik (which is touched on in *Talabot*), the Eskimo child who discovered that the skeleton exhibited in the Museum of Natural History in New York was his father's, is a particularly unflattering instance of anthropological cannibalism.

Cannibalism was *my* category of thought, however. Their questions were concrete. 'What did you sing as a child?' 'How did you call for the cows in Iceland?' 'Which shoes do you normally wear?' These were simple questions that were, nevertheless, difficult to answer because in general we are not used to verbalizing the obvious. I was somewhat confused until Eugenio finally told me, in a more precise manner than he had previously, that they were going to use even the details of my biography in the performance about the woman anthropologist. Otherwise they knew very little about the performance so far.

To impose a certain systematic method onto the enquiry, Eugenio asked me to tell the group about the 21 most important events in my life. Imagine that question on an ordinary weekday in Holstebro, Denmark. As I got started, time disappeared. The events poured out in no obvious pattern, and I saw how my life had indeed been a process and not only a series of sequences. In the recollection of childhood episodes, I saw their projections in other times, other situations. The dream of becoming a Polar explorer, which was nurtured by my reading of Knud Rasmussen and others, had come true in Iceland, I realized, although my entrapment in violent fishing life at the world's end in winter Iceland, at the time, had seemed far away from the glorious expeditions of earlier eras.

The explorer now found herself among a group of strangers taking notes on her story. The recollection was easier than I had anticipated, and doubtlessly the episodes recorded did reflect a real significance. In a holographic manner, each of the events reflected my whole life. I was fascinated with this discovery and wanted to share my delight with the group. After all, they were the ones who had asked about my self. Although I had already perceived of the situation in terms of an inverse fieldwork, I had not realized that 'the questioner, the question and the questioned are one', as Sartre had once said (quoted in Rabinow 1982: 185). They were not really interested in me; they had their own world to discover, not mine. In a strange way, they had taken on the collective plight of anthropology presented as social theatre: 'men in dark times representing to themselves images of their own work' (Rabinow 1982: 177). My subject had become an object of their theatre, to be represented as an image of their own work. I did not see it in these terms at the time, but I remember my feeling of waste in the absence of any reactions on their part to me and my rediscovered story. Their faces showed only professional interest in 'me'. Masked I went forward.

Eugenio asked me to write a series of autobiographical texts covering my entire life, from childhood to adulthood, and including private and professional events. The masking had to uncover my true story.

Writing oneself is not so different from the writing of cultures. It is an essentially creative process in which discovery merges with definition. My recollections made me discover a person who was defined as such at the same stroke. The stories often seemed to write themselves through me, and they were certainly personal. Yet upon reflection I cannot claim absolute authenticity. Intervening in the world of play and performance, I was caught between two worlds; my life history was already implicated by Odin's search for a main character. To some degree, at least, this made my story 'un-authentic'. It was still true, of course.

To clarify this I shall mention one example. Most of the self-images produced displayed Kirsten as the lonely rider in a vast wilderness of other people, other worlds. At the first meeting with the actors, one of them had remarked that among the episodes I had chosen to speak about, practically none referred to my closest personal relations. My marriage had passed unnoticed, for instance; what did that mean? I answered that I had always felt alone, and had had to fight for at least temporary sensations of belonging to a 'we'. That would still be part of my answer.

There is more to it. It is part of the anthropological condition to be alone among strangers. In the field and in the research process, one is permanently in a kind of exile. And possibly it has become, or has always been, part of my 'personality' to live in, or at least sometimes to retreat to, an internal exile, whether as a response to, or as the explanation for, my disrupted experiences with other people. It is part of the fieldwork condition to be unknown, and sometimes invisible; but it is also part of the game gradually to establish a position to speak from – that is, an identity. I realized that this, perhaps, was not exclusively related to fieldwork but was a general human condition: identities are invented, not given.

Whatever the ultimate truth about my personal or psychological condition, the general feeling of exile was to be emphasized further in my autobiography, precisely because of the theatrical intervention into my life. The group searched for a main character and, like any other informant, I had presented my self in a form that already was a dramatization (cf. Griaule 1957: 92). As Griaule – who was also a character in Leiris' *L'afrique fantôme* – points out, informants make implicit choices between stories to be told and points to remain unspoken. These choices are partly responses to the ethnographer's questioning. Similarly in my own case, there was not only power but also dialogue involved in the eliciting of my biography, as in any ethnography.

Writing myself produced me both as a text and as a person. The obtrusive presence of Odin Teatret made me tell my story, but at the same time this story transcended me. Like the anthropologist Crapanzano's informant, Tuhami, I thereby became a figure within an imposed allegory that in a very real sense bypassed me (Crapanzano 1980: xi). What is more, by writing myself, I had engaged in a risky process. Moroccan Tuhami had died when the anthropologist left him, leaving his trace only in text. And the wise old Shmuel, who had just given away his Jewish life history to young anthropologist Myerhoff, told her to leave because now he was tired; he died the same night (Myerhoff 1978: 74–75). What would happen to me, when my observers had finished their play about me?

Without realizing all this at the time, I was, nevertheless, shaky when I sent off the first 100 pages of selected dramas from my life history. In the autobiography my life had become text for somebody else to read. In the first place, it was addressed to Eugenio, who seemed to 'like' it – meaning that it suited his purpose. The process could proceed to the next stage, which implied transformation of the text into a new kind of life.

The most dramatic sequence was right ahead.

Third stage: seeing myself

More meetings were held, more questions put, and more details exchanged. As the group became increasingly focused on the performance, I experienced an increasing degree of off-centredness and could not see what role Kirsten was going to play. I was not given any clues about the actual performance, although we talked about various characters and their features. I had a feeling that 'Kirsten' was taking on a life of her own. The group would occasionally consult me on biographical or anthropological matters, but there was a veil of secrecy between the theatre and the rest of the world.

After some months of silence, during which the group had been in Mexico to rehearse far away from public curiosity, I was invited to a rehearsal. The performance was beginning to take shape, and Eugenio wanted my 'approval'. I watched, laughed, and cried. My fists were clenched and my shoulders stiff. My whole body reacted violently to the play. Seeing Kirsten in all too familiar situations of fear, joy and pain freed a set of feelings in which I would not normally allow myself to indulge. Familiarity was also belied, of course, because the context was alien, and because the dramatic effects used to stress particular points transcended my imagination. Most important, I was represented by another woman, and the representation denied my presence in my own story. I was extremely surprised that they used my proper name and my own wordings in such a literal manner. It occurred to me that I had in some ways repressed my knowledge that 'I' was actually the central character. Eugenio had told me, of course, but I had not known what it meant, or I had not wanted to see the implications. As it happened, when I first saw 'Kirsten' on stage, she was no longer me. She was not-me.

Later, I saw more rehearsals, with new details added, and was asked about my reaction. Generally, and as the tears in my eyes would reveal, I was overwhelmed by the precision with which the group had grasped the essence of my stories. They told the truth about Kirsten, yet she was still not-me. The play evoked my biography within the context of world history as suspended between violence and science. It made me see myself more clearly than before. Through the selective fiction of not-me, my reality became focused.

The observation has been made that the theatre director and the fieldworker are like one another because both are evoker-observers (Schechner 1982: 80). Seeing myself on stage, represented by another woman who bore my name and lived my life, made me experience the truth in this. Eugenio's fieldwork with me had yielded a result: a play that evoked my reality. The evocation had the shape of a performance, and unlike ordinary ethnographic monographs that are nothing but texts, this was also a restoration of behaviour.

Restored behaviour is a key element in theatrical performance (Schechner 1982: 40). However, 'performance is not merely a selection from data arranged and interpreted; it is behavior itself and carries with it a kernel of originality, making it the subject for further interpretation, the source of further history' (ibid.: 43). In that way the dramas of my own life had become independent of me. The play mirrored a real social space, but there was a crack in the mirror allowing a separate reality to be seen: a reality of not-me. I was enchanted by it.

A remarkable change occurred when, in the middle of an audience on the opening night, I saw the performance again. In the audience there was a good number of well-known faces: colleagues from the university, students and family. They knew me, but they did not know my story. Once again I was absolutely caught by the magnificent play, the brillance of the actors and the ingenuity of the direction. My involvement was clearly shared by the audience, who responded intensely to the drama before their eyes. Yet amidst it all, something significant happened. The presence of other spectators entailed an astonishing reorientation of my own view of Kirsten on stage: she was no longer not-me, but had become not-not-me.[3] In the eyes of the audience, distance was denied; Kirsten came dangerously close to me.

Afterwards, during the opening-night celebration, to which the entire audience was invited, many people commented on my 'courage'. I wondered what that could mean – irresponsibility, perhaps? Anyway, I had nothing to say. There was no way to speak from a doubly negated position. I could hardly be spoken to either. When I heard that a group of Italian dramatists wanted to see me, I went into their room to say hello, and they just looked at me. I wonder whom they saw. A local newspaper smelled a 'story' and wanted to interview me about 'how it really was'. I told them off and asked them to see the play once more. That was how it really was.

It was a strange night. I was present but non-existing. The performance-made-public transformed me. The illusion of my own otherness had been represented as a fact – even to me. It was only among the actors and their director that I felt on my own.

I saw the performance three times within a week. Each time I saw more details and grasped more meaning of the parts. The play had become a self-defined entity, and only then did the parts gain their full meaning. I was in a peculiar state of mind when, on the last night, I saw the group pack up their impressive costumes, masks and so forth, already on their way to Italy, Latin America and the rest of the world to show *Talabot*. What about me, or not-me, or not-not-me? How could they just leave me? I had to be among them to see who I was. As professional strangers they departed, carrying with them the meaning of my life.

My panic was acute, and in retrospect I know it was related to the fact that 'meaning is connected with the consummation of a process – it is bound up with termination, in a sense, with death' (Turner 1986a: 97). Through the restoration of my life history, *Talabot* had created a whole out of biographical fragments. Its meaning implicated my death. Alive as I was, no one understood my agony.

During the following weeks I was caught in the void between two histories, one that was terminated and another that had yet to begin. The experience of having been 'fieldworked upon' made me realize that I could no longer be an anthropologist. Since important parts of my history had been given away, I also knew that I could no longer be me. The theatre had left, and there was no way to live the mythical life of Kirsten that they had created. The only answer was to vanish. Unlike Tuhami and Shmuel, who vanished forever when they had been written, I am only temporarily underground – trying to write back. On the other side of the globe a new kind of strangeness may eventually permit *me* to re-enter the world.

Who will be there to meet me?

II: THE OUTCOME

It is a general truth about performances that they catch their audiences by being not-real and not-not-real at the same time; the 'as if' of the rehearsals becomes subjugated to the 'is' of the performance (Schechner 1982: 70–72; 1985: 102ff.). When the show opens, it becomes almost real; good actors convince the audience of the reality of the restored behaviour by their 'presence'. The not-real is thereby negated. At the first performance of *Talabot*, I had sensed this intensely. Kirsten, who until then had not really been me, now presented herself as *not* not really me. She in fact came so close to me that I had no longer any place in the world.

Because the main character of the play bore my name and restored my biography, the play implicated my destruction. This may now be rephrased at a more general level; although I cannot speak back as a character, I may still write back as an anthropologist.

Myth: unmasking history

Talabot features several 'mythical' characters who, one way or another, mirror elements in Kirsten's life. They are mythical in the sense that they are all dead, and that they are remembered as images rather than individuals. In the play they wear masks in contrast to Kirsten's naked face, which becomes covered in ashes only after the breakthrough (or breakdown) in the field. One of the characters is Knud Rasmussen, the famous Danish Polar explorer, who was very much a part of Kirsten's own mythological world during her childhoood. He is featured as a man who 'drives his dogs further ahead' at whatever cost. He has accepted the role as explorer-hero, and suppresses his individual desires to satisfy the world's thirst for knowledge about the Eskimos. He lured amulets from them in order to exhibit them at the National Museum in Copenhagen, and he was elected honorary doctor as a matter of course. His mythical position is based on the fact that in the end his individual desires converged with the public's desires. The rest was made silence.

Kirsten is different from Knud Rasmussen, mainly in the fact that she is a living person whose history, therefore, cannot yet be silenced. There are other conspicuous differences, such as Kirsten breaking down when she knew she had stolen the dignity of her impoverished friends in the Icelandic fishing village. But again, the differences may be owed to the fact that we know of her feelings, whereas we only know about Knud Rasmussen's dogs and his achievements. For both, the exploration of other worlds has become an existential as well as a scientific necessity. Thus, in spite of the differences, Knud Rasmussen's story reflects Kirsten's own fate in the mirror of another time and another sex. Sameness, or otherness in this case, is a matter of definition and of separating myth from history.

In the case of Che Guevara, another character in the play, the separation between myth and history is explicit. He is introduced as myth, wearing a beautiful purple dress and a mask. He undresses and becomes 'historical', and we learn how his experience with his father and the local upper class made him a revolutionary. Ultimately, it is this unmasked reality that led to the masked, or mythical truth, of posteriority. Whereas Kirsten chose anthropology to defend the weaker cultures, Che chose revolution. His death for this cause made him eligible for myth. In the play, having met Kirsten as a real unmasked person, Che once again dresses in purple, takes up his mask, and joins the merry land of the dead – including his Indian nanny who had been raped and killed by *blancos*. As myths, people may live beyond their deaths as masked truths.

A third character of mythical proportion in *Talabot* is Antonin Artaud, the French surrealist poet who foreshadowed ethno-graphic surrealism (Clifford 1981). In an intense scene, he speaks about the theatre and the plague (which, in fact, he did at the Sorbonne), and in his madness he breaks through to the agonized Kirsten, who after fieldwork is caught in a spider's web of sepa-rate realities. He provides the answer to her implicit question of why she must suffer so much from her knowledge: the plague makes you see who you really are – just as theatre does. Conceal-ment and revelation are twin birds.

Kirsten also has a twin in the play, Trickster, who binds together the scenes with grotesque gestures and speeches about the cruelty of the world. Trickster is a mirror in which the world is confronted with its own repressed knowledge of itself. Trickster is not only the world's conscience, but also the one to teach the world to play tricks upon conscience. The anthropologist is like the trickster in many ways; he or she promises not to lie, but never tells the whole truth either (Crapanzano 1986). In both cases, the 'rhetoric empowers *and subverts* their message' (Clifford 1986a: 6). As clown and storyteller respectively, Trickster and Kirsten achieve their identities by exploiting the ambiguities of their cultural and social position (cf. Crapanzano 1980: 61). In *Talabot* they play complementary roles; as Kirsten's 'twin', Trickster reveals what she conceals, and vice versa.

The point is that the mask is not only a concealment, but also a revelation. Masks are like myths in that they cannot be treated as separate objects hiding a face or a history behind a metaphor. They derive their sense from their relationship to a wider seman-tic space (cf. Lévi-Strauss 1988: 13–14). The mask gives away part of this space – thus also for the masks used in *Talabot*.

At a another level this implies that becoming a myth gives one a true history. I experienced this through the reactions to the play of some of my students: for the first time they realized I was human. Until then I had been a figure with no apparent humanity, quite irrespective of the fact that my writings had become increasingly personal. Like the Brazilian *Carnaval*, the performance had transcended the systematic inequality between us – as teacher and students – and given way to a feeling not only of equality but also of identity (cf. DaMatta 1984). As humans, we were free to choose our own masks. I sensed that myth and history implied each other, as do concealment and revelation.

Myth and history are equally true renderings of the past; they differ mainly in their being two distinct modes of representation (Hastrup 1987d). Myth is an allegorical representation of the past, whereas history is perceived as literal. In our culture we have given priority to literal-mindedness and have largely relegated metaphor to a parasitic position upon literal language. We have repressed the knowledge that metaphors induce action, and thus *are* history. We have also conceived of the world in terms of a hierarchy between literate and oral forms of communication. In our ethnocentric view of the world, all this has implied that history has been given priority over myth as a charter for reality. I have argued against that view on theoretical grounds (Hastrup 1987d).

Talabot confirms my argument on an experiential level: when my history became mythical, it became real. On his death, Che Guevara became eligible for allegorical representation, and the meaning of his life history became crystal clear. It was only at that time that the 'events' in his life could be singled out from the mass of happenings that we are all involved in. If events are happenings of significance also in biography, only death or myth allow us to sort out the significant from the insignificant, because only then does a whole emerge.

When I became myth, the significant events of my life revealed themselves as historical densities, that is, points in time where there are clusters of memorable events. In the literal language of history, including life history, the memorable points cannot be distinguished from the forgettable ones, because densities are not part of language. Only metaphor reveals what is otherwise concealed from language: experiential densities.

The mask uncovers your true face.

Allegory: cracking the mirror

There has been a continuous struggle over the definition of the anthropological object of study. One suggestion is to see it in terms of performances. Performances are processes with particular diachronic structures that reveal distinct patterns of social relationships. By studying 'social dramas', the anthropologist gains access to the alien world as it is enacted in practice rather than as an abstract system. Practice always puts structure at risk and, at any time, the event observed by the anthropologist may prove to engender change in the system. Focusing on events, therefore, facilitates our apprehension of other cultures as life rather than as text. The same applies to biographies.

In addition to this, the explicit focus on performances emphasizes the inherent reflexivity of the event. The performance arouses people's consciousness of themselves; it reveals them not only to the world but also to themselves (Turner 1982b: 75; 1986a: 81). It is the reflexive nature of social performances that ultimately makes them the source of the theatre. Both kinds of performance represent particular dramatizations of culture. One outcome of this convergence is the suggestion that anthropology in general moves toward a 'theatrical paradigm' (Schechner 1982: 51; Turner 1986a: 75). This implies a concentration on the processes of social dramas and an abandonment of the timeless patterns of culture. Although my own concept of the anthropological object is different, I still find it true that the reflexive trends in anthropology certainly challenges the traditional view of cultures and their reproduction in texts. Part of this discussion is of immediate relevance for the theatre and its restoration of behaviour.

We realize now that all ethnographic writings (and plays) are in some sense allegorical. Allegory designates a narrative practice in which the text continually refers to another pattern of ideas or events without assuming identity with it. Recognizing the allegorical nature of ethnography, therefore, is an acknowledgment of the *story* aspect of representation. It is worth emphasizing here that not only anthropologists but also their studied subjects may invoke allegories to construct their identities (Lavie 1989). The recognition of the power of allegory, therefore, transcends the realm of the anthropological discourse and reaches back into the structure of the reality to which this discourse refers. In brief, acknowledging the allegorical nature of ethnography implies a view of representation – of both selves and others – as a creative process rather than as a substantive category. That is the relevance of present-day anthropology – although substantially foreshadowed by Griaule, for instance.

The representation of 'the others' is not a mirror reflection of their social space, the accuracy of which can be measured against reality. It is a process of reenactment that, like the theatre, presupposes both actors and audiences. Still truthful to reality, the allegorical process allows greater freedom of expression than the realist paradigm in anthropology because the goal is no longer seen as reproduction but as evocation of the alien social space.

Although presence in the field is no longer an absolute source of ethnographic authority, it is still a precondition for the evocation of a probable world beyond the limits of the known. The ethnographic presence implies much more than the physical presence in the field – the 'I was there and I saw it myself' source of authority. It is also the degree to which the fieldworker impresses herself upon the alien culture and participates in its reflexivity. The acknowledgment of this kind of presence is a precondition for representation proper.

The theatre has its own rules of representation. Metaphor is taken to the extreme; allegory may reach the proportions of the grotesque. It is the grotesque in particular that binds the audience in a dual relationship to the play: it is not-real and not-not-real at the same time. In *Talabot*, the flow of grotesque, or at least exaggerated, reenactments of biographical events was the main reason for the acute schizophrenia in my concept of self. The experience of an allegorical 'me' made form and content fight each other, leaving me in a strange void *within* the dramatic sign.

Because representation is not merely a substantive category whose 'success' is measurable in terms of accuracy, but a creative process defining worlds as they are discovered, I could neither identify with nor distance myself from Kirsten on stage. She was neither my double nor an other. She restored my biography in an original way, being not-me and not-not-me at the same time. I was not represented, I was performed.

The performance was painfully reflexive.

Authority: voicing the unspeakable

Pain is a recurrent theme in these thoughts about *Talabot*. The process entailed fascination, pleasure and insight as well, but retrospectively (and still at a very short distance), the sense of loss dominates my feelings. It is less clear what I have lost, apart from a vague notion of 'me' and, possibly, some relationships that were dependent on that notion. However, tentatively, I think another aspect of the loss is the loss of an illusion of authority in anthropology. It was discussed briefly above and linked to a redefinition of the ethnographer's presence in the field. With what kind of authority can one ever speak about the other culture, if your being within it has already violated it? My experience of someone else running away to Italy and the rest of the world with the meaning of my life – my 'soul' – and giving away my passions stripped me of my concept of self. The pain made me understand all informants' latent loss at the departure of the ethnographer, who for awhile forced them to see who they were. Without comparison of the depth of the pain, my situation resembled Rosaldo's, whose personal grief finally enabled him to understand the Ilongot headhunters' rage (Rosaldo 1984). In his case, the anthropologist's personal costs in doing fieldwork made him question the meaning of anthropology at a fundamental, existential level. In my case, the informant's feeling of violation by the ethnographer made me pose a similar question, but from the reverse side. In both cases the immediate answer was to abandon anthropology, but this was to be replaced by perhaps an even stronger conviction about its necessity, irrespective of the costs on both sides. The illusions may be broken, but the reality is still there for us to comprehend.

The loss of illusions about anthropological authority is connected to my personal experience of the fundamental truth: one cannot learn what is systematically hidden in any culture or biography by mere presence; one has to exert a kind of violence to make the informants talk about themselves. As we have discussed before, the ethnographer must keep up the pressure to elicit any information (Griaule 1957: 14). This also applied to my ethnographer: Eugenio Barba kept up the pressure to the extent that he asked me to write about the process once it was over. I 'write back' on my own, of course, but the inner motivation to do so is seconded by a strong external pressure. Eugenio never went beyond our agreement, but to make me speak and write myself he had to be in some sense violent. Ultimately, it is this violence that is the source of *his* authority in relation to me.

On the surface of it, the implied violence may seem prohibitive to doing ethnography (or biography) of any sort; yet it is not. The violence is symbolic rather than physical, and the asymmetrical relationship between the anthropologist as author and the informant as contributor is of a peculiarly creative nature, provided it is recognized. The ethnographer's presence, however violent, is in some way the only alternative to silence about the other worlds, because her sharing of this world is a source of authority about its objective reality; no reality can ever be exhaustively apprehended within its own categories. Thus, it was also Eugenio's 'presence' in my life that made him the author of my biography.

Realizing this, the question of identity or opposition in my relationship to Kirsten on stage must be rephrased. Given the source of ethnographic authority, we are forced to admit that sameness and otherness are not objective qualities but categories of throught. During my fieldwork in Iceland I had experienced the fluid boundaries between subject and object; 'I' had become redefined as 'she' in an alien discursive space. With Talabot I experienced the truth of this from the informant's point of view. Both I and she disappeared in the pragmatic reflexivity of performance, leaving me with nothing but a body of my own. With no clear *concept* of my self, my sense of person could not be expressed in language. I could move about as an individual, but my identity was muted.

This experience confirms the point that identities are always relational and inventive. There is no essence of 'self' except as an invention made to meet particular tactical ends. Seeing myself performed by another woman in a strange context forced me to question my authenticity. I became an invention even to myself. Consequently, the traditional categories of thought broke down. Self or other, I or she, subject or object, were dichotomies of no relevance. Losing my identity implied a complete loss of confidence in the world.

My childhood fear of darkness came back upon me.

'LA FEMME NUE': CONCLUDING REMARKS

We do not *have* identities, we invent them. In writing this, I am trying to reclaim a position in the world in spite of the fact that *Talabot* left me naked. Thrown back to my nature, I realize that I am neither me nor not-me because 'I' am not. Only myth provides us with life: 'Where historical life itself fails to make cultural sense in terms that formerly held good, narrative and cultural drama may have the task of *poeisis*, that is, of remaking cultural sense'

(Turner 1982b: 87). Such is also the lesson of *Talabot*, and of anthropology.

In this personal account, I have attempted to practise anthropology, namely to 'faire de la subjectivité la plus intime un moyen de démonstration objective' (Lévi-Strauss 1973: 25). The story goes on, and the lessons are many. Most of them are yet to be learned, but I first felt an intense need to reclaim my biographic presence in my own history, and to close the void between the separate realities. Understanding my position as an object of dramatic representation was a precondition for redressing the person left naked by the theatre.

Out of anthropology – my self.

AFTERTHOUGHTS 1994

At six years' distance, the experience of having been fieldworked upon is no longer painful, yet there is no doubt that it left its mark in my personal history. Like any representation of human life – whether in the singular or the plural – the play on me intervened into my self-understanding. *Talabot* extended and challenged my identity in ways that are barely knowable, but which surely led me onto courses of action that I would not otherwise have considered possible. Possibly, I had actually become more of a character. In the present context, I am particularly aware of the impact it had upon my feeling of anthropology as a forceful practice of intersubjectivity.

Talabot was a dramatic echo of the profound insight that theories about social life change their object in the process of theorizing itself. This is no reason to stop theorizing, only to stop modelling the idea of social and human science on the ideal inherited from the natural sciences – i.e. operating on an object that largely remains unaffected by theory – and to revise the sense of purpose.

This revision needs taking into account in the proposition that the identities of people emerge in a process of reflection and action, a process that is part and parcel of being human. All selves are continuously both searching for an identity and trying to form it in accordance with their imaginative ideals of what it might be (Johnson 1993: 149). Anthropological practice affects both of these processes, by providing contextual knowledge on the one hand and contributing to a cross-cultural sense of shared moral deliberations on the other. This explodes the Enlightenment sense of scientific purpose as a matter of clarification, as well as the folk model of the Moral Law as prescriptive. The former recedes to a purpose of making sense, the latter to a view of moral principles as summaries of collective experience.

The route to this field of force goes by way of subjects, possibly experiencing a degree of pain at the loss of preconceived notions of self, yet also potentiated by the telic demand to redress a painless state, where the self may once again recede into unawareness. The recessive self embodies the marks left by the loss; its learning about itself changes it. The ecstatic self, literally the self that 'stands out', is exposed to symbolic violence, yet through this exposition the individual gets access to another world. Anthropology is instrumental in this by its staging an experience of intersubjectivity.

Chapter 8

The native voice
On taking responsibility

In ethnographic fieldwork, silence is not the sole feature of the encounter with 'the natives', be they neighbours, friends or more distant persons. They also have a distinct voice – each one of them – to which the ethnographer must listen carefully. Of late, a debate on the place of the native voice in anthropology has led to a reconsideration of the dilemma between the local and the anthropological claims to speaking the truth. It is to a discussion of this dilemma that this chapter is addressed.[1]

THE NATIVE POINT OF VIEW

It was Malinowski (1922: 25) who first claimed that anthropology was concerned with an understanding of other cultures from the 'native's point of view', as was discussed in the prologue. Since then, there has been an expectation that ethnographers learn to think, feel and often even behave like a native. Because this can only be achieved through prolonged communication with the natives, an extensive period of fieldwork has been essential to the profession. The necessity of a close association with the natives to acquire anthropological knowledge has been expressed in different ways according to paradigm. Margaret Mead, who is more renowned for her fieldwork than for her theories, has it thus: 'As the inclusion of the observer within the observed scene becomes more intense, the observation becomes unique' (Mead 1977: 6). Rosalie Wax went a step further when she stressed that it is in the 'areas of mutual trust and, sometimes, affection that the finest fieldwork can be done' (Wax 1971: 373). The examples are legion, and although it has been claimed that the notion of 'immersion' in the foreign culture is most often totally unwarranted (Crick 1982: 21), no anthropologist seems to deny that 'the closer the better'. To 'know' another world, one must associate with the natives of that world, even possibly become one of them, at least temporarily.

The first obvious question is 'who are the natives?'. A quick answer is that by natives we simply refer to people who at some point are studied by social anthropologists as inhabitants of a particular social space. All of us are natives in this sense; we may even declare ourselves as belonging to a particular people, of the kind and magnitude studied by anthropologists – the Nuer, the Ilongot, the Icelanders. Natives name themselves in this way, and anthropologists have taken to these names. On closer inspection, *naming* peoples only begs the question of nativeness. Through their naming practice, anthropologists have invented peoples where none existed before; the Tallensi, described – and defined – by Meyer Fortes are a case in point (Fortes 1945, 1949). There was a 'population', of course (that is, children and adults milling around) but no sense of a shared name – not a 'people' (cf. Ardener 1975). In other cases there may have been a shared name, but too many aspirants to that name through history to give it a precise referent; the 'gypsies' studied by Judith Okely is an example (Okely 1983).

A more recent but no less complicated case is provided by Maryon McDonald, whose work on the Bretons speaks loud and clear about the problems inherent in naming (McDonald 1989a). In Brittany, a radical nationalist movement of mainly intellectuals who were born French-speakers now claim to speak (in their acquired second language) on behalf of the 'Bretons' – including many Breton-speaking peasants who feel completely alienated from the movement. Who are 'the Bretons' then? More generally, who are the natives? Whose voice is representative, and who are we to listen to for our anthropology not to be repressive?

In the postmodern condition it has been claimed that there are no natives left, meaning that there are no cultural isolates of which one can claim to be indigenous. We all live in a global village, where the speed of communication and the range of possibilities open to anyone (at least theoretically) makes all talk about cultures meaningless. While not incorrect, the global argument takes us nowhere beyond the obvious, and it cannot, therefore, claim any status as scientific truth.

More to the point in the present connection is a less often

drawn conclusion: all of us are natives in some world. In spite of the obvious globalization, there are still parts of the world where people are 'at home', in the sense that they *know* the social space – even if they do not actually *understand* it. And that is the point; the difference between knowing and understanding amounts to a difference between an intimate and implicit native knowledge and an external and explicit expert understanding. Evidently, the native is a practical expert on local lifeways, and is constantly engaged in self-description. Yet the point of anthropology is to transcend self-description – not through a bypassing of it but by way of incorporating it into a language of a higher-order generality.

Our claims to a native knowledge of other cultures may be questioned, from both a factual and an epistemological perspective; there are limits to empathy. But it is important to stress, that whatever we might know, a genuinely anthropological understanding is different from mere knowing. When assessing the tone of the native voice raised in critique of particular results this is an important thing to remember. When an Icelandic critic of some of my own observations on Iceland claims that it is the fact of his being 'a product of the culture involved . . . that gives [him] the background and the right to comment on the work involved' (Einarsson 1990: 69), I would retort that the right to comment belongs to everyone, while – of course – the backgrounds for commenting may differ. The native background is one; anthropology is another.[2] If nothing else, anthropology gives another version of reality (Cohen 1987: 3–4). This version is not necessarily one that makes the native 'happy with the results', nor need it be (*pace* Einarsson 1990: 69). There is no need to reverse ethnocentrism.

An interpretive social science like anthropology cannot, of course, bypass the agents' self-understanding, since this is a precondition for the identification of the social space under study. But to assimilate interpretation with the adoption of the agents' point of view is crippling to theory (Taylor 1985b: 118). In anthropological practice, the problem is further complicated by the fact that we cannot know in any absolute manner who the natives are. In connection with advocacy, anthropologists engaged by indigenous populations to fight governments or oil companies have often noted that opinions may be divided locally, and that problems of representativeness are often acute (Maybury-Lewis

1985). Factions may hold absolutely irreconcilable viewpoints (Hastrup and Elsass 1990).

While, evidently, anthropologists must gracefully face the criticisms made by subjects of study and colleagues alike, there still is no simple truth to be told. Given the nature of our scientific endeavour, there is no absolute, objective world to be reported. Consequently, the point that natives have privileged access to the truth about their worlds does not stand for closer inspection. 'The native point of view' is part of the ethnography, of course, but should not be conflated with anthropology, as I have argued in more detail elsewhere. The essence of the native critique against my own work, for instance, is that the Icelanders never 'speak of' this or that, and that it cannot, therefore, be true. Again, this is missing the point – even in the case that my conclusions will not stand for closer anthropological scrutiny; anthropology is so much more than a recording of words. As we have discussed before, local categories do not exhaust the world, and native voices never tell the full story about the world. This is related to the fact that for natives, their culture is referentially transparent. It is not 'seen' but 'seen with'.

I have claimed that part of the ethnographer's task is to 'know' another culture. Fieldwork and the sharing of experience are key elements in this. The notion of fieldwork has changed, however. The observationist stance has been abandoned; fieldwork is not only a means to observation at the closest possible distance, as implied by Malinowski, Mead and Wax above. We have realized that fieldwork itself may generate the events, that are then portrayed as facts. In this perspective, the native point of view is never unmediated in anthropology. What the informants tell us is produced in the liminal space of the encounter with the ethnographer; it is self-reflexive to a degree of a 'doubling of consciousness' (Rabinow 1977: 119).

The nature of ethnographic fieldwork makes reflexivity an essential, even constitutive, feature of anthropology, as we have seen in a previous chapter. However, reflexivity

> does not leave the subject lost in its own concerns; it pulls one toward the Other and away from isolated attentiveness toward oneself. Reflexiveness requires subject and object, breaking the thrall of self-concern by its very drive toward self-knowledge

that inevitably takes into account a surrounding world of events, people and places.

(Myerhoff and Ruby 1982: 5)

Thus, reflexivity in anthropology is far from that culture-specific kind of self-centredness we know by the name of narcissism – which seems to be part of present western culture, as was said before.

The restoration of subjectivity implied in the reflexive mode means that at the level of ethnography, no one can claim privileged access to knowledge. The pronouns engaged in the ethnographic dialogue speak on equal terms. In the colloquial situation of fieldwork there are speakers and listeners, I's and you's. Identities are construed reciprocally; selves and others are mutually implicated and objectified. Given the interlocutory nature of fieldwork, the reciprocal identities of speakers and listeners embody the essence of subjectivity. As anthropologists we still have a problem of objectification, that is, a demand of transcending the dialogue – not by taking sides between I and you, but by positing both in a discursive space that positions them equally. In spite of their claims to the contrary, advocates of admitting the native voice *into the anthropological text* miss the point of equality: it is a strategy of incorporating the others into a decidedly western kind of logocentrism.

Equality – and respect for the constitutive voice of the native subject (Page 1988: 164) – is not to assume that all native worlds can be rendered in our language, even if one of the most powerful implicit features of our mental landscape 'is the assumption that nearly everything we might want to say in words can be said adequately – and in fact *should* be said – in the alphabetically written prose of journal articles and other scholarly forms' (Tedlock 1982: 150).

The alleged lack of respect for the native who is imported into our scheme as a legitimizing voice is related to a failure to comprehend that the first person singular is irreducible. It follows that 'the authenticity of the historical subject may not be fully captured from the outside even by way of direct quotes' (Trouillot 1991: 39). In short, the accommodation of the natives into the anthropological discourse is not done by the recipe of 'add native, stir, and proceed as usual' (ibid.: 44 n. 20). The revision of anthropology needs something more than this kind of reconstitutive surgery, and the natives deserve better than giving voice to our theories. The responsibility belongs to no one but in the anthropologists who make them up (cf. Geertz 1988: 140).

Thus, I would second Stephen Tyler when he claims that 'representing native dialogue has no ethical import', because it functions totally within our own discourse based on pure reason. 'For this reason, dialogical representation must make its claim, not from the value of ethical recuperation – the anticolonial freeing of the native's voice – but from the imperialistic claim of enlightened representation' (Tyler 1987b: 338). To me, this is not only the point about representation through dialogue but also of anthropology in general. Cultural relativism is not about 'different worlds' (to a point of caricature) but more importantly about different ways of communicating worlds. This is not achieved by arranging a textual space for informants to have their own voices (*pace* Marcus and Fischer 1986: 67). Once the natives are construed as 'informants', their voices are already edited. As a strategy of textualization, no dialogue can overcome its own textualization (Tyler 1987b: 339). The text remains text, at one remove from life. From this position we can see that the call for native voices in ethnography is not a solution to the epistemological dilemma in anthropology.

AUTO-ANTHROPOLOGY

Taken at face value, the canon that anthropology is about understanding the world from the native point of view makes it absurd not to grant the natives themselves privileged access to their own culture. After all, they were there first and stayed longer than even the keenest of anthropologists.

If the natives are really privileged knowers, we should immediately direct our entire professional attention towards 'home'. An important question remains, however: how does one *know* when one is at home, as Marilyn Strathern has pointed out (Strathern 1987: 16). Where are the boundaries of one's 'home-culture', once culture has been dismantled as an entity and rediscovered as an analytical perspective? As anthropologists we are keenly aware of social and cultural differences within *soi-disant* nation-states, and we cannot overlook the fact that wherever we go, the problems of representativity, typicality and degrees of generality are always acute once we give up on the idea of culture as essence and the others as an entity. 'Home' seems virtually boundless from the postmodern perspective.

Even linguistic boundaries seem to dissolve at this stage. Global communication blurs the boundaries from outside, while, conversely, recent sociolinguistic studies have shown that within one language there is a wide variety of differing practices of speaking that makes the view of language as an entity highly dubitable. Language cannot be taken for granted; as pointed out by Judith Okely, for instance, she 'had to learn another language in the words of [her] mother tongue' when studying traveller gypsies in Britain (Okely 1984: 5). Apparently these people spoke English words but the meanings were different. Recently, Angel Díaz de Rada and Francisco Cruces have shown how they uncovered new meanings in their native Spanish, once they turned their professional ethnographic gaze towards contemporary compatriots (Díaz de Rada and Cruces 1994). And Pavlos Kavouras has convincingly shown how he, a native speaker of Greek, was taken aback when after a couple of years of fieldwork in Olympos, he discovered the full semantic, and indeed practical, range of the concept of *trimistiro* (a polysemic word for transgressor and storyteller) (Kavouras 1994).

The general point is that whatever language is spoken, the anthropologist cannot take the words at face value. Actual social experience is always included in the category system which therefore becomes marked by irregularities of meaning and particular semantic densities. In anthropology, therefore, it is not the personal credentials and linguistic competence that determines whether a particular ethnographer works 'at home' or elsewhere. 'Home' is a conceptual category with shifting reference. The only way to measure or define an anthropology at home seems to be by way of the resulting writings. They alone show 'whether there is cultural continuity between his/her labours and what people in the society being studied produce by way of accounts of themselves' (Strathern 1987: 17). It is this continuity which marks a proper auto-anthropology: the adoption of appropriate local genres of representation, which is not at all a direct consequence of simply being a 'member' of the overarching culture or society in question. The ultimate consequence of auto-anthropology would be, say, a Greek anthropological discourse in Greek about the Greeks and for the Greeks (cf. Gefou-Madianou 1993: 162).

In this sense, auto-anthropology is radically different from 'tribal ethnography', defined by Edmund Leach as ethnographies that

> concentrate their attention on communities in which the level of literacy among the older members of the adult population is very low and in which there is a very marked gap between the technological sophistication and resources of the ethnographers themselves and those whom they are studying.
>
> (Leach 1989: 34)

If auto-anthropology, as the only logically conceivable form of anthropology 'at home', is defined in terms of continuity, not only of knowledge but also of conventions of representation, tribal ethnography is as far from home as possible in both ways. It is doubly marked by a discontinuity that must still be the the the hallmark of a scholarly discipline; scholarship is irreconcilable with discursive self-containment, auto-validation and closure.

The fact of separate experiential spaces and the solid documentation of different epistemologies always made anthropologists acutely aware of possible misunderstanding. Unlike the folklorist, the anthropologist cannot begin to study even the quasitextual elements in the field (such as myths) without the recognition that his or her understanding may be inadequate and perfunctory (Ardener 1989b: 174). *Ignorance* has to be presumed from the outset. On this presumption, auto-anthropology is unconvincing.

The preliminary conclusion is that concerning the 'natives' you do not have to *be* one to *know* one: anthropological interpretation cannot and should not be imprisoned within the mental horizons of others (whoever they are), like 'an ethnography of witchcraft as written by a witch' (Geertz 1983: 57). The fieldwork experience may draw the ethnographer into a web of witchcraft, because there are no neutral positions in the local discourse, as ferociously demonstrated by Jeanne Favret-Saada in her study of witchcraft in rural France (Favret-Saada 1980). But in analysis and writing, one must distance oneself and step out of the local discourse. The point is that witchcraft is not practised by way of scholarly analysis, but through secret practices. 'Understanding someone cannot simply mean adopting his point of view, for otherwise a good account could never be the basis of more clairvoyant practice' (Taylor 1985b: 118). And, withholding the better part of

Enlightenment ethics, anthropology and other human sciences
should aim at widening horizons.

THE OBJECT OF INTEREST

One of the criticisms raised against anthropology, also by natives,
is the standardized concept of culture. The concept allegedly blurs
the selves and personalities of the natives in the search for a
common cultural denominator. By their practice of writing cultures anthropologists have levelled individual difference and blurred internal inconsistencies and disorder. It has been suggested
that the particular task of native anthropologists, therefore, is to
'write against culture' (Abu-Lughod 1991).

While each one of us would admit that today 'more persons in
more parts of the world consider a wider set of "possible" lives
than they ever did before' (Appadurai 1991: 197), we would be
deceiving ourselves (and the 'natives') if this was presented as an
actual choice of culture. The images conveyed by the mass media
may give us a sense of a shared world, but one's social space is
not reducible to images. The imagined worlds may feed into and
blur the boundaries of culture through processes of mimicry, but
people still live in real worlds that are socially constrained – also
by their own definitions.

While we cannot claim social spaces to be closed or isolated
communities, since postmodernity has made their interchange-
ability manifest, this does not necessarily invalidate all claims to
holism, once the uncontested hallmark of the anthropological
method. Holism was not solely a corollary to the now disclaimed
genre of realism, and one among other false representations. Like
realism itself, 'holism' is both a genre convention and a particular
kind of epistemology. While the first has lost its credibility, the
latter is still possible – and necessary. We have to somehow bound
our object of interest; even the most radical of interpretations
has its limits.

To invoke holism is not only to save a methodological foothold
against theoretically unwarranted assumptions of totalitarianism;
more importantly, it is to acknowledge the fact that people live
in real worlds, which may be made up, temporary, blurred, global,
narcissist or whatever, but which nevertheless still ground them,
connect them to other people, and make sense of the everyday
as well as the unprecedented. In that sense, all of us *know* –

through experience – a particular world. As natives to some world of that order, all of us have an intimate and largely implicit knowledge about how to act in daily life; we even have some implicit knowledge of how to react to the non-routine, the unprecedented, the disorderly. But this does not imply that we know how culture is constituted. This would be anthropological knowledge.

We are facing a paradox, however; while native anthropologists stand up and argue against the concept of culture, more and more 'anthropological natives' declare their own autonomous and inviolable culture. While native anthropologists react against the stereotyping of their people, these people themselves transform their cultures into clichés, which may be spoken, performed and worn at festive occasions. In other words, at a point in time where anthropologists are finally ready to admit that 'our ability to interpret culture from the standpoint of tradition or continuity over time is undermined by the force of colonially imposed difference' (Urban and Sherzer 1991: 3), increasingly articulate native voices invoke tradition and culture as a means of resistance. The anthropological and the native voices again seem dissonant.

It is in the nature of 'ethnicity' to be past-oriented; 'time-honoured' practices are invoked to establish present-day singularity (Nash 1989: 14). Generally, indigenism is based in the paradox of colonially imposed difference and change, and situatedness within a state, on the one hand, and a claim to stability and continuity on the other. The inventory of culturally 'distinct' traits has largely been produced by interaction with a hegemonic structure (Jackson 1991; see also Rappaport 1990). This is an anthropological point, however. It can never be part of the native discourse. The voice that purports to speak cultural truths and the ritual specialist who performs traditional rites have no interest in this kind of knowledge, which would be directly counterproductive as far as claims to autonomy go. For the natives (of whatever order), consciousness of difference has to be embodied, lived, taken for granted; culture must be implicitly known. Only anthropologists can afford to 'disembody' it in their aim at understanding. If invited, however, they can also afford to collaborate with the locals in their performances, their struggles and their general quest to save the authenticity of their own world.

The dichotomy between native and anthropologist remains; our task is not to provide ethnographies that question this through an admission of 'native voices' into our texts, but to provide a kind of anthropological knowledge that offers new entries into the world in which 'nativeness' is premised and exploited as a symbolic resource. The process of globalization has a counter-effect of producing remarkable strategies of localization and ethnicity, stressing the uniqueness of a particular locality. Indeed, it appears that the manifest process of globalization generates an increasing number of 'remote areas' – whose prime feature it is to stress their own singularities, as will be recalled (Ardener 1987). In the process, the culturally 'banal' is transfigured as the significant; the old language is stretched to perform new tasks. The definitional space is transformed accordingly.

In the world system, 'remote areas' can make a general claim to minority status. This is a matter of acquiring symbolic capital. Marginality is a symbolic resource, which centrality is not. Minorities may even compete in terms of accusing one another of majority links and qualities; in the process the 'majority' world itself seems to empty as a category of self-ascription; no one wants to be the 'majority' (McDonald 1989a: 143, 309). The contextual emptiness of the majority category puts an even stronger pressure on the minority to declare itself. Hence the structural propensity towards the paradox inherent in the creation of an increasing number of 'remote areas' in the postmodern global village.

While anthropology has become historicized and globalized to a point where all talk about continuity or cultural difference is eligible for the classification as treason, natives tend to folklorize and exoticize their worlds. They make a claim to totality where possibly there is none, and where even native anthropologists advocate a study of 'the particular' rather than the common and shared (Abu-Lughod 1991). Instead of focusing on general features, anthropologists have been directed towards a study of 'the everyday' (Taussig 1991). I would argue that while, certainly, the particular and the everyday is part of ethnography, it cannot by itself be theory and thus satisfy the anthropological project. Once culture is deconstructed into persons living unique lives, 'people' can have no common referent; consequently, anthropology itself dissolves as a theory and vacates the field.

This is important: the claim to represent individuals in an ethnography of the particular amounts to a deconstruction of the inviolable subjects. We can never 'know' individuals as subjects; nor can we 'understand' them, as if they were truly objects; what

we, as ethnographers, can know, is the space that they are prepared to share with us.

This has an important consequence for our notion of holism.
In (postmodern) ethnographic texts there can be no claim to
totality or to have exhausted 'reality'; there is an admission of
fragment and relativity, of disorder and instability. There must
also be a claim to a kind of whole, however, without which
ethnography remains just another figment of the deconstructed
narrative about the world. This whole is a space of which the
ethnographer is part; it is the shared experiential space of
the field. The whole is no longer seen from outside; it is experienced from inside with the aim of learning how people construct,
change and deconstruct their own social spaces. By way of understanding *their* self-descriptions, we may formulate a new way of
comprehending the way in which the world moves. Our theoretical account amounts to a recontextualization that may easily
involve a challenging of the native self-understanding, including,
of course, our own.

The key thing is not to dismantle holism through an individual-
ization of the social space, but to realize that it is inhabited
by subjects who have their own understanding of the world. A
theoretical concept of social spaces that admits individual discon-
tinuites makes room for a renewed concept of holism, which is
no longer about a totalitarian and stable world, but about the
integrity of anthropological research – including the acknowledge-
ment of the essential reflexivity and relativity inherent in ethnography.

NATIVE ANTHROPOLOGY

We are now in a position to rethink the issue of native anthropology. On the surface of it, and judging from recent debates,
there seem to be both gains and losses from being a native
anthropologist. Among the gains reported is a possibly privileged
access to certain aspects of local culture, notably the emotive and
other intimate dimensions (Ohnuki-Tierney 1984). It has also
been suggested that a native anthropologist possibly 'feels' the
subtle links and nuances within a culture more easily than a
foreigner (Gefou-Madianou 1993: 167). Among the losses is the
immediate positioning of the anthropologist within known social
categories (Mascarenhas-Keyes 1987), a greater pressure to con-

form to local social norms (Gefou-Madianou 1993: 168), and a certain propensity towards preconceived notions (Limón 1991).

Whether privileged or inhibited by local social boundaries, for the native anthropologist there remains a problem of transforming self-evident cultural knowledge to genuine anthropological understanding. As forcefully demonstrated by Dorinne Kondo (1984), the very success of participation may even lead to momentary losses of orientation due to the breakdown of the ascription as anthropologist. Kondo's collapse of professional identity led

> to a sense of vertigo, and to a fear of the Otherness – in the self. Though participation and rapport are highly laudable goals for the anthropologist in the field, in my case participation to the point of identification led also to a disturbing disorientation, and uncertainty as to which role I was playing.
>
> (Kondo 1984: 79)

The symbolic violence attributed to anthropologists is reversed here; the informants demand of their allegedly native anthropologist that she identifies herself with them. However, the main problem is not whether this or that particular observer's position is more or less privileged, because this is unmeasurable anyway, but to be sufficiently aware of whatever position one has in the social space under study (cf. Loizos 1992: 170).

As a scholarly discipline, anthropology truly *disciplines* its practitioners. By inscribing oneself into anthropology one submits to particular rules. The rules are largely implicit and become part of the internalized, unquestioned practical knowledge of the trained anthropologist. They may change over time and vary between particular institutions. But there is no way to be or to become a professional anthropologist without implicit acknowledgements of certain standards of scholarship. One of them is the obligation to verse onself in earlier literature on and previous arguments about the area one is going to study. By consequence, later anthropologies always encompass earlier ones, and all of them encompass and transcend local knowledge. This implies that anthropology will always by definition encompass native understanding. The two belong to separate registers and must be measured on distinct scales of value. As a theoretical mode of knowledge, anthropology is opposed to the practical mode of knowledge that is the basis of ordinary social experience of the social world. Instead of submitting to a kind of auto-anthropology, which is unable to distinguish between ethnographic *sources* and ethnographic *descriptions*, we must meet the challenge posed by the discontinuity between local knowledge and anthropological understanding. Only then can we expand the field of significance of anthropology.

This is the point: there is no way in which one can simultaneously speak from a native and an anthropological position. It is logically impossible to speak from an inside and an outside position at the same time. It is not a matter of Icelandic citizens not being capable of studying fellow Icelanders, or Greek speakers being excluded from the study of familiar linguistic communities. It is a much more profound epistemological matter of acknowledging the inherent process of 'othering' in anthropology. As I have argued in the prologue to this volume, we are now in a position to turn the concept of othering towards ourselves. It is for anthropology to assume the position of the 'radical other' in the world.

It is a particular epistemological position in which we renounce continuity between our own words, conceptions, theories and conventions of representation and those of the people studied, whoever they are, and to whatever world they are native. The anthropological practice presupposes discontinuity, where a truly 'native' anthropology would require an essential continuity between the social space studied and the anthropological knowledge project. For the anthropological results to be theoretically and historically significant, one must reflect upon the objective conditions for the production of knowledge itself. For the native there is no way of incorporating such an objective viewpoint and still speak as 'native'.

'Native anthropology', indeed, is a contradiction in terms.

RESPONSIBILITY

In the preceding section, I have argued that the native point of view should not be conflated with the anthropological vision, and I have dismantled the notion of native anthropologist in the process. While all of us are natives of some social space or other, there is no way in which one can claim privileged access to *anthropological* knowledge – except by being native to anthropology. This implies that one, through extensive enculturation in theory and practice, has come to 'know' anthropology – not just to understand a few of its words.

Reflexivity is an integral part of what must be 'known' about anthropology. It is a kind of reflexivity that theoretically acknowledges the world of betweenness established in the field, while also admitting the distinctness of the interlocutors. In anthropology there can be no claim to know the other as subject; he or she can be known only as part of a communicative space. The native voice must be heard and respected, not violated by textual mercy. Subjects are irreducible; anthropological ethics demands that we aknowledge this.

Natives may objectify themselves as such, by forcefully declaring the uniqueness and continuity of their space. Anthropologists, however, must both make relative and contextualize this space – as a first step towards scientific objectification. Part of our 'objective' knowledge about the world today is that histories are irreducible, because all of them are fragmented and implied in one another. Anthropology seeks to understand the process of fragmentation and of cultural implication. From the ethnographies of the particular, anthropologists condense a general knowledge about the world.

What distinguishes anthropology from native declarations of culture is both a sense of cumulative knowledge and a keen awareness of heterotopia. Anthropological scholarship is cumulative, not in the simple sense of being additive, but in that the results of our precursors in the discipline work themselves into our conception of the field. There is no way in which we, professionally, can unlearn the wisdom of our precursors. We may refine, reshape, deconstruct, reject or discredit their work, but no native to anthropology can take pride in *not* knowing it without losing his or her birthright. By contrast to those natives whom we study, anthropologists can not stand up and declare 'culture' from scratch – independently of those processes that (seen from outside) permanently put this culture at risk, including those processes by which language is stretched to perform new tasks of self-declaration. However much we wish to de-essentialize our object of study, anthropological theory must be able to contain and explain local essentialisms.

The sense of accumulation as interacting knowledge is backed by an awareness of heterotopia, which any internal view of culture denies. While native declarations of culture firmly territorialize it, anthropology moves towards a kind of juxtaposition and comparison conceived in terms of heterotopia, which firmly deterritorializes culture. 'The whole' constructed in anthropology is an emergent space (of shared social experience), not a territory. For once, we are approaching a position where we no longer mistake map for territory, or space for place. If ethnography creates worlds 'out of time', it also creates worlds out of place. This is a precondition for creating a general anthropological knowledge that is not outdated the moment it is written, and which may move.

To arrive there, however, we must still take our point of departure in the realities of particular people. We must share their experience. In spite of anthropological knowledge transcending the individual instance of fieldwork, it still has a real referent – a world of which we are part. The traditional *mise-en-scène* of anthropology, in terms of fieldwork as observation at the closest possible distance, and of the monograph reflecting an objective and total world, has broken down. But anthropology stands, because, epistemologically, it has changed to meet the challenges of the real world. The admission of individuals as both definers and defined gives us a new sense of the social.

In contrast to ethnic discourses, anthropology is not oriented towards a past, in which culture was seen as a stable and bounded form. Today we have broken away from this illusion. The vision of anthropology is to embrace the multiplicity of selves and communicate the processes that at some point in time may compel them to collectiviely stress their singularities and to essentialize their culture. The process of enquiry has the nature of a recontextualization. This is where the anthropological responsibility begins.

Chapter 9

The realist quest
On asking for evidence

In Chapter 3 I argued that the world of study is no less real for our being part of it. I rejected the contention that we can only speak of the empirical in quotation marks even if anthropologists still gain their knowledge about social relations and cultural spaces by intervening into them. Direct experience is not opposed to rational thinking; they are indistinguishable in practice. There is no way to learn about the world from outside it, no possibility of adopting a God's Eye view once we have rejected the ontological dualism between mind and body and, by implication, between subject and self.

The Cartesian split between subject and self placed rationality in the subject, and resulted in a procedural rationality and a quest for instrumental control over the object world. The growth of science epitomized this, and obviously science thrived within the Enlightenment cosmology, which alienated people from themselves while promising emancipation and freedom of thought. Psychoanalysis was a timely answer to this, splitting people even further while promising insight and freedom of will. The present therapy culture is the last vestige of a structure that was born a ruin: the world split into essence and appearance. Much effort has been invested in embellishing the remains; the natural sciences adorned essence, or reality, while the human sciences, or arts, were left with the niceties of appearances.

Anthropology has vacillated between the two. At some points in time it wanted to pass for a natural science, at others it posed as one of the humanities. Today, we realize that the wavering of the discipline, in fact and somewhat paradoxically, may be read as a token of its composure, which we may only now back epistemologically. Reality and appearance are one, and upon this unified whole scholarship erects a hypothetical imagery based on radical interpretation rather than clarification. If, however, realism does not consist in clarification of essence, we have still to discuss the kind (or degree) of realism to be expected from anthropology. In this chapter I shall pursue that question from various angles in order to show that, although realism as a genre and as an instance of a correspondence theory of truth must be abandoned, realism is still the only possible epistemology for purported scholarship.

Realism as a genre confounded the world and the image of the world; thus the 'ethnographic present', where we started this tour towards a redefined realism, was confused with the lack of history in 'primitive' society. So strong was this image that it took ages to realize that even continuation or permanence takes an effort, and is therefore as historical as anything. Evidently, there is nothing wrong with holding particular images of the world; we all do, and anthropology is good for delivery of more. There is a problem, however, if we mistake our own image for reality itself. This mistake is related to the fallacy of regarding language as transparent. Just as embodied and imaginative structures appear transparent because (or when) they operate non-problematically in our ordinary experience, so also the words we have been using.

The Objectivist idea that there is a fixed relation between sentences and objective reality may be a motivated misreading, but a misreading it is. There is no fixed meaning except for certain sediments from previous events of understanding, as will have become clear from the preceding argument. Understanding is an imaginative event; it implies human agency. Meaning is not given by or derived from a preexisting scheme. It occurs in practice.

In anthropology, as in linguistics and philosophy, we have come to the end of 'the dream of a description of physical reality as it is apart from observers, a description which is objective in the sense of being "from no particular point of view" ' (Putnam 1990: 11). To see why this does not imply giving up a notion of truth altogether or succumbing to a kind of radical relativism, we shall first scrutinize the notion of reference.

REFERENCE

The question of reference has been raised mainly in linguistics and in linguistic philosophy. It has also been implicit in most recent discussions of representation in anthropology. In fact, reference and representation are often used interchangeably and as more or less synonymous with the older notion of denotation (cf. Putnam 1981: 1). All of these terms have pointed to a relation between words and something that actually exists outside them. This is the basis of the correspondence theory of truth in anthropology and elsewhere.

As we saw in Chapter 2, the view that categories 'map' worlds can no longer be entertained; shifting prototypes and varying semantic densities constantly displace the relationship between meaning and reference. Representation is not possible; yet we still have to produce a kind of knowledge with some degree of fit with a 'shared' world. To communicate this we are bound to use a 'public' language. No speaker can use words with unique reference and expect them to be meaningful. What no one else can figure out cannot be part of meaning. Even without an idea of reference or representation, anthropology must still entertain a notion of reality, which may be communicated.

The language of communication cannot be directly observational, which presupposes transparency. No language is transparent in this sense; in natural language as in scholarly discourse we can no longer claim that to each meaningful expression corresponds an entity, which is its 'meaning'. The central role of reference in linguistic, and other, theory must be given up as part of the cost of going empirical (cf. Davidson 1984: 223). This implies a profound shift in our view of meaning, which we may name a shift from a semantic to a pragmatic view. The first, which has been the cornerstone of much symbolic or semantic anthropology, presupposes a meaning-space with fixed coordinates. The coordinates frame a map, which the anthropologist may then reproduce in her rendering of the local culture. The pragmatic perspective is different; it is more of an itinerary, meaning it is relative to people in motion. Their selves are at all times at the centre. There are no preestablished charts of meaning, no semantic space prior to experience; if a map can be retrospectively drawn it is of a corporeal field. Reference, then, plays no essential role in exploring the relation between language and reality. Words have no function, save in sentences, and sentences have little function apart from their part in helping people achieve their goals or realize their intentions (Davidson 1984: 220). The net result is not a constitutive theory of the world, however. When epistemology, and the human sciences in general, took the linguistic turn, the idea of observable objects gave way to a discussion of observation terms and constructed realities. As a temporary correction this was a sound move, but it will not do. The world is there all right and more or less independent of our words upon it; as we know, we only have words for the smaller part of the knowledge stored in our social selves.

Nature itself leaves reference indeterminate; what determines it is human action. This essential indeterminacy of reference implies that the 'question of reference' only makes sense *within* a language (Putnam 1981: 52). It follows that reference is *not* the point of contact between linguistics and events (cf. Davidson 1984: 219), or the relation between a word and an object in the one and only admissible model of the world (cf. Putnam 1981: 48). In other words, reference is no direct road to ontology. Those observational and theoretical sentences that anthropologists may choose for their descriptions of worlds are not direct lines to truth, they are invocations of it, arabesques upon it, or extensions from it; as such their truth warrantability rests upon a degree of acceptability that has more to do with our experience of the world than with our words for it. 'Man proposes, the world disposes' (Quine 1992: 36). Anthropology makes its own propositions upon the world, which, again, disposes its scholars in a particular way. Reference is inscrutable, yet our theories still have to be based on evidence.

EVIDENCE

In so far as anthropology is concerned with *human* knowledge, this knowledge is positioned. Understanding is an event, implying a human agent or a mediation by a subject. This subject is *not* a disengaged rational subject, even if we have been led to believe that this is so. Meaning cannot be flattened into reference; there is nothing to 'discover' that is not simultaneously defined. The distinction between fact and definition has collapsed. This has two important consequences for our conception of 'evidence'. While it must still be asked for in any science, we have to realize, first, that pure observation can only lend negative evidence to our hypothetical statements, and, second, that evidence hinges on a relation of implication rather than reference. In turn, this implicational relationship presupposes a kind of holism that is not 'out there' but is part of the theoretical argument (cf. Quine 1992: 13ff.). Or, if it is permissible to extract one sentence from a long argument on epiricism, 'the unit of empirical significance is the whole of science' (Quine 1953: 42).

The simultaneity between discovery and definition has often been noted in anthropology, but the full implications of this have yet to be made out. If reality is in some way conventional, we have to discuss its nature in a new manner. A first step is to recognize how 'elements of what we call "language" or "mind" *penetrate so deeply into what we call "reality" that the very project of representing ourselves as being "mappers" of something "language-independent" is fatally compromised from the very start'* (Putnam 1990: 28, emphasis original).

In so far as anthropology is 'like' a language, and as its theories are but sentences, we have to acknowledge the reverse insight as well: experience is not the sole subject matter of language. Language contains its own automatisms, imposing its own appearances upon reality. The problem of 'fit' between language and experience takes on a new meaning in this light. Experience may provide the *evidence* for the (public?) acceptance of sentences as meaningful; but there is no presupposed correspondence or 'fit' between the words and the world of experience.

Philosophically, this leads to a rejection of the externalist perspective implied by metaphysical realism, seeking for (and claiming that there is) one true and complete theory of the world. Instead, we are drawn towards an internalist perspective (Putnam 1981: 49ff.). From this perspective, the question of 'what objects does the world consist of' only makes sense *within* a particular theory or description. This implies that there can be more than one true theory of the world, each drawing upon evidence defined within a particular holistic view.

A crucial problem remains of deciding rational grounds for adhering to one theory or the other, or for bounding one analytical space at the expense of another that may equally be said to incorporate the element in question. We generally appeal to evidence, but once this has been deemed relative to scheme, we are left with a severe problem of language. The contingency of language (and the inscrutability of reference) has made us stop thinking about it as a direct medium for reality, even if it is still a medium for interpretation. Thus, we need a theory of interpretation that makes no a priori assumptions about shared meanings, concepts or beliefs (Davidson 1984: 198), and which is able to incorporate the 'knower' as an experiencing subject. The knower asserts the truth of a particular point by means of a correlation between words and experiences, even if this correlation can never be perfect. There is always a possibility of error in one's *representation* of the experience, maybe even delusion, as we saw for the hunger-stricken shanty town dwellers in Brazil discussed in Chapter 6.

We attend to the world through experience, not through its representation in language, however. Anthropologists coming to the field with limited knowledge of the local language know this perfectly well; the force of first experiences and their powerful mark upon later reflections bear witness to the unmediated, non-linguistic nature of the cultural encounter.[1] Strangely enough, so far we have not taken this particular knowledge at face value, so to speak. In the process of transmutation from a first-person experience (event) of understanding to an objectified, impersonal mode of comprehension, the actual *experience* of understanding without words has been glossed over as irrelevant. The procedural rationality has required a degree of disengagement that has violated the nature of human understanding in the name of objectivity and intellectual control.

There is still a question of truth, however, in the sense that there are more or less acceptable theories, more or less adequate 'wholes' to evidence. In a post-objectivist scheme, truth denotes a kind of rational acceptability in a (scholarly) community of potential dissenters, which again is based upon a degree of coherence with experience. A theory of radical interpretation, of which I see anthropology as an example, must fulfil two demands: '[F]irst, it must specify the kinds of empirical evidence that a successful meaning theory may be required to account for. In this context, "empirical evidence" includes *any contingent propositions that the radical interpreter may legitimately appeal to to warrant his interpretation*' (Fodor and Lepore 1992: 71, emphasis original). The constraint must be substantive, and must entail that there are true propositions that are unavailable to the interpreter; otherwise 'there will be no content to the insistence that his epistimological situation is "radical" ' (ibid.). Second, since different ways of constraining or defining the evidence will lead to different theories, a theory of radical interpretation must justify the imposition of one set of evidential constraints in preference to others.

In so far as the loci of those experiential worlds that we purport to study are not minds but selves, the evidence for our theories is not to be found in reference, then, but in resonance.[2] It is by way of resonance that we begin to understand what life is 'like' elsewhere. This parallels the fact that empathy dominates the learning of language, both by child and field linguist (Quine 1992: 42). While observational propositions may serve as entries into the conversational community by the not-yet-speaker, fluency in communication exceeds far beyond even the most extensive dictionary; there is no meaning which is not also oriented in a social and moral space, in which motives and values are premissed.

It is the resonance between our 'own' and 'their' experiences that gives evidence to our imaginative understanding of 'other cultures'. Words (and pictures) have no intrinsic connection to what they purport to represent; possessing a concept is not only to possess a word, but to have the ability to use sentences and images appropriately (Putnam 1981: 19). Achieving this ability is what fieldwork amounts to. It is not a matter of being able to properly translate the odd word in use elsewhere, but to be able to sense its experiential implications and put it to use in the interpretative context. We note in passing how the idea of cultural translation is (also) incompatible with the notion of radical interpretation.

Thus, 'the option for an epistemology which privileges disengagement and control isn't self-evidently right', to put it in the mild terms of Charles Taylor (1989: 164). Only engaged exploration of resonated evidence takes us further towards a true knowledge of what it means to be human, that is, towards a more pregnant event of anthropological understanding. By approaching 'evidence' in this fashion, we begin to comprehend cultures, not as schemata or fixed semantic spaces, but as plot-spaces, inhabited by real persons, making choices of relevant actions and words, and within which meaning cannot be separated from motive. Briefly: speaker's meaning must be substituted for sentence meaning (Putnam 1990: 298).

Without an idea of the 'plot' we cannot make a coherent story out of the multiple incidents we witness, to invoke a concept proposed by Ricoeur (1991: 21). The concept of emplotment is useful in relation to ethnographies; emplotments are what make it possible to compose a story, or an ethnography, in which one draws a configuration out of a succession. In the composition of ethnographies, from which we still require a kind of fit with reality, evidence is established imaginatively by way of a particular kind of inference. It is an inference based on what Donald Davidson has named 'the principle of charity'.[3] This implies a double strategy of maximizing agreement on the one hand, i.e. of assuming commensurability of thoughts and words – if at the risk of *not* making true sense of what the other is thinking or saying – and, on the other, of maximizing the degree of self-consistency we attribute to him, on pain of not understanding *him*.

The principle of charity is of pertinence to an anthropology that defines itself as a kind of radical interpretation, and whose practice is based in a performative paradox of being one with the others and making their world comprehensible in terms that transcend it. In the first capacity, we maximize internal consistency; we cannot intelligibly attribute any motive or attitude to an agent except within a framework of a theory of the world-view to which his beliefs and decisions are relative. Global confusion is impossible; if everything were out of place, there would be nothing to be confused about. In the second capacity, we maximize commensurability; we assume that other worlds may be accountable for in terms that bypass them. The principle of charity guides the definition of 'evidence' in anthropology, which by implication may supply us with new beliefs about the world.

According to Richard Rorty, there are three ways to add new beliefs to current ones: perception, inference and metaphor (Rorty 1991b: 12). All of them are relevant to anthropology. Perception changes our beliefs by intruding unprecedented experiences into our network of beliefs; inference changes our beliefs by forcing us to rethink them in view of the unfolding consequences of our previously held beliefs. Both of these modes of changing belief largely leave our language unchanged. By contrast, 'metaphor as a third source of beliefs, and thus a third motive for reweaving our networks of beliefs and desires, is to think of language, logical space, and the realm of possiblity as open-ended' (Rorty 1991b: 12). It therefore suggests that cognition is not always recognition, and makes us reject the idea that the aim of thought is the attainment of the God's Eye view. Meaning is not a result of position but of intention.[4] Science is not about clarification but about imaginative extension of reality by way of a metaphorical scholarly language.

RELATIVISM

What will be clear now is that in spite of all the rightful (sometimes righteous) criticisms levelled against realism, scholars are still committed to some notion of truth, or more modestly 'of being right' (cf. Putnam 1990: 40). Being right does not imply the old objectivist notion of correct representation of reality. It is, rather, a matter of assertion and hence of (public) acceptability. Truth is not a 'property' at all, as the theory of direct reference would have it. It is a matter of convention, or, if you wish, of conceptual relativity. This is where the divergence of metaphysical and internal realism manifests itself most clearly; while the metaphysical realist cannot recognize the phenomenon of conceptual relativity, the internal realist judges right and wrong by the standards appropriate to the scheme itself (Putnam 1990: 96–97).

Truth, then, is not absolute correspondence to reality; it can be no intrinsic property of particular images or interpretations of the world. In the view I am advocating here, truth is not substantive. It is 'adjectival'. To paraphrase Putnam, to be true is to be warrantable on the basis of experience and intelligence (Putnam 1990: 41). Giving up Realism, with a capital R, is not to abandon the quest for true knowledge about the world. Truth may be relative to embodied understanding, but this does not entail a radical relativism, as some scholars, including some anthropologists, seem to think. In the words used earlier, the manifest conceptual relativism in the world is no argument for an ontological Relativism (with a capital R). The performative paradox inherent in anthropology straddles the gap between the conceptually relative and the ontologically real.

Relativism, therefore, is no self-evident conclusion to the anthropological search for understanding the real worlds of other people. Yet its insistent adhesion to the image of the profession (not least in the field of philosophy) makes it pertinent to discuss its implications a bit further. As demonstrated by Putnam (1981: 119ff.), Relativists cannot make sense of the distinction between 'being right' and 'thinking one is right'. Since there is no possibility of seeing the world from Nowhere, and because Relativists can have no objective criterion of rightness, they land in a logically inconsistent position: if reality is relative, the Relativist position must in itself be relative. The principle of Relativism clearly is self-refuting. 'Relativism, just as much as Realism, assumes that one can stand within one's language and outside it at the same time' (Putnam 1990: 23). This inconsistency undermines both R's and any other correspondence theory of the world.

It is tempting to fall back into a constitutive theory of the world and, with self-congratulation, declare that 'we make the world'. Of course, we do not. Even if cultures are always to some extent written, people live real lives, as I have argued before in this work. Although it can be maintained that fiction is an irreducible dimension of self-understanding by its providing imaginative variations of the self (Ricoeur 1991), we do live facts. The world is no imaginary product; our experience is evidence to the contrary. The world enthuses and hurts.

Relativism in the extreme (ontological) sense violates the nature of human understanding as much as Realism does since it requires belief that we can actually understand culture from 'native's point of view', unmediated by our own sensations and categories. Methodologically, we must suspend judgement and initially privilege the local communicative space, seeking to present it in a way that does not violate local perception, but there are limits to our becoming at one with (any) 'other'. Somewhat paradoxically, the Relativist point of view, claiming to reflect the natives', is strangely and most often unknowingly positivist (cf. Putnam 1990: 106). Conversely, a completely consistent positivist must end up a total relativist (ibid.: 116). The claim to represent accurately another space from somebody else's point of view makes Relativism but another version of Realism, in the sense that both are based on the premiss that the object of enquiry has a context *of its own*. In Realism, the context is an absolute and permanently fixed real world; in Relativism, it is a 'context which is privileged by being the object's rather than the inquirer's' (Rorty 1991a: 96). Even if privileged in the name of anti-ethnocentrism, this context is no less unrealistic than the God's Eye perspective of Realism, and it fails to recognize that the criteria of theoretical acceptability or reasonableness are neither given by God nor by the natives. They are posed in a scholarly community of possible dissenters and depend on a degree of fit with experience. The world cannot be made up in theory.

My contention is that there is no conflict between a cultural relativism and a search for a more general truth, be it named objectivist, rationalist, universalist or whatever has been used to disclaim the relativist view – more often than not presented as a caricature of the anthropological enterprise. These polemic polarities are reflections of Realist concerns that have lost interest. After years of intensive debates with philosophy,[5] anthropology has finally realized that its scope is not to solve a western philosophical dilemma, but to pursue its own knowledge interests that have to do with an understanding of the theories and practices of other cultures rather than a defending of a particular kind of preestablished western rationality.

REASONABLENESS

It is within the knowledge interests of anthropology to contribute to new canons of reasonableness in a world that is becoming increasingly marred by the consequences of procedural rationality. Reasonableness is based in a view of a rational acceptability, which incorporates evaluation and feeling in the empirical world we study and attribute with sense.

The recognition of the empirical equivalence of alternative reference schemes and the coexistence of different epistemologies may have led to a dislocation of the notion of reference, but certainly not of reality. Further, even if human nature is not surveyable from nowhere in particular – which undermines old notions of the anthropological object – this does not leave us with no world to study. If these were the conclusions, we would still not have gone beyond the notion of interpretation as correlation with objects in themselves. This is not the only notion of interpretation available to us, however. We can still seek to correlate discourse with discourse, or construct a meaningful comment on one discourse in another (Putnam 1990: 122). With the notion of radical interpretation this possibility is taken to its conclusion, far beyond old notions of justification. With the notion of interpretative charity in mind it would be utterly inconsistent to restrict our practice of interpretation to an abstract epistemological principle of correspondence, or object-intrinsic evidence.

The justification of any interpretative scheme is that it renders the behaviour of others at least minimally reasonable by our lights (Putnam 1981: 119). Reasonableness in this sense is a public criterion for the rightness of a particular interpretation, or of a particular theory of truth. This presupposes a degree of commensurability that relativism would denigrate; realities cannot be absolutely incommensurable. Indeed, the doctrine of incommensurability is as self-refuting as other versions of Relativism. Comparison presupposes *some* compatibility. Thus, there is no intelligible way of relativizing reality that justifies a concept of ontological relativity (Davidson 1984: 238). The world that anthropologists study is comprehensible in a particular language of theoretical knowledge that applies globally, if neither absolutely nor eternally. Knowledge, including anthropological knowledge, is not a story with no constraints except internal coherence. There are requirements of coherence and fit, amounting to a canon of reasonableness and of situated objectivity, even if rational acceptability is both tensed and relative to person.

To summarize, there is a profound need to get beyond Cartesian epistemology, which called for a complete disengagement from the world, and for the assumption of an instrumental stance towards it. One of the profound consequences of this epistemology was a kind of rationality that could not be defined substantially, but which had to be defined procedurally, in terms of standards by which we constructed orders of science and life (Taylor 1989: 156). It is this procedural rationality more than anything else that we have to evince from anthropology where it has reigned supreme for a century, since Durkheim's disengaged and 'objective' stance towards society. Like other scholars in his time, he positioned himself outside his object of study, by bounding it in the first place. An enormous achievement at one level, the separation from psychology in other ways proved a drawback – to anthropology as well as psychology, that is. The separation of the personal from the social was counterproductive as far as lasting theories of people's attention to the world was concerned. A similar outside standpoint is part and parcel of most semantic anthropology to this day. But, as there is no disengaged standpoint of knowing, the former hero of science, who gained control through disengagement, has to be replaced by a scholar who achieves understanding by way of involvement.

In the process, we are bound to question the old cultural institution of western science, namely that there is an absolute distinction between a 'statement of fact' and a 'value judgement' (Putnam 1981: 126–127). Without values we would have no facts, not even a world. We would also have no science:

Bereft of the old realist idea of truth as 'correspondence' and of the positivist idea of justification as fixed by public 'criteria,' we are left with the necessity of seeing our search for better conceptions of rationality as an intentional activity which, like evey activity that rises above the mere following of inclination or obsession, is guided by our idea of the good.

(Putnam 1990: 139)

Whatever criteria of relevance we might establish, they are imbued with value. Values are collective, just like meanings are, because values are integral parts of meanings and hence must be shared.

The anthropological search for real knowledge about the world must be guided by a standard of scholarly reasonableness, of which truth is the idealization. If scholarship holds anything important, it must strive to be faithful to something – just like local cultural modes of acting. This something is not an independent object with a fixed degree and manner of evidence, but rather a largely inarticulate sense of what is of decisive importance (Taylor 1985a: 38). And as we saw for 'culture' so also for theory: the articulation of the 'object' tends to change it.

Cross-cultural understanding, or sameness of meaning, is the reasonableness of ignoring local differences in scheme. Anthropology advances in a permanent internal debate on such questions, and this debate mimes the fact that anthropology is not about establishing yet another regime of truth in a Foucauldian sense, which would presuppose the view that all epistemic orders are equally possible. To repeat the words of Charles Taylor, the

point of view from which we might constate that all orders are equally arbitrary, in particular that all moral views are equally so, is just not available to us humans. It is a form of self-delusion to think that we do not speak from a moral orientation which we take to be right.

(Taylor 1989: 99)

This orientation forms an integral part of our motivation – to practise culture as well as anthropology.

THE HARDNESS OF FACTS

Implicitly I have advocated a view of social science which derives as much from romanticism as from Enlightenment notions of rationality. From this point of view, I shall now briefly discuss the relative 'hardness of facts'.[6] From what I have said before it follows that relative 'hardness' is not located in the facts themselves, but in the community that agrees upon it, that is, the community governing the politics of explanation.

In this community some theories have been accredited with more 'power' of explanation than others. Bruno Latour has made a scale ranging from the most powerful, deductive models to the least powerful, descriptive models (Latour 1988). The natural sciences largely belong to the first kind, history and ethnography to the second. This is related to the kind of facts they analyse; natural facts seem so solid that we may generalize them beyond history. By contrast, historical coincidences appear so soft that they are hardly generalizable at all. In this sense, the subjective experience as part of ethnography is hardly a scientific datum at all. This is a *trompe-l'oeil*, however, owing to our own beliefs about the world. The degree of certainty about facts, or of centrality to our belief system, is not correlated with different relations to reality (Rorty 1991a: 52).

It is with science as with reality in general; science cannot escape the conditions of an essential reflexivity, as we have seen in previous chapters. This reflexivity also implies that the hardness of facts is an expression of social agreement rather than a quality of the facts themselves. As Rorty has it: 'The hardness of fact . . . is simply the hardness of the previous agreements within a community about the consequences of a certain event' (Rorty 1991a: 80). Thus, facts may be 'hardened' in the process of (scholarly) exchange (cf. Latour 1987: 211). There is hope, then, for the social sciences.

We can discuss the implications of this by comparing some well-known phenomena. It is one of the hard facts of contemporary human life that people in vast areas suffer from recurrent famine. It is also part of the anthropological legacy that hunger and other symptoms of suffering and disorder have been externalized from the dominant discourse, which has been based on assumptions of an essential social order and stability, while disorder is temporary (cf. Davis 1992b). Hunger has been left to medical and other hard sciences such as economics; the 'softer' consequences have been neglected.

From our present perspective the relative 'hardness' of hunger must be questioned. There is uncontestably general agreement about the sad consequences of famine; the disaster is immediately visible in the thin limbs, the grey skin and the lifeless eyes of the starving. The slow death is immediately imaginable. Hunger qualifies as a hard fact, but only in a world that no longer has any subjective experience of the degree of individual pain, social disruption and emotional catastrophe that famine entails.

Another example is 'evil'. Why does evil seem less 'hard'. As recently testified to by a volume entitled *The Anthropology of Evil*, it is a slippery category, talk about which 'ranges over the terrible and serious as well as the playful and creative' (Parkin 1985: 1). What is evil and what is not is open to a wide range of interpretation. Again, we can see how the relative hardness is owed to the degree of agreement in a wider social context, within which the nature of reality is premissed.

In between the hardness of hunger and the softness of evil, we find such a category as 'violence'. Covering a vast range of phenonema, and certainly open to definition, it nevertheless seems possible to agree upon its two-dimensionality: it has both an instrumental and an expressive function (Riches 1986: 25). It is less certain that we will agree that the instrumental (physical) function is the more important, however. As Parkin argues, there is a wide gap between violence as physical destruction and violence as metaphysical desecration (Parkin 1986: 205). We still recognize it as violence, however.

Hunger, violence and evil are, all of them, brutal facts of social life. Their brutality is non-linguistic, however, and there is no way of transferring non-linguistic brutality to 'facts', or to the truth of sentences (Rorty 1991a: 81). That is why it is difficult to reach a new agreement on relative hardness, because such agreement is established within a scientific frame of reference that has already marked its own areas of hard and soft concerns.

Once we acknowledge that the hardness of facts is not inherent in the facts themselves but a quality attributed to them by a particular social community, we may also realize the fundamental equality of sciences. All sciences are equal with respect to the reality of the facts they deal with, just as all cultures have equally good reasons for promoting their own view of the world. Only it seems that in some domains of reality it is easier to reach an agreement on the desired goals. This is where prediction and control may reign. In anthropology, the quest for predicting the world has been replaced by the wish to enlarge it by widening the range of possible definitions; the future is implicated in our contribution to the ethnographic present.

When dealing with famine, the anthropology of violence and evil must stand on its own feet. While there is no way of borrowing authority from 'harder' sciences, anthropology should not accept scientific disqualification by its being soft, either. Anthropology itself must aim at producing hard facts, i.e., facts about which it is possible to achieve agreement; that is what objectivity is all about, as stated before. 'The idea of truth as correspondence to reality might gradually be replaced by the idea of truth as what comes to be believed in the course of free and open encounters' (Rorty 1989: 68).

Truth is in one sense beyond language, however. The very literality of words makes language only partially suitable for the purpose of trading truth. Language introduces its own appearances upon a reality that by itself is non-linguistic, as we have discussed before. In a non-Platonist view of science, language and mind do not relate to reality as scheme to content (Davidson 1984: 183ff.). Rather, it is like the measuring rod to the measured, as will be recalled. This is actually the main reason why we must abandon both the correspondence and the constitutive theory of the world, of which scholars are of necessity part but not creators.

THE FORCE OF ARGUMENT

Above, I made the case that hardness of certain facts could be argued for, implying that an important part of scholarly practice consisted in arguments over relative hardness, in pursuit of at least a temporary agreement about truth. Generally, I would contend that what there is no argument for, there is no reason to believe. Argument, therefore, is vital to the publicizing of scientific results. And the force of the argument is instrumental to its acceptability.

The focus on experience, and by implication on agency, also leads to another point of profound epistemological impact upon anthropology, namely the reinstalment of responsibility (Johnson 1987: 15; Taylor 1985a). In the current mode of anthropology people do not merely *react* to external events, they *respond*. In contrast to reaction, response involves an awareness of oneself as a centre capable of action. The more experience comes to the fore as the locus of apprehension, the more we realize that all people are in some greater or smaller way responsible for what happens to them. The interaction between people or between people and the environment is always somehow forceful. This is part of our embodied experience.

The agent experiences as a whole person, a subjective self. This is ultimately what makes us abandon the old dualism of objective and subjective knowledge, between scheme and world. We do not give up the world of course, rather we 're-establish unmediated touch with the familiar objects whose antics make our sentences and opinions true or false' (Davidson 1984: 198).

Actually the most radical consequence is that we give up the idea of the 'punctual self' – that is, the extensionless being who is nowhere but in his or her power to objectify and remake the world (Taylor 1989: 171–172). This gives way to the experiencing, embodied self in direct touch with reality and able to make true judgements of both facts and values. This 'being in touch with reality' is all the realism we need, in anthropology too (cf. Johnson 1987: 302).

The positive qualification of the anthropological project possibly implies that the human sciences *should* look different from the natural sciences, because they have a different concept of purpose. To the extent that natural scientists are interested primarily in predicting and controlling the behaviour of things, prediction and control may not be what we want from the social sciences (Rorty 1991a: 40). In the (pragmatic) view of social science, 'the image of the great scientist would not be of somebody who got it right but of somebody who made it new' (Rorty 1991a: 44).

If, by force of argument, we can convince the world that most of what we respond to in the world (and what we speak about in anthropology), is placed ontologically not in things themselves but in our experience of it, we may open new doors of perception. To the extent that properties are 'subject-referring', they are no more fixed than the subject herself. As such they are part of the anthropological force field, in whose power it is to demonstrate that there is a difference between what is physically impossible and what is only epistemically impossible in a global perspective. After all, reality is what resists the trials of time and argument.

The anthropologists' competence in different worlds privileges their knowing and compels them to speak up about the actual nature of self-description and about those processes that reproduce or transform them. This is a theoretical project with wide claims to solidarity, by now part and parcel of objectivity in anthropology – in quest of the real world.

Epilogue
Returning Home

With realism regained, we have completed our pilgrimage, and
time has come to recuperate what has been achieved. The excursions were determined yet they brought no solutions, and provided no securities. They posited demands and gave only flashes
of the promised land – which is still to conquer by individual
anthropologists' own efforts and to understand by their own
lights.

One of the ambitions of my invitation to touring was to show
that common sense and critical intelligence have to be brought
to anthropology; they cannot simply be purchased from it – if I
may once again echo Hilary Putnam on science in general (1990:
162). In other words, anthropology provides no fixed set of prov-
erbial understandings, no immediate tool kit for repairing the
world. What we inherit is a field, not authority, and my aim has
been to ground this field in a wider epistemological space. As
practising anthropologists confronted with a world in flux, we
may collectively aspire not only to temporary flashes of insight
but also to more solid theories of fluctuation itself. The explicit
process of enculturation to which professional anthropologists are
exposed in the field is a cornerstone in the scientific comprehension of processes of incorporation and creativity in the world.
With this in mind we may return home and reestablish our scholarly credentials on a new basis.

Returning home means returning to the theoretical project of
anthropology that has been fading from view during the past
decade due to qualms that were at one and the same time epistemological and ethical. As will have become clear in the course
of my argument, I believe that these two issues cannot be separated at all. The task, therefore, is to incorporate both in a new

kind of theory-building based on radical interpretation and charity – or, more profoundly, on objectivity and solidarity. A balance between them has to be maintained; objectivity without solidarity is prone to dehumanizing the field, while solidarity without objectivity risks posing cultures and individual actions as beyond correction.

Thus, the theoretical project of anthropology is reducible neither to behaviourism nor to ventriloquism. We cannot just map behavioural units in linear sequences, nor should we simply give voice to other people by way of our own lips. By involving ourselves in the field our task is to identify connections that are not linear, and which may not be spoken at all. Such connections are real, yet they are also theoretical in that they are constructed in theories that are but sentences, internally linked by logic, proposing particular interpretations of the world. Theories are ways of making the constitutive self-understandings explicit, of articulating motivations, of recontextualizing the world of experience; articulation is different from clarification in that it is also always definition. In that sense, anthropological theory is about raising awareness, of explicating the inexplicable, of plotting successive impressions in a story form that exposes the simultaneities of culture in a context that incorporates the practice of theorizing itself.

Theories may be either designative or expressive (Taylor 1985a: 218ff.). The former are relatively straightforward in their pointing out certain qualities of the object; with such theories, the object tends to be naturalized and meaning to be unmysterious. Such were the correspondence theories that we have now largely left behind. The problem is that with them we have left behind also part of the popular appeal of direct designation – and latent behaviourism as far as the human sciences are concerned. A more rewarding path is opening for us to explore, however, namely, the path cleared by the development of expressive theories making the world manifest in embodying it. As an expression in this sense, anthropological theory may be partly enigmatic, and may often present only a fragment of the reality it embodies. Yet, the point is that what is expressed is made manifest only by this expression. However imperfect, expressions cannot be replaced by other kinds of presentation. As expressive theory, anthropology maintains some of the mystery surrounding language as a field of indeterminacy. Expressive meaning is subject-related because it makes something manifest for someone. As we have said before, there is no knowledge independent of a knower.

Designative theories point to, and propose; expressive theories make manifest, and realize. No doubt our general cultural strategies for coping with the world include both dimensions, just like our ways of using language are both propositional and evocative. For anthropology to exploit its own full potential, it will have to cultivate the expressive dimension of its theorizing, thereby opening up a new dimension of understanding and articulating a new awareness that not only brings new abilities to describe but also facilitates new ways of responding.

Like art, anthropology was once conceived in terms of mimesis; both imitated the real – by way of designation. The Romantics – of past intellectual history and present-day anthropology – have a different conception of their artistry. In the words of Charles Taylor, 'the artist strives to imitate not nature, but the author of nature' (Taylor 1985b: 229). I contend that this applies to the scientist as well; there is no mirroring but an attempt to understand how the world is disposed in the first place.

Thus, anthropological theory must strive to realize the world in its own terms, and we are back to metaphor as a domain of language use, highlighting the fact that language is virtually inexhaustible. There is a surplus of meaning in the chaotic parts of language, just like there is a surplus significance in any event, and a surplus historicity in any moment. The 'surplus' is the potential, the not yet, or not ever, manifest: the possible. Physical possibilities are one thing, epistemic possibilities another. Anthropology may influence the latter by showing, first, how certain things are or are not possible *given the current knowledge conditions*, and second, by extending the knowledge conditions by articulating theories that realize the world in unprecedented ways. Like metaphorical reasoning in general, anthropology makes it possible to learn from experience (cf. Johnson 1993: 3).

Anthropological theory is not only subject-referring, it is also in an important sense 'social'; as such it is a particular kind of practice. It is theorizing in a context of which the practitioners are irrevocably part.[1] There is no illusion of distance between anthropology and the world of study. Anthropological theories are articulations, and as such they may influence, confirm, or alter the constitutive self-description of particular people. In that sense, theories do not only make the constitutive self-descriptions explicit, they also extend, criticize and even challenge them. This makes social theory radically different from natural science, and poses distinct problems of validation.

The alteration of awareness that anthropological theory may bring about also changes the object, which is partly constituted by self-understanding. Evidently, there are a number of features in the world that – like the object of natural science – can be described independently of people's self-interpretation; but in so far as we conceive of the anthropological object as *human* life (at whatever scale), self-interpretation is part of it. One yardstick of validity is, therefore, the measure of change that can be agreed upon as a change – not only for the better – but for the common good. Scholarship is profoundly moral, and it is time to acknowledge this fact.

Theories are public and open for inspection and dissent, and the degree to which anthropological theories are valid to a large extent hinges upon the extent to which they can be shared. As we have discussed before, they must have some coherence with experience to be rationally acceptable. The sharing of significance is related to the sharing of experience; this is the basis for learning from the cross-cultural encounter.

There are other measures to theoretical adequacy, however, even when questions of reference (and ontology) have been defused. Theory, as an expressive practice, is not only about realizing something but also about making inactive the false implications of particular statements. Illusions have to be broken, presupposing that we have standards – if not for right and wrong then at least for better or worse interpretations.

Theories are not synonymous with the world, yet there are limits to licence. No interpretation is wholly subjective, because meaning must in some ways be shared for it to be meaning at all. There are limits to which questions make sense in a community of conversational partners. If theory posits reality, this still has to 'resist' the trial of intersubjectivity and intertextuality. Theories (and we might wish to recall that they are but sentences) may be logically incompatible, yet still empirically equivalent, meaning that they may sum up experiences in equally acceptable ways.[2] In this case, the incompatibility is one of vocabulary rather than reality, and is related to the construction of evidence. 'Incompatibility', therefore, may be translated into complementarity and read as a result of scholarly freedom to propose. Allegedly irresolvable rivalries between theories about human life stem from a failure to acknowledge the nature of theory as subject-referring and social. This has to be sorted out before one can adequately compare theoretical propositions and correct, refute or hierarchize them – showing that a particular theory can in fact be seen as just a singular case of a more general theory.

Because theory is not about reference but about interpretation, the research process is as important as the results; in fact, there is no way of distinguishing absolutely between them. The process is part of the result; the field of study is an experiential space. Most of what we see as significant data in anthropology are ontologically not in the things themselves but in our experience of them. So also for the social spaces that bound our studies. Therefore, or in that sense, anthropology is more about competence and doing than about facticity and knowing. This is a feature of 'becoming' in the field, as well as presenting it in a discursive mode afterwards. Competence makes the present accessible for intervention, which nostalgia brakes.

When the itinerary was set out at the beginning of this tour, the imperialist nostalgia within anthropology was mentioned as one of the reasons for our seeking new directions. It was seen as related to an apocalyptic imagery of a world on the wane. The interconnectedness of these two feelings has not been cast in doubt. On the contrary, during our tour, we have constantly reaffirmed the profound continuity between anthropology and the world. The above brief discussion of the theorizing practice of anthropology adds a new dimension to this, which may rearticulate the continuity in positive terms. We may mourn the lost world, but our theoretical interest must be to potentiate the ethnographic present. Realizing that each moment has a surplus historicity, a statement that is the result of anthropological theorizing, means that articulation is simultaneously such potentiation.

The imperialist nostalgia, and the accompanying sentimental pessimism on anthropology's behalf, can now be seen for what it is: an *in*ability to mourn.[3] The regressive melancholy of an anthropology lost in its own reminiscences of a long-dead love-object turns towards itself as apocalyptic imagery. The world is falling apart, and anthropology along with it. The lost object continues to be an object of investment, and the loss keeps informing the regressive sentiment. By way of contrast, proper mourning implies a reworking of lost material, a recognition of the past as *past*, and a gradual return to an unending present as the target of emotional and theoretical investment. The lost object is not obliterated but it is reinstalled as something no longer obtainable, and in the process it gives way to new objects of investment. What I am saying is that the mourning of the loss of the particular world that inspired our forebears to sire anthropology is not the end of theoretical desire; there is still a world to comprehend.

With anthropology this world is comprehended from a position of eccentricity. The conscious choice of a scholarly perspective beyond the western centre makes room for an attitude of non-ethnocentricity. This may seem somewhat paradoxical for a science like anthropology, which is identified as a kind of radical interpretation. Is not interpretation unavoidably committed to ethnocentricity?[4] While any interpretation is, of course, vulnerable and open to criticism, it is not, however, particularly prone to ethnocentricity. This would be the case of any Realist or Relativist theory, as discussed in Chapter 9. The former would appeal to a neutral scientific language, while the latter would objectify any local language. Both positions are untenable and essentially self-refuting, as we have seen.

The error in assuming that radical interpretation by definition is ethnocentric is to think that the language of our cross-cultural cultural therories has to be either theirs or ours.

> If this were so, then any attempt at understanding across cultures would be faced with an impossible dilemma: either accept incorrigibility, or be arrogantly ethnocentric. But as a matter of fact, while challenging their language of self-understanding, we may also be challenging ours.
>
> (Taylor 1985b: 125).

In other words, the theoretical language of anthropology is a language of perspicuous contrast, which is neither theirs nor ours, but a separate language in which we can formulate both their and our lifeways as alternative possibilities.

With this view of the anthropological language we do not indulge in a mindless anti-ethnocentricism in which judgement is precluded.[5] The formulation of alternatives presupposes a common scale against which they can be compared. The language of contrast may show either their or our language to be distorted or illusionary in some respects, by some scale that we can agree to formulate. The strength of the anthropological language lies in its being able to construct such a scale on the basis of an explicit fusion of horizons, while also avoiding the pitfalls of the 'incorrigibility' thesis, requiring that we explain each society in its own terms, and thus ruling out an account that shows them to be wrong, confused or deluded (Taylor 1985b: 123). There are corrections or supplementary understandings to be made everywhere, and judgements to pass; self-understandings are not incorrigible. What we should evince from anthropological theorizing is the 'rationalist theory of rationality', namely 'the idea that you are being irrational, and probably viciously ethnocentric, whenever you cannot appeal to neutral criteria' (Rorty 1991a: 208).

While anthropological theory, like any other social theory, extends and challenges self-understanding, it avoids criticizing it on irrelevant grounds because it never just bypasses self-understanding. Theorizing in anthropology is not solely about understanding the others, because the language of contrast presupposes that we understand ourselves as well – from the same critical perspective. The theoretical language of anthropology thus brings the manifest reality of the contact zone to discursive effect. Articulating the anthropological insight in a language of contrast means understanding human practices in relation to each other. This is the only passable route between the Objectivist refutation of real differences on the one hand, and the Relativist view of absolute incommensurability on the other. Understanding is an event of juxtaposition. Radical interpretation thus brings about the opposite of ethnocentrism.

The performative paradox of anthropological practice, dealt with at the beginning of our tour, in theory transforms into what I have called the performative parallax. The parallactic power is related to the eccentricity of anthropological theory that explicitly challenges western self-understanding, including Enlightenment notions of rationality and reason, and brings it into a zone of performative indeterminacy, from where new kinds of action may sprout. Just like a poem may have a surplus meaning, reflecting the indeterminacy of words, so ethnography may have a surplus significance, reflecting the surplus historicity in any moment. Social change may result from the creative imagination that emerges in the language of contrast. From the chaos of the contact zone, anthropology alchemizes a general theory that expands on the world.

With the notion of the performative parallax we are led back to the idea of anthropology being in a prophetic condition, expanding the horizon by way of an expansion of a language of contrast. This potential is owed to the implicitly metaphorical nature of ethnographic reasoning. As will be recalled, metaphors are literal; their efficiency is owed to the way particular words are *used* rather than to what they might mean. From the position of the radical other, the anthropologist may create a field of argumentative force, if not of empowering knowledge.

The notion of force field explodes the narrowness inherent in the disciplinary field. The passage to anthropology has been made when it is realized that it is not principally an exclusive territory of knowledge but a particular way to the world.

Notes

PROLOGUE

1 Quoted from the Penguin edition (Forster 1974: 317).
2 My use of the notion of performative contradiction is inspired by Johannes Fabian (1991: 197).
3 For an extensive discussion of the moral ambiguity of the present I refer to John Casey (1990).
4 For an elaboration of the distinction between map and itinerary I refer to Michel de Certeau (1984: 118ff.).

1 THE ETHNOGRAPHIC PRESENT: ON STARTING IN TIME

1 Part of the following argument on the ethnographic present has been published previously in Hastrup (1990c).
2 Fieldwork in Iceland was carried out over a total of 13 months in 1982–83, and for shorter dispersed periods since then. It was supported by the Danish Research Council for the Humanities and by the Icelandic Ministry of Education.
3 We shall discuss 'realism' in more depth in chapter 9; here I shall just stress the importance of distinguishing between realism as a genre and realism as an epistemological imperative. The former may be criticized without necessarily affecting the latter.
4 The ideas on ritual expounded here are owed to Edwin Ardener (1993).
5 This loss has been dealt with by Dan Sperber (1985: 6).
6 I cannot pursue these points here, but have to refer to James Clifford (1985) for an important discussion of heteroglossia in anthropology, and to Shirley Ardener (1975) for a discussion of mutedness.
7 The notion of betweenness – as applied to fieldwork – is owed to Dennis Tedlock (1983: 323).

2 THE LANGUAGE PARADOX: ON THE LIMITS OF WORDS

1 In 1975, Geertz wrote: 'The culture of a people is an ensemble of texts, themselves ensembles, which the anthropologist strains to read over the shoulders of those to whom they properly belong' (Geertz 1973: 452). At the time, 'reading' was used metaphorically, while here I use it literally. The point is, however, that the easiness by which the metaphor was taken to heart, and by which, indeed, 'text' was used as a sign of 'culture', points to the priority given to the literary over the oral in the West. It is this priority that now also seems to make anthropologists jump to 'native texts' as privileged clues to culture.

2 My discussion of 'classical' vs. 'new' theories of language is based on Lakoff (1987), to whom I shall refer on a number of specific points. While much of his and his associates' work has been influenced by anthropological studies of classification (colour categories are a notable example), it by no means exhausts the anthropological implications. Quite the contrary, because linguistics has now developed along its own path from the anthropological stimulus (among other things) the pendulum may swing back and linguistics may provide a renewed source for anthropological thought.

3 I certainly do not want to belittle the significance of an anthropological analysis of a textual corpus, as is frequently done in historical anthropology, also by myself (Hastrup 1985a, 1990a). Nor am I criticizing academic disciplines that are not experientially based. I am just arguing that literary or textual analysis is based on a different premist than fieldwork, which may, therefore, potentially yield a different kind of insight. The *process* towards the understanding of other cultures cannot be separated from understanding itself.

4 My discussion of etymology was originally inspired by a paper given by John Davis at the Institute of Social Anthropology, University of Oxford, in May 1991, on 'Words and Institutions'. I wish to thank him for allowing me to listen to his thoughts on work in progress, even if our views on etymology deviate.

5 The translation goes: 'Whoever wishes to write today the etymology of a word must not be content to note the disappearance of a meaning or the addition of a new meaning. He must also ask himself which is the lucky rival, the heir to the meaning which has disappeared, or which is the word from which the term in question has taken a new meaning. The first condition for conducting this kind of research is an exact understanding of semantics and of the circumstances governing the life of words' (Wartburg 1946: 104; translation from Ullmann 1972: 241).

3 THE EMPIRICAL FOUNDATION: ON THE GROUNDING OF WORLDS

1 For a discussion of the relationship between philosophy and language I refer to Taylor's essay on 'Language and Human Nature' (1985a: 215–247).

2 The notion of 'remote area' as a theoretical construct is owed to Edwin Ardener (1987).

3 The distinction between 'fieldnotes' and 'headnotes' is owed to Simon Ottenberg (1990).

4 The insistence upon explanation as the aim of anthropology is not to distantiate it from hermeneutic understanding or 'mere' description, let alone interpretation. Rather it is to insist upon a mode of comprehension that is not coterminous with local conventions.

4 THE ANTHROPOLOGICAL IMAGINATION: ON THE MAKING OF SENSE

1 Part of my discussion of the anthropological imagination was originally given as a speech to the Association of Social Anthropologists Decennial Conference at Oxford, July 1993. I wish to thank Marilyn Strathern for inviting me to speak.

2 The tale is quoted from *The Complete Illustrated Stories of Hans Christian Andersen*, translated by H.W. Dulcken, first published in 1889, and published in a facsimile edition by Chancellor Press, London 1983 (and since).

3 The notion of 'scopic regime' is owed to Martin Jay (1993: 114ff.), to whose work I refer for a more elaborate assessment of its implications for the intellectual history of the West.

4 For a highly readable account of the sources of the self in European thought I refer to Charles Taylor (1989; see also 1985c). In anthropology, the recent book on 'self consciousness' by Anthony Cohen (1994) bridges the gap between the plurality of selves and the unity of society. Unfortunately, the book was published too late for me to be able to take its significant insights into account.

5 In chapter 9 we shall have a more substantial discussion of relativism.

5 THE MOTIVATED BODY: ON THE LOCUS OF AGENCY

1 Karen Blixen's autobiographical novel, *Out of Africa*, was first published in 1937. The quote here is from the Penguin edition (1954: 191).

2 By 'theatre anthropology' I refer to the theories and research conducted by ISTA, the International School of Theatre Anthropology, founded by director Eugenio Barba of Odin Teatret, in Denmark. For a presentation of this school I refer to Barba (1979, 1986), Exe Christoffersen (1989), Watson (1993) and Barba and Savarese (1991).

I take the opportunity to express my gratitude for having been given the opportunity to participate in several sessions of the ISTA, and thus to learn about the works of Odin Teatret and Eugenio Barba by way of my own experience, as well as from books.

3 Part of the argument of the present section on 'The absent body' is unfolded also in Hastrup (1994a), where it is explicitly developed in relation to the anthropological knowledge project.

4 The notions of assimilation and accommodation are used here in the sense suggested by Piaget (1962).

5 The notion of being 'decided' is owed to Niels Bohr, but has been further elaborated by Barba (1991).

6 THE INARTICULATE MIND: ON THE POINT OF AWARENESS

1 The lines quoted are from the poem 'Burnt Norton', the first of Eliot's *Four Quartets* (London 1944: Faber and Faber, p. 15).

2 Part of this chapter was given to the Association of Social Anthropologists Conference on 'Questions of Consciousness', held at the University of St Andrews, Scotland, March 1993. I want to thank the convenors, Anthony Cohen and Nigel Rapport, for creating a stimulating event. The present chapter has developed and parted company from the ASA paper, yet a proportion of the central argument remains the same.

3 I am in no position to evaluate the actual ethnography presented by Scheper-Hughes, but I remain impressed by her will to combine analysis with compassion, and see her work as a forerunner of badly needed anthropological works that explicitly seek to combine objectivity and solidarity.

4 I refer to Hastrup (1985a, 1990a, 1990b) for a substantiation of Icelandic history in anthropological terms. For a brief discussion of the relationship between history and anthropology I refer to Hastrup (1992d).

5 For an extended discussion on the interrelationship between social experience and anthropological knowledge, see Hastrup and Hervik (1994).

7 THE SYMBOLIC VIOLENCE: ON THE LOSS OF SELF

1 This chapter is a reframed and slightly edited version of an article previously published by *Cultural Anthropology* under the title of 'Out of Anthropology. The Anthropologist as an Object of Dramatic Representation' (Hastrup 1992c). It was originally written at University of California, Santa Cruz, in 1988, right after the event portrayed.

2 Odin Teatret is an internationally renowned group theatre established some 30 years ago. Its leader is Italian-born Eugenio Barba, who also directed *Talabot*, and the actors are from all over the world. Odin is Danish, therefore, only in the sense that it has its base in Denmark, which is where I met the group.

3 Afterwards, in reading about the anthropology of performance to better understand what had happened to me, I realized that this is exactly the process the actor goes through from rehearsal to actual performance (cf. Schechner 1982). Unknowingly, I had already formulated my own experience in those terms.

8 THE NATIVE VOICE: ON TAKING RESPONSIBILITY

1 The main bulk of this chapter has been published in two separate articles addressing closely connected issues, one in *Social Anthropology/Anthropologie sociale* (Hastrup 1993a), another in *Folk* (Hastrup 1993d).
2 I have answered Niels Einarsson directly and more explicitly in Hastrup (1990e).

9 THE REALIST QUEST: ON ASKING FOR EVIDENCE

1 For a particularly illustrative example of the first encounter in the field and the significance of non-linguistic learning I refer to Tamara Kohn (1994).
2 The notion of resonance has been explored by Unni Wikan (1992) with particular reference to the nature of the fieldwork. I am taking it a bit further here, and proposing it as an epistemological concept.
3 The notion of interpretive charity has been developed and discussed in many parts of Davidson's work. In connection with my brief description of its significance in the present paragraph I refer particulary to Davidson (1984: 27 and 1980: 221).
4 For an elaboration of this on philosophical grounds I refer to Hilary Putnam (e.g. 1981: 2, 29; 1990: 107)
5 The debate has been particularly conspicuous in the volumes edited by Wilson (1970), Hollis and Lukes (1982) and Overing (1985a).
6 For a fuller argument on this theme I refer to Hastrup (1993b).

EPILOGUE

1 My argument on theory in this paragraph is inspired by Charles Taylor's article on 'Social Theory as Practice', published in Taylor (1985b: 91–115).
2 I refer to Quine (1990: 95ff.) for some of the background inspiration for the discussion of theoretical equivalence.
3 The inspiration for some of the phrasing of this paragraph stems from Martin Jay's article on 'The Apocalyptic Imagination and the Inability to Mourn', published in Jay (1993: 84–98).
4 I refer to Charles Taylor's essay on 'Understanding and Ethnocentricity' for a fully fledged discussion of this (1985b: 116–133).
5 In his essay 'On Ethnocentrism: A Reply to Clifford Geertz', Richard Rorty has made a convincing case for an anti-anti-ethnocentrism, which does not land us in an ethnocentric position (1991a: 203–210).

References

Abrahams, Roger D. (1986) 'Ordinary and Extraordinary Experience', in Victor Turner and Edward Bruner (eds) *The Anthropology of Experience*, Urbana and Chicago: University of Illinois Press.

Abu-Lughod, Lila (1991) 'Writing Against Culture', in Richard G. Fox (ed.) *Recapturing Anthropology. Working in the Present*, Santa Fe: School of American Research Press/University of Washington Press.

Alpingisbækur Íslands (1912–82) 15 vols, Reykjavík: SögufélagiD.

Andersen, Hans Christian (1983 [1889]) *The Complete Illustrated Stories of Hans Christian Andersen*, trans. by H. W. Dulcken, London: Chancellor Press.

Appadurai, Arjun (1991) 'Global Ethnoscapes: Notes and Queries for a Transnational Anthropology', in Richard G. Fox (ed.) *Recapturing Anthropology. Working in the Present*, Santa Fe: School of American Research Press/University of Washington Press.

Ardener, Edwin (1971a) 'Introductory Essay', in E. Ardener (ed.) *Social Anthropology and Language*, London 1971: Tavistock (ASA Monographs 10).

— — (1971b) 'The Historicity of Historical Linguistics', in E. Ardener (ed.) *Social Anthropology and Language*, London 1971: Tavistock (ASA Monographs 10).

— — (1975) 'Language, Ethnicity and Population', in J. H. M. Beattie and R. G. Lienhardt (eds) *Studies in Social Anthropology*, Oxford: Clarendon.

— — (1982) 'Social Anthropology, Language and Reality', in David Parkin (ed.) *Semantic Anthropology*, London 1982: Academic Press (ASA Monographs 22)

— — (1985) 'Social Anthropology and the Decline of Modernism', in Joanna Overing (ed.) *Reason and Morality*, London 1985: Tavistock (ASA Monographs 24)

— — (1987) 'Remote Areas: Some Theoretical Considerations', in A. Jackson (ed.) *Anthropology at Home*, London 1987: Tavistock (ASA Monographs 25).

— — (1989a) *The Voice of Prophecy and Other Essays*, (ed.) by Malcolm Chapman, Oxford 1989: Blackwell.

—— (1989b) 'Comprehending Others', in E. Ardener, *The Voice of Prophecy and Other Essays*, ed. by Malcolm Chapman, Oxford 1989: Blackwell.

—— (1989c) 'The Construction of History: Vestiges of Creation', in Malcolm Chapman, Maryon McDonald and Elizabeth Tonkin (eds) *History and Ethnicity*, London: Routledge (ASA Monographs 29).

—— (1993) 'Ritual og socialt rum', *Tidsskriftet Antropologi*, no. 25: 23–28.

Ardener, Shirley (1975) 'Introduction', in Shirley Ardener (ed.) *Perceiving Women*, London: Malaby Press.

Artaud, Antonin (1958) *The Theatre and its Double*, New York: Grove Press.

Asad, Talal (1986) 'The Concept of Cultural Translation in British Social Anthropology', in James Clifford and George Marcus (eds) *Writing Culture. The Poetics and Politics of Ethnography*, Berkeley 1986: University of California Press.

Atkinson, Paul (1990) *The Ethnographic Imagination. Textual Constructions of Reality*, London: Routledge.

Barba, Eugenio (1979) *The Floating Islands*, Holstebro: Drama.

—— (1985) *The Dilated Body*, Rome: Zeami Libri.

—— (1986) *Beyond the Floating Islands*, New York: PAJ Publications.

—— (1991) 'Introduction', in Eugenio Barba and Nicola Savarese (eds) *The Secret Art of the Performer. A Dictionary of Theatre Anthropology*, London: Routledge.

Barba, Eugenio and Savarese, Nicola (eds) (1991) *The Secret Art of the Performer. A Dictionary of Theatre Anthropology*, London: Routledge.

Barnes, Barry and Bloor, David (1982) 'Relativism, Rationalism, and the Sociology of Knowledge', in Martin Hollis and Steven Lukes (eds) *Rationality and Relativism*, Oxford 1982: Blackwell.

Bateson, Gregory (1972) *Steps to an Ecology of Mind*, New York: Free Press.

Berger, Peter L. and Luckman, Thomas (1967) *The Social Construction of Reality*, New York: Anchor Books.

Bernstein, Richard J. (1983) *Beyond Objectivism and Relativism*, Oxford: Blackwell.

Bjarnadóttir, Kristín (1986) 'Drepsóttir á 15. öld', *Sagnir*, vol. 7: 57–64.

Björnsdóttir, Inga Dóra (1989) 'Public View and Private Voices', in E. Paul Durrenburger and Gísli Pálsson (eds) *The Anthropology of Iceland*, Iowa City: University of Iowa Press.

Blacking, John (ed.) (1977) *The Anthropology of the Body*, London: Tavistock (ASA Monographs 12).

Blixen, Karen (1954) *Out of Africa*, Harmondsworth: Penguin.

Bloch, Maurice (1977) 'The Past and the Present in the Present', *Man*, vol. 12: 278–92.

Boon, James A. (1982) *Other Tribes Other Scribes*, Cambridge: Cambridge University Press.

—— (1983) 'Functionalists Write Too: Frazer/Malinowski and the Semiotics of the Monograph', *Semiotica*, vol. 46: 131–149.

—— (1986) 'Between the Wars – Bali. Rereading the Relics', in George

Stocking (ed.) *Malinowski, Rivers, Benedict and Others. Essays on Culture and Personality*, Madison: Univeristy of Wisconsin Press.

Bourdieu, Pierre (1977) *Towards a Theory of Practice*, Cambridge 1977: Cambridge University Press.

— — (1990) *The Logic of Practice*, Cambridge: Polity Press.

— — (1991) *Language and Symbolic Power* ed. and introduction by John B. Thompson, Cambridge 1991: Polity Press.

Bruner, Edward M. (1986a) 'Experience and its Expressions', in Victor Turner and Edward Bruner (eds) *The Anthropology of Experience*, Urbana and Chicago 1986: University of Illinois Press.

— — (1986b) 'Ethnography as Narrative', in Victor Turner and Edward Bruner (eds) *The Anthropology of Experience*, Urbana and Chicago 1986: University of Illinois Press.

Bulmer, Ralph (1967) 'Why is the Cassowary not a Bird?', *Man*, vol. 2: 5–25.

Burke, Peter (1978) *Popular Culture in Early Modern Europe*, London: Temple Smith.

Burkitt, Ian (1991) *Social Selves*, London: SAGE.

Caplan, Patricia (1988) 'Engendering Knowledge: The Politics of Ethnography', *Anthropology Today*, vol. 4: 8–12.

Casey, John (1990) *Pagan Virtue*, Oxford: Clarendon.

Casey, Edward S. (1987) *Remembering. A Phenomenological Study*, Bloomington and Indianapolis: University of Indiana Press.

Cavell, Marcia (1986) 'Metaphor, Dreamwork and Irrationality', in Ernest LePore (ed.) *Truth and Interpretation. Perspectives on the Philosophy of Donald Davidson*, Oxford: Blackwell.

Certeau, Michel de (1984) *The Practice of Everyday Life*, Berkeley: University of California Press.

Chapman, Malcolm (1978) *The Gaelic Vision in Scottish Culture*, London: Croom-Helm.

— — (1982) 'Semantics and the Celt', in David Parkin (ed.) *Semantic Anthropology*, London 1982: Academic Press (ASA Monographs 22).

Christoffersen, Erik Exe (1989) *Skuespillerens Vandring. Om Odin Teatrets Historie, Teori og Teknik*, Århus: Klim (English trans. by Richard Fowler: *The Actor's Way*, London 1993: Routledge).

Clifford, James (1981) 'On Ethnographic Surrealism', *Comparative Studies in Society and History*, vol. 25: 539–564.

— — (1982) *Person and Myth. Maurice Leenhardt in the Melanesian World*, Berkeley: University of California Press.

— — (1983a) 'Power and Dialogue in Ethnography: Marcel Griaule's Initiation', in George Stocking (ed.) *Observers Observed: Essays on Ethnographic Fieldwork*, Madison: University of Wisconsin Press.

— — (1983b) 'On Ethnographic Authority', *Representations*, vol. 1: 118–146.

— — (1985) 'On Ethnographic Self-fashioning: Conrad and Malinowski', in Thomas C. Heller, Morton Sosna and David Wellberg (eds) *Reconstructing Individualism: Autonomy, Individuality, and the Self in Western Thought*, Stanford: Stanford University Press.

— — (1986a) 'Introduction: Partial Truths', in James Clifford and George

Marcus (eds) *Writing Culture: The Poetics and Politics of Ethnography*, Berkeley: University of California Press.

—— (1986b) 'On Ethnographic Allegory', in James Clifford and George Marcus (eds) *Writing Culture. The Poetics and Politics of Ethnography*, Berkeley: University of California Press.

—— (1988a) *The Predicament of Culture. Twentieth Century Ethnography, Literature and Art*, Cambridge, Mass.: Harvard University Press.

—— (1988b) 'Identity in Mashpee', In J. Clifford, *The Predicament of Culture. Twentieth Century Ethnography, Literature and Arts*, Cambridge, Mass. 1988: Harvard University Press, pp. 277–346.

Clifford, James and Marcus, George (eds) (1986) *Writing Culture. The Poetics and Politics of Ethnography*, Berkeley: University of California Press.

Cohen, Anthony (1987) *Whalsay. Symbol, Segment and Boundary in a Shetland Island Community*, Manchester: Manchester University Press.

—— (1994) *Self Consciousness. An Alternative Anthropology of Identity*, London: Routledge.

Comaroff, Jean and Comaroff, John (1992) *Ethnography and the Historical Imagination*, Boulder, San Francisco and Oxford: Westview Press.

Connerton, Paul (1989) *How Societies Remember*, Cambridge: Cambridge University Press.

Cooper, David E. (1986) *Metaphor*, Oxford: Blackwell.

Crapanzano, Vincent (1980) *Tuhami: Portrait of a Moroccan*, Chicago: University of Chicago Press.

—— (1986) 'Hermes' Dilemma: The Masking of Subversion in Ethnographic Description', in James Clifford and George Marcus (eds) *Writing Culture. The Poetics and Politics of Ethnography*, Berkeley: University of California Press.

Crick, Malcolm (1976) *Explorations in Language and Meaning. Towards a Semantic Anthropology*, London: Malaby Press.

—— (1982) 'Anthropological Fieldwork, Meaning Creation and Knowledge Construction', in David Parkin (ed.) *Semantic Anthropology*, London: Academic Press (ASA Monographs 22).

Croll, Elisabeth (1991) 'Imaging Heaven. Collective and Gendered Dreams in China', *Anthropology Today*, vol. 7, no. 4: 7–12.

DaMatta, Roberto (1984) 'On Carnaval, Informality and Magic', in Edward M. Bruner (ed.) *Text, Play, and Story*, Washington DC: The American Ethnological Society.

D'Andrade, Roy (1992) 'Schemas and Motivation', in Roy D'Andrade and Claudia Strauss (eds) *Human Motives and Cultural Models*, Cambridge: Cambridge University Press.

Daniel, Valentine (1984) *Fluid Signs. Being a Person the Tamil Way*, Berkeley: University of California Press.

Davidson, Donald (1980) *Essays on Actions and Events*, Oxford: Clarendon.

—— (1984) *Inquiries into Truth and Interpretation*, Oxford: Clarendon.

Davis, John (1992a) 'Tense in Ethnography: Some Practical Considerations', in Judith Okely and Helen Callaway (eds) *Anthropology and Autobiography*, London: Routledge (ASA Monographs 29).

— — (1992b) 'The Anthropology of Suffering', *Journal of Refugeee Studies*, vol. 5: 149–161.

Descartes, René (1988) *Descartes. Selected Philosophical Writings*, trans. by John Cottingham, Robert Stoothoff and Dugald Murdoch, with an introduction by John Cottingham, Cambridge: Cambridge University Press.

Díaz de Rada, Angel and Cruces, Francisco (1994) 'The Incarnated Field: Some Problems of Analytical Language', in Kirsten Hastrup and Peter Hervik (eds) *Social Experience and Anthropological Knowledge*, London 1994: Routledge.

Douglas, Mary (1970) *Natural Symbols*, London: Tavistock.

Dumont, Jean-Paul (1978) *The Headman and I. Ambiguity and Ambivalence in the Fieldworking Experience*, Austin: University of Texas Press.

Dumont, Louis (1986) *Essays on Individualism. Modern Ideology in Anthropological Perspective*, Chicago: University of Chicago Press.

Duranti, Allessandro and Goodwin, Charles (1992) 'Rethinking Context: An Introduction', in A. Duranti and C. Goodwin (eds) *Rethinking Context. Language as an Interactive Phenomenon*, Cambridge: Cambridge University Press.

Dwyer, Kevin (1977) 'On the Dialogic of Fieldwork', *Dialectical Anthropology*, vol. 2: 143–151.

Einarsson, Niels (1990) 'From the Native's Point of View – Some Comments on the Anthropology of Iceland', *Antropologiska Studier*, no. 46/47: 69–77.

Einarsson, Oddur (1971 [1589]) *Íslandslýsing: Qualiscunque descriptio Islandiae*, ed. by Jakob Benediktsson, Reykjavík: Bokútgafa menningarsjoDs.

Eliot, T. S. (1935) *Four Quartets*, London 1944: Faber and Faber.

Fabian, Johannes (1983) *Time and the Other*, New York: Columbia University Press.

— — (1990) *Power and Performance*, Madison: University of Wisconsin Press.

— — (1991) 'Dilemmas of Critical Anthropology', in Lorraine Nencel and Peter Pels (eds) *Constructing Knowledge. Authority and Critique in Social Science*, London: Sage.

Fardon, Richard (ed.) (1990) *Localizing Strategies. Regional Traditions of Ethnographic Writing*, Edinburgh: Scottish Academic Press, and Washington DC: Smithsonian Institution Press.

Favret-Saada, Jeanne (1980) *Deadly Words. Witchcraft in the Bocage*, Cambridge: Cambridge University Press.

Fernandez, James (1986) *Persuasions and Performances. The Play of Tropes in Culture*, Bloomington 1986: Indiana University Press.

Finnsson, Hannes (1970 [1796]) *Mannfækkun á hallærum*, ed. by J. Nordal, Reykjavík: Almenna bókfélagiD.

Fodor, Jerry and Lepore, Ernest (1992) *Holism. A Shopper's Guide*, Oxford: Blackwell.

Forster, E. M. (1924) *A Passage to India*, Harmondsworth 1974: Penguin.

Fortes, Meyer (1945) *The Dynamics of Clanship Among the Tallensi*, Oxford: Oxford University Press/International African Institute.

—— (1949) *The Web of Kinship Among the Tallensi*, Oxford: Oxford University Press/International African Institute.

Foucault, Michel (1963) *Naissance de la clinique*, Paris: Plon.

—— (1984) *The Foucault Reader*, ed. by Paul Rabinow, New York: Pantheon.

Fox, Richard G. (ed.) (1991a) *Recapturing Anthropology. Working in the Present*, Santa Fe: School of American Research Press/University of Washington Press.

—— (1991b) 'Introduction' in Richard G. Fox (ed.) *Recapturing Anthropology. Working in the Present*, Santa Fe: School of American Research Press/University of Washington Press.

Friedrich, Paul (1986) *The Language Parallax. Linguistic Relativism and Poetic Indeterminacy*, Austin: University of Texas Press.

Geertz, Clifford (1973) *The Interpretation of Cultures*, London 1975: Hutchinson.

—— (1983) *Local Knowledge*, New York: Basic Books.

—— (1988) *Works and Lives. The Anthropologist as Author*, Stanford: Stanford University Press.

Gefou-Madianou, Dimitra (1993) 'Mirroring Ourselves Through Western Texts: The Limits of Indigenous Anthropology', in Henk Driessen (ed.) *The Politics of Ethnographic Reading and Writing. Confrontations of Western and Indigenous Views*, Saarbrücken: Verlag Breitenbach.

Gellner, Ernest (1982) 'Relativism and Universals', in Martin Hollis and Steven Lukes (eds) *Rationality and Relativism*, Oxford 1982: Blackwell.

—— (1992) *Reason and Culture*, Oxford: Blackwell.

Gíslason, Magnús (1977) *Kvällsvaka: En isländsk kulturtradition belyst genom bondebefolkningens vardagsliv och miljö under senare hälften av 1800–talet och början av 1900–talet*, Uppsala: Acta Universitatis Upsaliensis.

Goffman, Erving (1959) *The Presentation of Self in Everyday Life*, New York: Doubleday-Anchor.

—— (1961) *Asylums*, New York: Doubleday-Anchor.

Good, Mary-Jo Delvecchio, Brodwin, Paul E., Good, Byron J. and Kleinman, Arthur (eds) (1992) *Pain as Human Experience. An Anthropological Perspective*, Berkeley: University of California Press.

Goody, Jack (1987) *The Interface Between the Written and the Oral*, Cambridge 1987: Cambridge University Press.

Greenblatt, Stephen (1991) *Marvelous Possessions: The Wonder of the New World*, Chicago: Chicago University Press.

Griaule, Marcel (1957) *Methode de l'ethnographie*, Paris: Presses universitaires de France.

Grotowski, Jerzy (1969) *Towards a Poor Theatre*, London: Methuen.

Guttormsson, Loftur (1983) *Bernska, ungdómur, og uppeldi á Einveldisöld*, Reykjavík: Ritsafn SagnfræDistofnunar.

Hanks, William F. 1990, *Referential Practice. Language and Lived Space Among the Maya*, Chicago: University of Chicago Press.

Hastrup, Kirsten (1985a) *Culture and History in Medieval Iceland. An*

Anthropological Analysis of Structure and Change, Oxford 1985: Clarendon.
—— (1985b) 'Male and Female in Icelandic Culture', *Folk*, vol. 27: 49–64.
—— (1985c) 'Anthropology and the Exaggeration of Culture', *Ethnos*, vol. 50: 313–324.
—— (1986a) 'Veracity and Visibility. The Problem of Authenticity in Anthropology', *Folk*, vol. 26: 5–18.
—— (1986b) 'Text and Context: Continuity and change in Medieval Icelandic History as "said", and "laid down" ', in E. Vestergaard (ed.) *Continuity and Change: A Symposium*, Odense 1986: Odense University Press.
—— (1987a) 'The Challenge of the Unreal', *Culture and History*, vol. 1: 50–62.
—— (1987b) 'Fieldwork Among Friends', in Anthony Jackson (ed.) *Anthropology at Home*, London: Routledge (ASA Monographs 25).
—— (1987c) 'The Reality of Anthropology', *Ethnos*, vol. 52: 287–300.
—— (1987d) 'Presenting the Past: Some Reflections on Myth and History', *Folk,* vol. 29: 257–270.
—— (1989) 'The Prophetic Condition', in Edwin Ardener, *The Voice of Prophecy and Other Essays*, ed. by Malcolm Chapman, Oxford 1989: Blackwell.
—— (1990a) *Nature and Policy in Iceland 1400–1800. An Anthropological Analysis of History and Mentality*, Oxford 1990: Clarendon.
—— (1990b) *Island of Anthropology. Studies in Icelandic Past and Present*, Odense: Odense Universitetsforlag.
—— (1990c) 'The Ethnographic Present: A Reinvention', *Cultural Anthropology*, vol. 5: 45–61.
—— (1990d) 'Studying a Remote Island. Inside and Outside Icelandic Culture', in Kirsten Hastrup, *Island of Anthropology. Studies in Icelandic Past and Present*, Odense 1990: Odense University Press.
—— (1990e) 'The Anthropological Vision – Comments to Niels Einarsson', *Antropologiska Studier*, no. 46/47: 78–84.
—— (1990f) 'Videnskabens magi. En antropologisk diskussion af årsag og virkning i verden', in Hans Fink and Kirsten Hastrup (eds) *Tanken om enhed i videnskaberne*, Aarhus: Aarhus Universitetsforlag.
—— (1992a) 'Writing Ethnography: State of the Art', in Helen Callaway and Judith Okely (eds) *Anthropology and Autobiography*, London 1992: Routledge (ASA Monographs 29).
—— (1992b) 'Anthropological Visions. Some Notes on Visual and Textual Authority', in Peter Ian Crawford and David Turnton (eds) *Film as Ethnography*, Manchester: Manchester University Press.
—— (1992c) 'Out of Anthropology. The Anthropologist as an Object of Dramatic Representation', *Cultural Anthropology*, vol. 7: 327–345.
—— (1992d) 'Introduction', in Kirsten Hastrup (ed.) *Other Histories*, London: Routledge.
—— (1993a) 'The Native Voice and the Anthropological Vision', *Social Anthropology/Anthropologie Sociale*, vol. 1: 173–186.
—— (1993b) 'Hunger and the Hardness of Facts', *Man*, vol. 28: 727–739.

— — (1993c) 'Selvets Kilde. Mod en ny sexologi?', *Nordisk Sexologi*, vol. 11: 130–141.

— — (1993d) 'Native Anthropology: A Contradiction in Terms?', *Folk*, vol. 35: 147–161.

— — (1994a) 'Anthropological Knowledge Incorporated', in Kirsten Hastrup and Peter Hervik (eds) *Social experience and Anthropological Knowledge*, London 1994: Routledge.

Hastrup, K. and Elsass, Peter (1990) 'Anthropological Advocacy: A Contradiction in Terms?', *Current Anthropology*, vol.31: 301–311.

Hastrup, Kirsten and Hervik, Peter (eds) (1994) *Social Experience and Anthropological Knowledge*, London: Routledge.

Hastrup, Kirsten and Ramløv, Kirsten (eds) (1988) *Feltarbejde. Oplevelse og metode i etnografien*, København: Akademisk Forlag.

Hendry, Joy (1992) 'The Paradox of Friendship in the Field', in Judith Okely and Helen Callaway (eds) *Anthropology and Autobiography*, London 1992: Routledge (ASA Monographs 29).

Herzfeld, Michael (1987) *Anthropology Through the Looking-Glass: Critical Ethnography in the Margins of Europe*, Cambridge: Cambridge University Press.

Hirst, Paul (1985) 'Is it Rational to Reject Relativism?', in Joanna Overing (ed.) *Reason and Morality*, London 1985: Routledge (ASA Monographs 24).

Hobsbawm, Eric and Ranger, Terence (eds) (1983) *The Invention of Tradition*, Cambridge: Cambridge University Press.

Hollis, Mark (1985) 'Of Masks and Men', in Michael Carrithers, Steven Collins and Steven Lukes (eds) *The Category of the Person*, Cambridge: Cambridge University Press.

Hollis, Martin and Lukes, Steven (eds) (1982) *Rationality and Relativism*, Oxford 1982: Blackwell.

Irvine, Judith (1990) 'Registering Affect: Heteroglossia in the Linguistic Expression of Emotion', in C. A. Lutz and L. Abu-Lughod (eds) *Language and the Politics of Emotion*, Cambridge 1990: Cambridge University Press.

Jackson, Anthony (ed.) (1987) *Anthropology at Home*, London: Tavistock (ASA Monographs 25).

Jackson, Jean (1991) 'Being and Becoming an Indian in the Vaupés', in G. Urban and J. Sherzer (eds) *Nation-States and Indians in Latin America*, Austin 1991: University of Texas Press.

Jameson, Fredric (1991) *Postmodernism. Or, The Cultural Logic of Late Capitalism*, London and New York: Verso.

Jay, Martin (1993) *Force Fields. Between Intellectual History and Cultural Critique*, New York and London: Routledge.

Jenkins, Timothy (1987) 'Metaphor and Language', Ms.

Johnson, Mark (1987) *The Body in the Mind. The Bodily Basis of Meaning, Imagination and Reason*, Chicago: University of Chicago Press.

— — (1993) *Moral Imagination. Implications of Cognitive Science for Ethics*, Chicago: University of Chicago Press.

Kant, Immanuel (1991 [1781]) *Critique of Pure Reason*, trans. by J. M. D. Meiklejohn, London: Dent.

Kavouras, Pavlos (1994) 'Where the Community Reveals Itself', in Kirsten Hastrup and Peter Hervik (eds) *Social Experience and Anthropological Knowledge*, London 1994: Routledge.

Ker, W. P. (1923) *The Dark Ages*, Edinburgh and London: William Blackwood.

Kershaw, Baz (1992) *The Politics of Performance. Radical Theatre as Cultural Intervention*, London: Routledge.

Kleinman, Arthur (1988) *The Illness Narratives: Suffering, Healing, and the Human Condition*, New York: Basic Books.

Kleinman, Arthur and Kleinman, Joan (1991) 'Suffering and its Professional Transformation', *Culture, Medicine and Psychiatry*, vol. 15; 275–301.

Kohn, Tamara (1994) 'Incomers and Fieldworkers. A Comparative Study of Social Experience', in Kirsten Hastrup and Peter Hervik (eds) *Social Experience and Anthropological Knowledge*, London 1994: Routledge.

Kondo, Dorinne (1984) 'Dissolution and Reconstitution of Self: Implications for Anthropological Epistemology', *Cultural Anthropology*, vol. 1: 74–89.

Lakoff, George (1987) *Women, Fire and Dangerous Things. What Categories Reveal about the Mind*, Chicago: University of Chicago Press.

Lakoff, George and Johnson, Mark (1980) *Metaphors we Live By*, Chicago: University of Chicago Press.

Lasch, Cristopher (1978) *The Culture of Narcissism*, New York: N. W. Norton.

Latour, Bruno (1987) *Science in Action*, Milton Keynes: Open University Press.

— — (1988) 'The Politics of Explanation: An Alternative', in Steve Woolgar (ed.) *Knowledge and Reflexivity. New Frontiers in the Sociology of Knowledge*, London 1988: Sage.

Lavie, Smadar (1989) 'When Leadership Becomes Allegory', *Cultural Anthropology*, vol. 4: 99–136.

Leach, Edmund (1973) 'Ourselves and Others', *The Times Literary Supplement*, 6 July: 771–772.

— — (1989) 'Tribal Ethnography: Past, Present, Future', in Elizabeth Tonkin, Maryon McDonald and Malcolm Chapman (eds) *History and Ethnicity*, London 1989: Routledge (ASA Monographs 27).

Lecercle, Jean-Jacques (1990) *The Violence of Language*, London 1990: Routledge.

Leder, Drew (1990) *The Absent Body*, Chicago: University of Chicago Press.

Le Goff, Jacques (1988) *The Medieval Imagination*, Chicago: University of Chicago Press.

Leiris, Michel (1988 [1934]) *L'afrique fantôme*, Paris: Gallimard.

Lévi-Strauss, Claude (1963) *Totemism*, Boston: Beacon Press.

— — (1966) *The Savage Mind*, London: Weidenfeld and Nicolson.

— — (1973) *Anthropologie structurale deux*, Paris: Plon.

— — (1988) *The Way of Masks*, Seattle: University of Washington Press.

Lienhardt, Godfrey (1954) 'Modes of Thought', in E. E. Evans-Pritchard *et al.* (eds) *The Institutions of Primitive Society*, Oxford: Blackwell.

Limón, José E. (1991) 'Representation, Ethnicity, And the Precursory Ethnography. Notes of a Native Anthropologist', in Richard G. Fox (ed.) *Recapturing Anthropology. Working in the Present*, Santa Fe 1991: School of American Research Press/University of Washington Press.

Loizos, Peter (1992) 'User-Friendly Ethnography?', in J. de Pina Cabral and J. Campbell (eds) *Europe Observed*, Oxford: Macmillan.

Lovsamling for Island (1853–59) ed. by O. Stephensen and J. SigurDsson, 20 vols, København: Høst og Søn.

Lutz, Catherine A. and Abu-Lughod, Lila (eds) (1990), *Language and the Politics of Emotion*, Cambridge: Cambridge University Press.

McDonald, Maryon (1989a) *We are not French! Language, Culture and Identity in Brittany*, London: Routledge.

— — (1989b) 'Towards a Rigorously Empirical Anthropology', postscript to Edwin Ardener, *The Voice of Prophecy and Other Essays*, ed. by Malcolm Chapman, Oxford: Blackwell.

McDougall, Joyce (1986) *Theatres of the Mind. Illusion and Truth on the Psychoanalytic Stage*, London: Free Association Books.

Magnússon, Skúli (1944a [1785]) *Beskrivelse af Gullbringu og Kjósar syslur*, ed. by Jón Helgason, København: Munksgård.

— — (1944b [1786]) *Forsøg til en kort beskrivelse af Island*, ed. by Jón Helgason, København: Munksgård.

Malinowski, Bronislaw (1922) *Argonauts of the Western Pacific*, London: Routledge.

Marcus, G. E. and Fischer, M. J. (1986) *Anthropology as Cultural Critique*, Chicago: University of Chicago Press.

Mascarenhas-Keyes, Stella (1987) 'The Native Anthropologist: Constraints and Strategies in Research', in Anthony Jackson (ed.) *Anthropology at Home*, London: Tavistock (ASA Monographs 25).

Maybury-Lewis, David (1985) 'A Special Sort of Pleading – Anthropology at the Service of Ethnic Groups', in R. Paine (ed.) *Advocacy and Anthropology*, St Johns, New Foundland: Institute of Social and Economic Research.

Mead, George Henry (1934) *Mind, Self and Society*, Chicago: Chicago University Press.

Mead, Margaret (1977) *Letters from the Field 1925–1975*, New York: Harper Colophon Books.

Merchant, Carolyn (1980) *The Death of Nature. Women, Ecology, and the Scientific Revolution*, San Francisco: Harper and Row.

Merleau-Ponty, Maurice (1962) *Phenomenology of Perception*, London: Routledge and Kegan Paul.

Mills, C. Wright (1959) *The Sociological Imagination*, New York: Grove Press.

Moore, Sally Falk (1987) 'Explaining the Present: Theoretical Dilemmas in Processual Anthropology', *American Ethnologist*, vol. 14: 727–736.

Myerhoff, Barbara (1978) *Number Our Days*, New York: Simon and Schuster.

Myerhoff, Barbara and Ruby, Jay (1982) 'Introduction', in Jay Ruby (ed.) *A Crack in the Mirror. Reflexive Perspectives in Anthropology*, Philadelphia: University of Pennsylvania Press.

Nash, Manning (1989) *The Cauldron of Ethnicity in the Modern World*, Chicago: University of Chicago Press.

Ohnuki-Tierney, Emiko (1984) ' "Native" Anthropologists', *American Ethnologist*, vol. 11, no.3: 584–586.

Okely, Judith (1983) *The Traveller-Gypsies*, Cambridge: Cambridge University Press.

— — (1984) 'Fieldwork in Home Countries', *RAIN*, no. 61: 4– 6.

— — (1994) 'Vicarious and Sensory Knowledge of Chronology and Change. Ageing in Rural France', in Kirsten Hastrup and Peter Hervik (eds) *Social Experience and Anthropological Knowledge*, London 1994: Routledge.

Ottenberg, Simon (1990) 'Thirty Years of Fieldnotes: Changing Relationships to the Text', in Roger Sanjek (ed.) *Fieldnotes. The Makings of Anthropology*, Ithaca: Cornell University Press.

Overing, Joanna (1985a) 'Introduction', Joanna Overing (ed.) *Reason and Morality*, London 1985: Tavistock (ASA Monographs 24).

— — (1985b) 'Today I Shall Call him Mummy: Multiple Worlds and Classificatory Confusion', in Joanna Overing (ed.) *Reason and Morality*, London 1985: Tavistock (ASA Monographs 24).

Page, Helan E. (1988) 'Dialogic Principles of Interactive Learning in the Ethnographic Relationship', *Journal of Anthropological Research*, vol. 44: 163–181.

Pálsson, Hermann (1962) *Sagnaskemmtan Íslendinga*, Reykjavik: Mál og Menning.

Parkin, David (1982) 'Introduction', in David Parkin (ed.) *Semantic Anthropology*, London: Academic Press (ASA Monographs 22).

— — (1985) 'Introduction', in David Parkin, *The Anthropology of Evil*, Oxford: Blackwell.

— — (1986) 'Violence and Will', in David Riches (ed.) *The Anthropology of Violence*, Oxford: Blackwell.

Pettit, Philip (1976) 'Making Actions Intelligible', in Rom Harré (ed.) *Life Sentences. Aspects of the Social Role of Language*, London: John Wiley & Sons.

Piaget, Jean (1962) *Play, Dreams, and Imitation in Childhood*, New York: Norton.

Pratt, Mary Louise (1992) *Imperial Eyes. Travel Writing and Transculturation*, London: Routledge.

Putnam, Hilary (1981) *Reason, Truth and History*, Cambridge: Cambridge University Press.

— — (1990) *Realism With a Human Face*, Cambridge, Mass.: Harvard University Press.

Quine, W.V. (1953) 'Two Dogmas of Empiricism', in W. V. Quine, *From a Logical Point of View*, Cambridge, Mass.: Harvard University Press.

— — (1992) *Pursuit of Truth*, Cambridge, Mass.: Harvard University Press.

Quinn, Naomi and Holland, Dorothy (1987) 'Culture and Cognition', in

D. Holland and N. Quinn (eds) *Cultural Models in Language and Thought*, Cambridge: Cambridge University Press.

Quinn, Naomi (1992) 'The motivational force of self-understanding', in Roy D'Andrade and Claudia Strauss (eds) *Human Motives and Cultural Models*, Cambridge: Cambridge University Press.

Rabinow, Paul (1977) *Reflections on Fieldwork in Morocco*, Berkeley: University of California Press.

— — (1982) 'Masked I go Forward: Reflections on the Modern Subject', in Jay Ruby (ed.) *A Crack in the Mirror: Reflexive Perspectives in Anthropology*, Philadelphia: University of Pennsylvania Press.

— — (1986) 'Representations are Social Facts: Modernity and Post-Modernity in Anthropology', in James Clifford and George Marcus (eds) *Writing Culture. The Poetics and Politics of Ethnography*, Berkeley: University of California Press.

Rappaport, Joanne (1990) *The Politics of Memory. Native Historical Interpretation in the Colombian Andes*, Cambridge 1990: Cambridge University Press.

Riches, David (1986) 'The Phenomenon of Violence', in D. Riches (ed.) *The Anthropology of Violence*, Oxford: Blackwell.

Ricoeur, Paul (1979) 'The Model of the Text: Meaningful Action Considered as a Text', in P. Rabinow and W. M. Sullivan eds *Interpretive Social Science*, Berkeley: University of California Press.

— — (1991) 'Life in Quest of Narrative', in David Wood (ed.) *On Paul Ricoeur. Narrative and Interpretation*, London: Routledge.

Rorty, Richard (1989) *Contingency, Irony, and Solidarity*, Cambridge: Cambridge University Press.

— — (1991a) *Objectivity, Relativism, and Truth*, Cambridge: Cambridge University Press.

— — (1991b) *Essays on Heidegger and Others*, Cambridge: Cambridge University Press.

Rosaldo, Renato (1984) 'Grief and the Headhunter's Rage', in E. M. Bruner (ed.) *Text, Play and Story*, Washington DC 1984: American Anthropological Association.

— — (1989) *Culture and Truth. The Remaking of Social Analysis*, Berkeley: University of California Press.

Rosch, Eleanor (1978) 'Principles of Categorization', in E. Rosch and B. B. Lloyd (eds) *Cognition and Categorization*, New Jersey: Social Science Research Council Committee on Cognitive Research.

Rose, Dan (1982) 'Occasions and Forms of Anthropological Experience', in Jay Ruby ed. *A Crack in the Mirror. Reflexive Perpectives in Anthropology*, Philadelphia: University of Pennsylvania Press.

Sahlins, Marshall (1976) *Culture and Practical Reason*, Chicago: University of Chicago Press.

— — (1985) *Islands of History*, Chicago: University of Chicago Press.

— — (1993) 'Goodbye to Tristes Tropes: Ethnography in the Context of Modern World History', *Journal of Modern History*, vol. 65, no. 1: 1–25.

Said, Edward (1978) *Orientalism*, New York: Pantheon.

— — (1989) 'Representing the Colonized: Anthropology's interlocutors', *Critical Inquiry*, vol. 15: 205–225.

— — (1993) *Culture and Imperialism*, London: Vintage.

Salmond, Anne (1982) 'Theoretical Landscapes', in David Parkin (ed.) *Semantic Anthropology*, London 1982: Academic Press (ASA Monographs 22).

Sanjek, Roger (1990) *Fieldnotes. The Makings of Anthropology*, Ithaca: Cornell University Press.

Sapir, Edward (1951) *The Selected Writings of Edward Sapir*, ed. by David G. Mandelbaum, Berkeley: University of California Press.

Schechner, Richard (1982) 'Collective Reflexivity: Restoration of Behavior', in Jay Ruby (ed.) *A Crack in the Mirror: Reflexive Perspectives in Anthropology*, Philadelphia: University of Pennsylvania Press.

— — (1985) *Between Theater and Anthropology*, Philadelphia: University of Pennsylvania Press.

Scheper-Hughes, Nancy (1992) *Death Without Weeping. The Violence of Everyday Life in Brazil*, Berkeley: University of California Press.

Scheper-Hughes, Nancy and Lock, M. (1987) 'The Mindful Body: A Prolegomenon to Future Work in Medical Anthropology', *Medical Anthropology Quarterly*, vol. 1: 6–41.

Schier, Kurt (1975) 'Iceland and the Rise of Literature in "Terra Nova"': Some Comparative Reflection', *Gripla*, vol. 1: 168–181.

Scholte, Bob (1980) 'Anthropological Traditions. Their Definition', in S. Diamond (ed.) *Anthropological Traditions, The Participants Observed*, The Hague: Mouton.

Shweder, Richard A. (1984) 'Anthropology's Romantic Rebellion Against the Enlightenment, or There's More to Thinking than Reason and Evidence', in R. A. Shweder and R. A. LeVine (eds) *Culture Theory. Essays on Mind, Self, and Emotion*, Cambridge 1984: Cambridge University Press.

Shweder, Richard (1991) *Thinking Through Cultures. Explorations in Cultural Psychology*, Cambridge, Mass.: Harvard University Press.

Sousa, Ronald de (1990) *The Rationality of Emotion*, Cambridge, Mass.: MIT Press.

Sperber, Dan (1982) 'Apparently Irrational Beliefs', in Martin Hollis and Steven Lukes (eds) *Rationality and Relativism*, Oxford 1982: Blackwell.

— — (1985) *On Anthropological Knowledge*, Cambridge: Cambridge University Press.

Stanislavski, Constantin (1963) *An Actor's Handbook*, New York: Theatre Arts Books.

Stocking, George (1983) 'The Ethnographer's Magic: Fieldwork in British Anthropology From Tylor to Malinowski', in G. Stocking (ed.) *Observers Observed*, Madison: University of Wisconsin Press.

Stoller, Paul (1989) *The Taste of Ethnographic Things. The Senses in Anthropology*, Philadelphia: University of Pennsylvania Press.

Strathern, Marilyn (1987) 'The Limits of Auto-Anthropology', in Anthony Jackson (ed.) *Anthropology at Home*, London 1987: Tavistock (ASA Monographs 25).

— — (1992) 'Reproducing Anthropology', in Sandra Wallman (ed.) *Contemporary Futures*, London: Routledge (ASA Monographs 30).

Strauss, Claudia (1992) 'Introduction', in Roy D'Andrade and Claudia Strauss (eds) *Human Motives and Cultural Models*, Cambridge: Cambridge University Press.

Strauss, Claudia and Quinn, Naomi (1993) 'A Cognitive/Cultural Anthropology', in Robert Borofsky (ed.) *Assessing Developments in Anthropology*, New York: McGraw Hill.

Street, Brian (1984) *Literacy in Theory and Practice*, Cambridge 1984: Cambridge University Press.

Taussig, Michael (1991) 'Tactility and Distraction', *Cultural Anthropology*, vol. 6: 147–153.

— — (1992) *The Nervous System*, London: Routledge.

— — (1993) *Mimesis and Alterity. A Particular History of the Senses*, London: Routledge.

Taylor, Charles (1979) 'Interpretation and the Sciences of Man', in P. Rabinow and W. M. Sullivan (eds) *Interpretive Social Science*, Berkeley: University of California Press.

— — (1985a) *Human Agency and Language. Philosophical Papers 1*, Cambridge: Cambridge University Press.

— — (1985b) *Philosophy and the Human Sciences. Philosophical Papers 2*, Cambridge: Cambridge University Press.

— — (1985c) 'The Person', in Michael Carrithers, Steven Collins and Steven Lukes (eds) *The Category of the Person*, Cambridge: Cambridge University Press.

— — (1989) *Sources of the Self*, Cambridge: Cambridge University Press.

— — (1991) *The Ethics of Authenticity*, Cambridge, Mass.: Harvard University Press.

Tedlock, Barbara (1991) 'From Participant Observation to the Observation of Participation: The Emergence of Narrative Ethnography', *Journal of Anthropological Research*, vol. 47: 69–94.

Tedlock, Dennis (1982) 'Hermeneutics and Alphabetic Literacy', in J. Ruby (ed.) *A Crack in the Mirror. Reflexive Perspectives in Anthropology*, Philadelphia: University of Pennsylvania Press.

— — (1983) *The Spoken Word and the Work of Interpretation*, Philadelphia: University of Pennsylvania Press.

Trouillot, Michel-Rolph (1991) 'Anthropology and the Savage Slot: The Poetics and Politics of Otherness', in Richard G. Fox (ed.) *Recapturing Anthropology. Working in the Present*, Santa Fe 1991: School of American Research/University of Washington Press.

Turnbull, Colin (1990) 'Liminality: A Synthesis of Objective and Subjective Experience', in R. Schechner and W. Appel (eds) *By Means of Performance*, Cambridge: Cambridge University Press.

Turner, Victor (1974) *Dramas, Fields and Metaphors*, Itacha: Cornell University Press.

— — (1982a) 'Dramatic Ritual/Ritual Drama', in Jay Ruby (ed.) *A Crack in the Mirror: Reflexive Perspectives in Anthropology*, Philadelphia: University of Pennsylvania Press.

— — (1982b) *From Ritual to Theatre*, New York: PAJ Publications.

— — (1986a) *The Anthropology of Performance*, New York: PAJ Publications.

— — (1986b) 'Dewey, Dilthey, and Drama: An Essay in the Anthropology of Experience', in Victor Turner and Edward Bruner (eds) *The Anthropology of Experience*, Urbana and Chicago 1986: University of Illinois Press.

— — (1990) 'Are there Universals of Performance in Myth, Ritual and Drama', in Richard Schechner and Willa Appel (eds) *By Means of Performance*, Cambridge: Cambridge University Press.

Turner, Victor and Bruner, Edward (eds) (1986) *The Anthropology of Experience*, Urbana and Chicago: University of Illinois Press.

Tyler, Stephen (1978) *The Said and the Unsaid. Mind, Meaning, and Culture*, New York and London: Academic Press.

— — (1986) 'Post-Modern Ethnography: From document of the occult to occult document', in James Clifford and George Marcus (eds) *Writing Culture*, Berkely 1986: University of California Press.

— — (1987a) *The Unspeakable*, Madison: University of Wisconsin Press.

— — (1987b) 'On "Writing-up/off" as "Speaking-for" ', *Journal of Anthropological Research*, vol. 43: 338–342.

Ullmann, Stephen (1972) *Semantics. An Introduction to the Science of Meaning*, Oxford: Blackwell.

Urban, Greg and Joel Sherzer (1991) 'Introduction', in G. Urban and J. Sherzer (eds) *Nation-States and Indians in Latin America*, Austin: University of Texas Press.

Varela, Francisco J., Thompson, Evan and Rosch, Eleanor (eds) (1992) *The Embodied Mind. Cognitive Science and Human Experience*, Cambridge, Mass.: MIT Press.

Vendler, Zeno (1984) 'Understanding People', in Richard A. Shweder and Robert A. LeVine (eds) *Culture Theory. Essays on Mind, Self, and Emotion*, Cambridge 1984: Cambridge University Press.

Wagner, Roy (1975) *The Invention of Culture*, Englewood Cliffs: Prentice-Hall.

Wartburg, W.V. (1946) *Problèmes et méthodes de la linguistique*, Paris.

Watson, Graham (1987) 'Make Me Reflexive – But Not Yet: Strategies for Managing Essential Reflexivity in Ethnographic Discourse', *Journal of Anthropological Research*, vol. 43: 29–41.

— — (1991) 'Rewriting Culture', in Richard G. Fox (ed.) *Recapturing Anthropology. Working in the Present*, Santa Fe: School of American Research Press/University of Washington Press.

Watson, Ian (1993) *Towards a Third Theatre. Eugenio Barba and the Odin Teatret*, London: Routledge.

Wax, Rosalie H. (1971) *Doing Fieldwork. Warnings and Advice*, Chicago: Chicago University Press.

Weber, Gerd Wolfgang (1981) 'Irreligiösität und Heldenzeitalder: zum Mythencharcter der altisländischen Literatur', in Ursula Dronke, Gudrun P. Helgadsttir, Gerd Wolfgang Weber and Hans Bekker-Nielsen (eds) *Speculum Norroenum: Norse Studies in Memory of Gabriel Turville-Petre*, Odense: Odense University Press.

Whorf, Benjamin Lee (1956) *Language, Thought and Reality: Selected Writings of Benjamin Lee Whorf*, ed. by John B. Carroll, Cambridge, Mass. 1956: MIT Press.

Wikan, Unni (1991) 'Toward an Experience-Near Anthropology', *Cultural Anthropology*, vol. 6: 285–305.

— — (1992) 'Beyond the Words: The Power of Resonance', *American Ethnologist*, vol. 19: 460–482.

Wilson, Bryan (1970) *Rationality*, New York: Harper and Row.

Wolf, Eric (1982) *Europe and the Peoples Without History*, Berkeley: University of California Press.

Woolgar, S. and Ashmore, M. (1988) 'The Next Step: An Introduction to the Reflexive Project', in S. Woolgar (ed.) *Knowledge and Reflexivity. New Frontiers in the Sociology of Knowledge*, London 1988: Sage.

Index

oneself 133–6; theatres of 90–3; writing oneself 129–33
self-fulfilment 72
self-interpretation 182–3
semantic density 30–1
sentimental pessimism 4–5, 184
sexuality/sex 93, 103
shanty town 102–4, 105–6, 118, 119
shared experience 17–19, 31–2, 51, 56, 183
Sherzer, J. 155
Shweder, R. 12, 50, 57, 68, 76
sinker lines 110
social construction 74
social drama 81; *see also* theatre anthropology
social experience 84; Iceland 107–11
social habit memory 41, 42
social process 27, 36–7, 41–4
social theory 182–3
sociological imagination 65–7
solidarity 5, 181
Sousa, R. de 73
Sperber, D. 22, 42
staging 91; *see also* performance, theatre anthropology
Stanislavski, C. 78, 80, 91
starvation 102–7, 119, 175–6
stereotypes 30–1
Stocking, G. 14, 20
Stoller, P. 32, 33, 48
Strathern, M. 9, 76, 151, 152
Strauss, C. 80, 90, 118
Street, B. 43
structuralism 35
subjectivity 150
superstition 69–70
symbolic capital 97
symbolic violence 142–3

Talabot 123–39, 141, 143–4, 144
Tallensi 147
Taussig, M. 10, 72, 74, 93, 156
Taylor, C. 16, 100, 101, 120, 168, 177; agency 84, 85–6, 86, 94, 97, 105–6; anthropological language 185, 186; art 182; articulation 12, 118–19; designative and

expressive theories 181; desires 118; identity 11, 118; imagination 67; interpretation 148; procedural rationality 173; punctual self 178; self-fulfilment 72; subjectivity 13, 174; understanding native voice 153
Tedlock, B. 19, 150
text *see* writing
theatre anthropology 77–8; lived experience 81–4; mind-body dualism 86–7; self 90–3; *see also* performance
theatrical paradigm 140
theory 5, 180–7; anthropology's shortcoming 10; imagination and 61–3; self-reflection 120–1
Thompson, E. 87
time: consciousness and 101; fieldwork and 21, 25; performance and 91; *see also* ethnographic present
training 88–9, 91
transformation 96
translation, cultural 22–4, 43–4
transparency 164
tribal ethnography 153
Trickster 138
Trouillet, M.-R. 6, 49, 150
Turnbull, C. 20
Turner, V. 77, 83, 140, 143–4; 'experience' and 'an experience' 84; meaning and death 136; performing and learning 78, 84; social drama 81; time 91
Tyler, S. 42, 151

Uchronic visions 112–15, 116, 117
Ullmann, S. 29
understanding: auto-anthropology 153; knowledge and 56, 148; and meaning 163
Urban, G. 155

values 118, 173–4
Varela, F.J. 87
Vendler, Z. 31, 50, 101